The Sixties in America

Biographies

The Sixties in America

Biographies

**Tom Pendergast
and Sara Pendergast**

Kathleen J. Edgar,
Project Editor

U·X·L

*An imprint of Thomson Gale,
a part of The Thomson Corporation*

THOMSON
GALE™

Detroit • New York • San Francisco • San Diego • New Haven, Conn. • Waterville, Maine • London • Munich

THOMSON

™

GALE

The Sixties in America: Biographies

Tom Pendergast and Sara Pendergast

Project Editors
Kathleen J. Edgar and Allison McNeill

Editorial
Jennifer York

Permissions
Mari Masalin-Cooper

Imaging and Multimedia
Denay Wilding, Lezlie Light, Mike Logusz

Product Design
Kate Scheible and Pamela Galbreath

Composition
Evi Seoud

Manufacturing
Rita Wimberley

LIBRARY OF CONGRESS CATALOGING-IN-PUBLICATION DATA

Pendergast, Tom.
    Sixties in America. Biographies / Tom Pendergast and Sara Pendergast.
        p. cm.
    Includes bibliographical references and index.
        ISBN 0-7876-9247-6 (hardcover : alk. paper)
    1. United States—History—1961–1969—Biography—Juvenile literature. I. Pendergast, Sara. II. Title.

E841.P3825 2004
920.073'09'046—dc22   2004016600

Printed in the United States of America
10 9 8 7 6 5 4 3 2 1

Contents

Reader's Guide

Many Americans realized by the middle of the 1960s that their nation was going through a period of intense change and disruption. The decade had begun in relative peace, with the election of a vibrant, young president, John F. Kennedy, a Democrat. Yet Kennedy faced several key issues that would come to define the decade. First, he clashed with the Soviet Union over the spread of communist influence in Europe and in Cuba. Then, he also faced domestic tensions as the civil rights movement in the South grew increasingly intense and even violent. When Kennedy was assassinated in November of 1963, the nation was shocked and saddened, for they had invested great hopes in Kennedy.

Kennedy's successor, Lyndon B. Johnson, struggled with the existing tensions and new pressures as well. He had an ambitious agenda for domestic policies that he called the Great Society, which included passing civil rights legislation, using federal funds to wage a "war on poverty," and creating programs to support public education, housing, and jobs. He succeeded in passing many of his programs. But Johnson's political career was undone by American involvement in the expanding war in Vietnam, which American combat troops entered in 1965. A powerful grassroots movement rose up against the war, and its dramatic demonstrations helped turn public sentiment against the war. Johnson did not seek reelection in 1968. Republican Richard M. Nixon won a hard-fought election by promising to return law and order to what he depicted as an unruly nation.

Domestic and international politics were not the only source of high drama in the 1960s. The colorful hippie subculture emerged as a growing youth movement, bringing changes in music, education, fashion, art, and other areas of culture. Thanks to television, American sports became more commercial and more dramatic, and American sports figures like Muhammad Ali, Vince Lombardi, and Joe Namath became important cultural figures. Riots in major cities and the assassinations of the Rev. Dr. Martin Luther King Jr., Malcolm X, and Robert Kennedy caused many Americans to worry about rising violence in their society. An increase in sexual content in books and movies, as well as a new openness about homosexuality at the end of the decade, raised worries about declining morality. There was, of course, much, much more, as changes in one area of American society encouraged or clashed with other movements and trends.

The dramatic, stirring, and sometimes violent events of the 1960s make it an important decade for students to study in their quest to understand American society as it exists today. Many aspects of American culture in the 2000s can be traced back to that era. In some ways, the 1960s are still close at hand. Classic rock radio stations continue to play music from the decade. In fact, The Beatles remain one of the top-selling bands, just as they were in the 1960s. Fashion trends introduced in the 1960s—bell-bottoms and paisley fabric, for example—make periodic comebacks. Politicians continue to refer to the legacy of President John F. Kennedy and civil rights leader Martin Luther King Jr. to inspire audiences. Political leaders and activists also point to the lessons of the Vietnam War to help Americans understand foreign policy. Many Americans who experienced the 1960s firsthand are in positions of power in American society in the 2000s, and their experiences of that decade inform their actions.

In some ways, however, the 1960s can seem quite distant. For example, during that era, television was still a relatively new phenomenon. Nightly coverage of war on television was something new to Americans. In addition, the Cold War (1945–91) between the United States and the Soviet Union—and the threat of nuclear war—informed every decision about foreign policy. And, sexuality, especially homosexuality, was never discussed in polite company, much less on television. One of the features that make this decade so fascinating is the fact that the 1960s are so close, yet so far away.

The Sixties in America: Biographies contains twenty-six biographies of men and women who played crucial roles in the social, cultural, and political developments of the 1960s. Readers will find coverage of the most notable figures of the decade, including John F. Kennedy, Lyndon B. Johnson, Martin Luther King Jr., and Malcolm X. Essays are also provided on a number of lesser-known though no less interesting figures, including labor activist Dolores Huerta, atheist activist Madalyn Murray O'Hair, scientist Frances Oldham Kelsey, feminist author and activist Betty Friedan, and Native-American activist Richard Oakes, who led a takeover of Alcatraz Island.

Features

The entries in *The Sixties in America: Biographies* contain sidebar boxes that highlight topics of special interest related to the profiled individual. Each entry also offers a list of additional sources that students can go to for more information. More than fifty black-and-white photographs help illustrate the material. The volume begins with a timeline of important events in the history of the 1960s and a "Words to Know" section that introduces students to difficult or unfamiliar terms. The volume concludes with a general bibliography and a subject index so students can easily find the people, places, and events discussed throughout *The Sixties in America: Biographies*.

Sixties in America Reference Library

The Sixties in America: Biographies is only one component of the three-part U•X•L Sixties in America Reference Library. The other two titles in this set are:

- *The Sixties in America: Almanac* (one volume) presents, in fifteen chapters, a comprehensive overview of events that occurred within the United States during the 1960s. The introduction asks readers to consider the themes that make the decade worthy of study. This includes: the unfolding dramas of the civil rights movement, the Vietnam War, and anti-war movement; the expansion of the federal government under Democratic presidents; the birth of a counterculture and its impact on American entertainment; and a variety of other cultural developments. These issues and others are considered closely in the thematic chapters that follow. Finally, the conclusion asks readers to consider the extent to which the experiences and events of the 1960s shaped American society in the years that followed. The volume contains more than seventy black-and-white photographs as well as a list of further readings related to the topic.

- *The Sixties in America: Primary Sources* (one volume) tells the story of the 1960s in the words of the people who lived and shaped the decade. The volume gives readers firsthand contact with some of the key documents of the era, including material pertaining to the civil rights movement, the formation of U.S. policy in Vietnam, the growth of the anti-war movement, the rise of feminism and the women's movement, and the emergence of television as a cultural force in the United States. Also included are expressions of political radicalism from such diverse groups and individuals as the Students for a Democratic Society, Young Americans for Freedom, Barry Goldwater, and the Yippies. Some of these primary sources use specialized or complex language, so efforts have been made to place these documents in context as well as define terms that may be otherwise inaccessible to young readers. The volume contains more than sixty black-and-white photographs as well as a list of further readings related to the topic.

- A cumulative index of all three titles in the U•X•L Sixties in America Reference Library is also available.

Special Thanks

The authors wish to thank the following talented and dedicated individuals for aiding in the creation of The Sixties in America Reference Library. At U•X•L, Allison McNeill has been the ideal editor for this set, pointing out pitfalls to avoid while ably steering us toward creating books that would best serve an audience of young readers. Special thanks also go to the skilled writers who contributed to the *Biographies* volume: Rob Edelman, Tina Gianoulis, Audrey Kupferberg, Mary Le Rouge, and Chris Routledge.

The authors note that work on this book was both enriched and complicated by the growing and diverse body of historical knowledge that exists on the 1960s. The 1960s may be considered a part of the distant past to many of the readers of this book, but many of those who have written about the period lived through it or, in the case of the authors of this book, had parents who lived through it. It was such a dramatic, eventful decade that those with direct experience have not always seen it clearly. As such, the authors have tried to develop an approach to the decade that is without undue bias, though it may take another generation before the decade is seen clearly.

Comments and Suggestions

We welcome your comments on *The Sixties in America: Biographies* and suggestions for other topics to consider. Please write: Editors, *The Sixties in America: Biographies,* U•X•L, 27500 Drake Rd. Farmington Hills, MI 48331-3535; call toll free: 1-800-877-4253; fax to (248) 699-8097; or send e-mail via http://www.gale.com.

Timeline

1960 Dolores Huerta and César Chávez form the United Farm Workers of America (UFW), an agricultural workers labor union.

1960 Berry Gordy founds the Motown Record Corporation in Detroit, Michigan. Motown goes on to become the most successful black-owned music business in history.

1960 Barry Goldwater publishes *The Conscience of a Conservative,* announcing his conservative political views.

January 4, 1960 The United Steel Workers agree on a settlement to end the longest steel strike in U.S. history. The strike had started in July 1959.

February 1, 1960 Four black students request service at a whites-only lunch counter at a Woolworth's store in Greensboro, North Carolina. They politely begin a "sit-in" to protest not being served. Their nonviolent protest sparks a new form of civil rights protest that quickly spreads throughout the American South.

May 1960 The oral contraceptive pill, known as "the pill," is approved for distribution throughout the United States.

May 6, 1960 The Civil Rights Act of 1960 is approved to protect black voting rights. However, the law's loopholes make it very difficult for blacks to register or to vote.

May 10, 1960 Nashville, Tennessee, becomes the first large city to desegregate public places.

May 13, 1960 College students protesting the House Un-American Activities Committee hearing outside the San Francisco, California, city hall are dispersed by police who blast the protestors with fire hoses.

July 25, 1960 The first African American eats a meal at the Woolworth's lunch counter in Greensboro, North Carolina.

September 1960 The Young Americans for Freedom, a group of conservative activists, release a set of principles known as the "Sharon Statement." This is considered the founding document on the modern conservative movement.

Fall 1960 Democrat John F. Kennedy and Republican Richard M. Nixon engage in a series of televised presidential debates, the first such debates to air on national television.

1961 Tom and Dick Smothers—known as the Smothers Brothers—release their first album, *At the Purple Onion,* which favors folk songs over the comedy for which they would later become famous.

January 3, 1961 The United States severs diplomatic ties with Cuba.

January 20, 1961 In his inaugural speech as president, John F. Kennedy urges Americans to "Ask not what your country can do for you—ask what you can do for your country." Kennedy takes office with Lyndon B. Johnson as vice president.

January 31, 1961 The United States launches a chimpanzee into space in a test flight of Project Mercury, a space mission of the National Aeronautics and Space Administration (NASA).

February 17-23, 1961 A six-day airline strike grounds flights by American, Eastern, Flying Tiger, National, and TWA airlines.

March 20, 1961 Louisiana's legislation enforcing segregation is deemed unconstitutional.

April 12-May 5, 1961 Two Soviet cosmonauts become the first men in space.

April 17, 1961 U.S.-supported Cuban exiles invade Cuba in the Bay of Pigs invasion. To the embarrassment of President Kennedy, they are defeated within three days.

May 4, 1961 Black and white civil rights activists begin their "freedom rides" to various southern cities in an attempt to end segregation in interstate transportation.

May 9, 1961 In a speech to the National Association of Broadcasters, Federal Communications Commission chairperson Newton Minow makes the famous statement that television is a "vast wasteland."

May 14, 1961 Ku Klux Klan members attack freedom riders and burn the riders' bus in Anniston, Alabama.

May 25, 1961 President Kennedy announces that the United States intends to land a man on the moon and return him safely, beginning the "space race" between the Soviets and Americans.

July 21, 1961 Astronaut Gus Grissom blasts off in the second American manned rocket flight, though he does not enter orbit.

August 13, 1961 East Germany begins construction of the Berlin Wall.

October 26-28, 1961 U.S. and Soviet tanks confront each other along the border of East and West Berlin.

November 3, 1961 U.S. government officials return from South Vietnam and suggest that decisive military action will lead to a quick victory.

December 1961 President Kennedy forms the Commission on the Status of Women to investigate barriers to women's full enjoyment of basic rights.

1962 Ken Kesey publishes *One Flew Over the Cuckoo's Nest*, which was partly written under the influence of hallucinogenic drugs.

1962 Folksinger Bob Dylan releases his first album.

1962 Harvard University psychology professor Timothy Leary takes his first dose of the hallucinogenic drug LSD and begins to conduct studies about the effects of the drug on volunteers, including Harvard students.

1962 Newsman Walter Cronkite begins his job as anchorman for the *CBS Evening News,* a position he holds until 1981.

1962 Nationally distributed *Harper's Bazaar* magazine includes a full-page color advertisement featuring a nude model, making nudity in advertising a subject of national discussion.

1962 Scientist Rachel Carson publishes *Silent Spring,* which is credited with giving birth to the modern environmental movement.

January 12, 1962 The U.S. State Department denies Americans who are members of the Communist Party the ability to travel abroad.

February 20, 1962 U.S. astronaut John Glenn is the first American to orbit the Earth; all three television networks cover the event.

February 26, 1962 The Supreme Court rules that segregation in interstate and intrastate transportation is unconstitutional.

June 1962 The Students for a Democratic Society (SDS) issues the "Port Huron Statement," a manifesto for the emerging New Left student movement.

June 25, 1962 The Supreme Court ruling in *Engel v. Vitale* holds that prayer in schools is unconstitutional.

July 8, 1962 The U.S. government initiates a study on the impact of television on young children.

July 9-August 1, 1962 Artist Andy Warhol exhibits a series of paintings of Campbell's soup cans at the Ferus Gallery in Los Angeles, California.

July 26, 1962 The public schools in Prince Edward County, Virginia, are opened by federal order after being closed for three years in an attempt to avoid desegregation. The schools remain closed on appeal, however, and the case is sent to the U.S. Supreme Court.

August 7, 1962 Food and Drug Administration (FDA) medical officer Frances Oldham Kelsey receives the President's Award for Distinguished Federal Civilian Service for her work in banning the drug thalidomide. Her work led to a law requiring that drug manufacturers prove that their drugs are safe for human use.

October 1962 President Kennedy faces off with Soviet Premier Nikita Khrushchev over the Soviets' placement of long-range missiles on the island nation of Cuba, eventually forcing the removal of the missiles.

October 1, 1962 James Meredith becomes the first black student to enroll at the University of Mississippi. The event sparks fifteen hours of rioting, leaving two dead. He had been blocked from enrollment by Mississippi governor Ross Barnett on September 24, by Lt. Governor Paul Johnson on September 26, and by riots on campus on September 30.

1963 Harvard professor Timothy Leary is fired from his job after he conducts a series of experiments with LSD. He travels to California to continue his experiments with the drug and becomes a kind of guru to hippie drug users.

1963 Betty Friedan publishes *The Feminine Mystique,* a major book on the role of women in U.S. society.

January 14, 1963 In his inaugural speech as governor of Alabama, George Wallace declares his support for "segregation now, segregation tomorrow, segregation forever!"

January 26, 1963 A New York City newspaper strike ends after 114 days with lost revenues of $100 million. It becomes the costliest newspaper strike in history.

January 28, 1963 The first black student enrolls at Clemson College in South Carolina—without incident.

April 2, 1963 The Rev. Dr. Martin Luther King Jr. and the Southern Christian Leadership Conference begin efforts to desegregate the city of Birmingham, Alabama.

June 11, 1963 Alabama Governor George Wallace blocks the steps of the University of Alabama to prevent the enrollment of two black students. However, a court order secures the enrollment of the students.

June 17, 1963 In the case of *Murray v. Curlett,* the U.S. Supreme Court issues a definitive ruling against prayer in public schools. The case launched the career of Madalyn Murray O'Hair, who became America's most vocal atheist activist.

June 26, 1963 President John F. Kennedy pledges that the United States will help West Germany resist communism, proclaiming "Ich bin ein Berliner" (I am a Berliner).

July 16, 1963 Barry Goldwater accepts the Republican presidential nomination, announcing that "extremism in the defense of liberty is no vice."

August 18, 1963 James Meredith becomes the first black to graduate from the University of Mississippi with a bachelor's degree.

August 28, 1963 At the March on Washington for Jobs and Freedom, attended by more than 100,000 supporters of the civil rights movement, the Rev. Dr. Martin Luther King Jr. delivers his "I Have a Dream" speech.

September 13, 1963 Mary Kay Ash forms Beauty by Mary Kay, one of the first woman-owned direct sales organizations in the United States.

September 15, 1963 Four young black girls are murdered when a bomb explodes under the steps of the Sixteenth Street Baptist Church in Birmingham, Alabama.

November 1, 1963 South Vietnamese president Ngo Dinh Diem is killed in a U.S.-backed coup.

November 22, 1963 President John F. Kennedy is assassinated in Dallas, Texas. Lyndon B. Johnson is sworn in as president.

December 16, 1963 President Lyndon B. Johnson signs an aid-to-higher-education bill into law as a "monument to President Kennedy."

1964 Ken Kesey and a group of friends calling themselves the Merry Pranksters cross the United States on a bus trip, introducing the nation to the first hippies. Tom Wolfe later chronicles this bus trip in his novel *The Electric Kool-Aid Acid Test.*

January 8, 1964 President Johnson declares a "War on Poverty."

February 1964 The Beatles begin their first U.S. concert tour.

February 1964 Boxer Cassius Clay defeats Sonny Liston to become world heavyweight champion. The next day he publicly changes his name, first to Muhammad X and then to Muhammad Ali. He also embraces the Nation of Islam as his religion.

March 1964 Black activist Malcolm X breaks with the Nation of Islam, a black separatist group, and begins his own group, the Organization of Afro-American Unity. The new association promotes peaceful coexistence between whites and blacks as well as equal rights for blacks.

May 25, 1964 The U.S. Supreme Court holds that the Prince Edward County, Virginia, schools must open.

June 1964 Three civil rights workers are killed during the voter-registration drive called "freedom summer" in Mississippi.

June 19, 1964 *Life* magazine runs a story calling atheist activist Madalyn Murray O'Hair "the most hated woman in America."

July 2, 1964 President Johnson signs the Civil Rights Act of 1964 into law.

July 18, 1964 Riots break out in the black neighborhoods of New York City.

August 3, 1964 North Vietnamese patrol boats attack U.S. ships in the Gulf of Tonkin.

August 7, 1964 The U.S. Congress passes the Tonkin Gulf Resolution, granting President Lyndon B. Johnson congressional approval to wage war in Vietnam.

August 30, 1964 President Johnson signs the Equal Opportunity Act, which provides $950 million for anti-poverty programs, small-business loans, and youth programs, and also forms the Job Corps.

September 1964 The Warren Commission issues a report declaring that Lee Harvey Oswald acted alone in the assassination of John F. Kennedy.

October 12, 1964 The first space flight with more than one man is launched by the Soviet Union.

December 3, 1964 Nearly eight hundred students sitting in at the administration building of the University of California, Berkeley, are arrested.

December 10, 1964 The Rev. Dr. Martin Luther King Jr. is awarded the Nobel Peace Prize for his work promoting equal rights for all Americans.

1965 Folksinger Bob Dylan upsets audiences at the Newport (Rhode Island) Folk Festival when he plays his songs with electric instruments.

1965 The rock band the Grateful Dead forms in San Francisco, California.

1965 *The Smothers Brothers Show,* featuring singer/comedians Tom and Dick Smothers, debuts on CBS.

1965 Consumer advocate Ralph Nader publishes *Unsafe at Any Speed: The Designed-in Dangers of the American Automobile.* The book launched his career as a champion of consumer issues.

January 25, 1965 The federal budget contains the largest increase in welfare and education spending since President Franklin Delano Roosevelt's New Deal of the 1930s.

February 8, 1965 The Soviet Union commits military support to the North Vietnamese.

February 21, 1965 Black leader Malcolm X is shot and killed after delivering a speech in Harlem, New York.

March 2, 1965 U.S. bombing campaigns begin over North Vietnam.

March 7, 1965 Civil rights activists, marching from Selma to Montgomery, Alabama, to protest the lack of voting rights for blacks, are attacked by Alabama state police.

March 8, 1965 The first U.S. combat troops leave for Vietnam; earlier on-ground personnel were advisers or other support personnel.

March 18, 1965 Soviet cosmonaut Aleksei Leonev walks in space for ten minutes.

March 25, 1965 Twenty-five thousand civil rights activists gather in Montgomery, Alabama.

April 17, 1965 The first mass protest against the Vietnam War is organized by Students for a Democratic Society and attracts more than 15,000 protestors to Washington, D.C.

April 25, 1965 The United States confirms that North Vietnamese troops are fighting within South Vietnam.

June 5, 1965 U.S. officials announce the active engagement of U.S. troops in combat in Vietnam.

June 18, 1965 Nguyen Cao Cy becomes South Vietnamese premier.

June 28, 1965 President Johnson increases the military draft from 17,000 to 35,000 men per month.

July 17, 1965 The first close-up photos of Mars taken in space are sent to Earth by U.S. spacecraft *Mariner 4.*

July 28, 1965 125,000 U.S. troops are committed to the fight in Vietnam.

August 6, 1965 President Johnson signs the Voting Rights Act of 1965 into law.

August 11-16, 1965 The Watts section of Los Angeles, California, erupts in riots that kill thirty-five people and damage $200 million in property.

September 16, 1965 Labor leader Dolores Huerta helps organize a strike of 5,000 United Farm Workers of America (UFW) farmworkers in Delano, California. The strike ends in 1970—following a two-year national boycott of grapes—with the recognition of the labor union.

October 15, 1965 Protests against the war in Vietnam spread to forty U.S. cities.

November 27, 1965 25,000 antiwar demonstrators converge on Washington, D.C.

December 20, 1965 U.S. field commanders pursue enemy troops into Cambodia, which borders South Vietnam.

December 21, 1965 The Soviet Union announces increased support for North Vietnam.

1966 The National Organization for Women (NOW), a political action group formed to win equal rights for women, is founded with author Betty Friedan as its first president.

1966 The Student Non-Violent Coordinating Committee (SNCC) changes its official policy from integration to separatism, changes its name to the Student National Coordinating Committee, and expels all whites from its organization.

January 1966 In the Haight-Ashbury neighborhood of San Francisco, California, a group of young people organize the Trips Festival, which is widely seen as the start of the hippie movement. Within months, Haight-Ashbury becomes the center of this loosely based youth movement.

February 3, 1966 The unmanned Soviet spacecraft, *Luna 9,* makes the first landing on the moon.

February 4, 1966 Televised congressional hearings on U.S. policy regarding the Vietnam War begin.

March 16, 1966 With *Gemini 8,* U.S. astronauts Neil Armstrong and David Scott perform the first space docking of an orbiting spacecraft.

April 3, 1966 The unmanned Soviet spacecraft, *Luna 10,* becomes the first man-made object to orbit the moon.

April 6, 1966 The National Farm Workers Union, headed by César Chávez, is recognized as the bargaining agent for farmworkers at Schenley Industries after nearly a year-long strike.

May 12, 1966 To protest the University of Chicago's cooperation with the military draft, students stage a sit-in at the administration building.

May 15, 1966 10,000 antiwar demonstrators picket the White House.

July 1, 1966 The first U.S. health-insurance plan for the elderly, Medicare, starts.

July 11, 1966 The Soviet Union refuses to send athletes to participate in the annual U.S.-Soviet track meet because of U.S. policy in Vietnam.

July 12, 1966 Riots erupt in Chicago, Illinois, and occur in twenty other cities during the summer.

August 30, 1966 Communist China agrees to send aid to North Vietnam.

September 1966 In a famous *Playboy* magazine interview, LSD advocate Timothy Leary urges Americans to "turn on, tune in [and] drop out."

September 1, 1966 French President Charles de Gaulle asks the United States to withdraw from Vietnam.

September 9, 1966 The Traffic Safety Act is signed by President Johnson. It enforces safety standards for automobiles.

October 1966 Huey P. Newton and Bobby Seale establish the Black Panthers, a militant black nationalist group.

1967 College student protests of the Vietnam War and the draft increase throughout the country.

1967 The Summer of Love begins when more than 75,000 young people migrate to San Francisco's Haight-Ashbury district with the hope of building a new society based on peace, "free love," and drugs. During the summer, bad drug experiences, crime, rape, and violence escalate in the district. The summer ends with a march proclaiming the death of the hippie movement.

1967 The North Vietnamese release three American prisoners into the custody of antiwar activist Tom Hayden, who has twice visited the country.

1967 The Maharishi Mahesh Yogi begins a world tour to promote his religious philosophy and the practice of transcendental meditation. Among his followers are the rock band The Beatles, philosopher Marshall McLuhan, and football star Joe Namath.

1967 *The Smothers Brothers Comedy Hour,* a variety program airing on CBS, becomes very controversial when its stars take an antiwar stance. Ultimately, the show is cancelled in 1969 when the brothers' satire grows too fierce.

1967 The use of LSD is made illegal nationwide.

January 15, 1967 Led by fiery coach Vince Lombardi, the Green Bay Packers win the National Football League's inaugural (first) Super Bowl.

January 27, 1967 Gus Grissom, Edward White, and Roger Chaffee are killed aboard the rocket *Apollo 1* after a fire on the launch pad.

April, 1967 Large antiwar protests occur in San Francisco and New York City.

April 1967 Boxer Muhammad Ali refuses induction into the U.S. military and, as a result, is stripped of his heavyweight crown.

May 13, 1967 New York City hosts a pro-Vietnam War parade that attracts 70,000 people.

June 23-25, 1967 In Glassboro, New Jersey, Soviet Premier Aleksei Kosygin and U.S. President Johnson discuss nuclear arms control, Vietnam, and the Middle East.

July 12, 1967 Riots break out in Newark, New Jersey.

July 23, 1967 Riots in Detroit, Michigan, kill forty-three people and damage $200 million in property; the National Guard is called in to restore order.

August 3, 1967 President Johnson announces plans to send 45,000 to 50,000 additional troops to Vietnam in order to raise troop strength to 525,000 by the end of 1968.

October 21-22, 1967 More than 250,000 people organized by the National Mobilization to End the War in Vietnam (MOBE) gather to protest the Vietnam War in Washington, D.C. The protest ends in a lighthearted attempt, led by activist Abbie Hoffmann, to levitate the Pentagon.

January 25, 1968 Secretary of Health, Education, and Welfare John Gardner's doubts about the "Great Society" lead him to resign.

January 31, 1968 The North Vietnamese army launches the Tet Offensive, a major military campaign against South Vietnamese and American forces in South Vietnam.

February 6, 1968 Sweden grants asylum to six American soldiers opposed to the war in Vietnam.

February 27, 1968 News anchor Walter Cronkite announces on national television that he believes the war in Vietnam has become a stalemate (a situation in which further action is blocked).

March 8, 1968 The first statewide teacher's strike in U.S. history ends after almost half of Florida's public-school teachers spend more than two weeks on picket lines.

March 16, 1968 The My Lai massacre leaves hundreds of South Vietnamese men, women, and children dead at the hands of U.S. soldiers. (Reports of the deaths are suppressed for more than a year.)

March 31, 1968 President Johnson announces that he will not seek reelection as president of the United States.

April 4, 1968 Civil rights leader Rev. Dr. Martin Luther King Jr. is assassinated in Memphis, Tennessee.

May 6-30, 1968 Student demonstrations in Paris, France, spark a general strike throughout the country that eventually involves 10 million workers.

May 12, 1968 Peace talks to end the Vietnam War begin in Paris.

June 3, 1968 Artist Andy Warhol is wounded by gunshots fired by one of his "superstars," Valerie Solanis.

June 5, 1968 Democratic presidential candidate Robert Kennedy is assassinated in Los Angeles shortly after winning the California primary.

August 26-29, 1968 At the Democratic presidential nominating convention in Chicago, Illinois, Vice President Hubert Humphrey secures the party's nomination. Protests rage, both inside and outside the convention center, and police and National Guard forces attack and beat demonstrators on national television. A radical group known as the Yippies nominates a pig for president.

September 7, 1968 More than one hundred women's liberation protestors gather outside the Miss America Pageant proceedings to throw out bras, girdles, and high-heeled shoes to protest women's subordination to men in American society.

October 14-28, 1968 American 200-meter dash gold medalist Tommie Smith and bronze medalist John Carlos bow their heads and raise their fists in a Black Power salute during the playing of the "Star-Spangled Banner" at the Olympic Games in Mexico. As a result, they are stripped of their medals and suspended from their team.

November 5, 1968 Republican Richard M. Nixon is elected president, defeating Democrat Hubert Humphrey and independent candidate George Wallace.

December 4, 1968 The U.S. government enforces the 1964 Civil Rights Act in the North by ordering the public schools in Union, New Jersey, to comply with desegregation.

December 21, 1968 With *Apollo 8,* the United States becomes the first to orbit a manned spacecraft around the Moon.

1969 The "Great Society" programs give educational aid to 9 million children from low-income families, offer Head Start primary care to 716,000, and support the vocational education of 4 million high school and 845,000 technical students.

1969 President Nixon continues negotiations to end the Vietnam War.

1969 The Supreme Court orders the immediate desegregation of all public schools.

1969 Betty Friedan becomes a founding member of the National Abortion and Reproductive Rights Action League (NARAL), a major women's rights organization.

June 8, 1969 President Nixon orders the removal of 25,000 American troops from Vietnam, thus beginning the American withdrawal from the war.

June 18-22, 1969 The Students for a Democratic Society holds its national convention, which concludes with the organization breaking up into the Progressive Labor Party and the Revolutionary Youth Movement (RYM).

June 27, 1969 Homosexuals and police clash at the Stonewall Inn in New York following a police raid on the bar; the Stonewall riot is the symbolic start of the gay liberation movement.

July 20, 1969 The United States lands the first manned spacecraft, *Apollo 11,* on the Moon. Neil Armstrong and Edwin "Buzz" Aldrin walk on the Moon's surface.

August 1969 Members of the Manson Family, a cult led by Charles Manson, murder seven people outside Los Angeles, California.

August 15-17, 1969 The Woodstock Music Festival is held in upstate New York, drawing more than 500,000 music lovers.

September 3, 1969 North Vietnamese president Ho Chi Minh dies at age seventy-nine.

October 15, 1969 Various antiwar groups label this day "Moratorium Day" and organize hundreds of thousands of marchers in protests across the United States.

November 15, 1969 250,000 antiwar demonstrators march on Washington, D.C.

November 21, 1969 A group of Native American activists, led by Richard Oakes, takes possession of Alcatraz Island in the bay near San Francisco, California. The event marks one of the most dramatic moments in the growing Native American rights movement.

1973 Following the landmark decision by the U.S. Supreme Court in *Roe v. Wade,* abortion is legalized in the United States. For many involved in the struggle for women's rights, particularly women's reproductive rights, this is a major victory for their cause.

April 23, 1975 President Gerald Ford, who succeeded Richard Nixon, announces that the war in Vietnam is "finished."

April 30, 1975 The South Vietnamese surrender to officially end the war in Vietnam.

January 21, 1977 President Jimmy Carter fulfills his campaign promise to pardon those who had peacefully avoided the draft during the Vietnam War. This allowed draft dodgers, who had fled the country to avoid mandatory military service, to return home to the United States without fear of being prosecuted for their actions.

1980 The conservative movement, begun under Senator Barry Goldwater, shows its strength as Republican

Ronald Reagan soundly defeats incumbent president Jimmy Carter in the presidential election.

December 8, 1980 John Lennon, singer, guitarist, songwriter, and former member of the legendary band The Beatles, is shot to death by a demented fan outside his home in New York City.

March 6, 1981 Walter Cronkite leaves his post as anchor of the *CBS Evening News* after nineteen years.

1982 The Equal Rights Amendment, which states that equal legal rights cannot be denied based on gender, fails to be ratified. Although the amendment passed in both the House and Senate in 1972, it needed to be ratified by three-fourths (thirty-eight) of the states before it could become part of the U.S. Constitution. The ERA fell three states short of ratification by its deadline in 1982. President Ronald Reagan was among those opposed to the amendment; earlier, he became the first major presidential candidate to voice his opposition to the ERA.

November 13, 1982 The Vietnam Veterans Memorial, also known as "The Wall," is dedicated in Washington, D.C. Designed by twenty-one-year-old artist/architect Maya Lin, the memorial records the names of the more than 58,000 American men and women who did not return from the war.

1984 Vietnam veteran John Kerry, who testified before Congress in April 1971 in an effort to end American involvement in the war, is elected to the U.S. Senate.

1991 The communist government of the Soviet Union collapses, thus ending the Cold War between the United States and the Soviet Union.

1992 Antiwar activist Tom Hayden is elected to the state senate in California.

1996 Muhammad Ali lights the torch signaling the start of the Summer Olympic Games in Atlanta, Georgia.

May 31, 1996 LSD advocate Timothy Leary dies from prostate cancer. Viewing his death as "the ultimate trip," he asks friends to document his passing on video. Leary's final words were reported to be "Why not? Why not? Why not?"

2000 Consumer advocate Ralph Nader runs for president of the United States on the Green Party ticket, receiving almost three percent of the vote. Some political observers believe that Nader's candidacy took votes away from Democratic candidate Al Gore, who ultimately lost the election to Republican George W. Bush.

November 2000 The first crew takes up residence on the International Space Station, a joint effort by the Canadian, European, Japanese, Brazilian, Russian, and U.S. space agencies. The crew consists of two Russians and one American.

August 2003 On August 20, Alabama Chief Justice Roy Moore refuses to abide by a U.S. District Court order to remove a Ten Commandments monument from the state's judicial building. The U.S. District Court had ruled that the monument violated the separation of church and state. On August 27, workers remove the monument from public view. Later, Moore loses his job for refusing to comply with the court order. The monument itself begins a tour of U.S. cities in mid-2004.

2004 Twin robots, part of NASA's Mars Exploration Rover program, transmit photos to scientists back on Earth as the agency studies the geology of the red planet.

2004 Senator John Kerry runs for president against incumbent George W. Bush.

August 2004 Interest in American women athletes soars during the Summer Olympic Games in Athens, Greece. U.S. women win gold medals in basketball, beach volleyball, gymnastics, softball, swimming, track, and other sports.

Words to Know

A

activist: A person who campaigns vigorously for or against a political, social, or economic issue.

authentic: True to one's spirit or character. In the 1960s, the idea of being authentic was important to many young people because they considered the behavior of their parents to be inauthentic or something that compromised their own values.

B

black nationalism: An ideology held among militant groups of American blacks that called for the formation of self-governing black communities that were separate from those of whites.

Black Power: A movement among American blacks to gain economic and political rights and improve their social condition.

C

civil rights: The legal, political, and human rights guaranteed by the U.S. constitution and various legislative acts, including the right to vote, the right to equal protection under the law, the right to equal use of public facilities, and the right to freedom of speech.

Cold War: A prolonged conflict for world dominance from 1945 to 1991 between the two superpowers, the democratic, capitalist United States and the communist Soviet Union. The weapons of conflict were commonly words of propaganda and threats, not military conflicts.

communal living: A shared living space formed by a group of like-minded individuals. Those living in communes work together for the common good of the group and share material possessions.

communism: A political system in which most aspects of social and economic life are dictated by the government. Under communism, all property is owned by the government and, theoretically, wealth is distributed evenly throughout society.

conservatism: A political ideology based on the concept of a limited federal government, one that protects individual's freedoms by maintaining domestic order, providing for national defense, and administering justice. This ideology is generally opposed to the use of federal powers for the protection or preservation of civil rights.

counterculture: Literally, a cultural group whose values run counter to the majority. In the late 1950s and through the 1960s, several distinct groups criticized developments in American society and worked for social change. Some historians use the term to refer only to hippies, but the counterculture also included groups such as the New Left and racial and ethnic political action groups.

D

democracy: A political system that places the power of the government in the hands of citizens. During the Cold

War, democracy was generally considered to include a capitalist economic system, in which individual property owners made the decisions that determined economic activities.

desegregation: To end the practice of separating races, as in schools, buses, restaurants, or other public facilities.

discrimination: The singling out of minority groups for unfavorable treatment.

draft (selective service): A system by which persons are chosen for mandatory service in a nation's military.

draft dodgers: Persons who hide in or flee from a country in order to avoid mandatory military service.

drop out: To reject the social and economic norms of society by living an alternative lifestyle.

E

establishment: A term used by members of the counterculture to refer to the established power structures and authority figures of the time, including parents, employers, and the government.

F

feminism: A theory and organized social movement based on the idea that male and female genders are socially, politically, and economically equal.

G

grassroots: An effort formed by ordinary people at a local community level.

Great Society: The social vision of President Lyndon B. Johnson that would use the federal government to improve the American quality of life. This would be achieved by enacting legislation to regulate air and water quality, to offer medical care, to provide civil rights, to enforce safety issues with regard to citizens and industry, and to support the arts and humanities, among other things.

H

hallucinogenic: A drug that disrupts the nervous system to produce perceptions of objects or sounds without regard to reality.

hippies: People, usually young, who rejected the established customs of society by engaging in such activities as taking drugs, living in communal societies, dressing in unconventional ways, and wearing their hair in long, flowing styles. Some historians refer to hippies as "the counterculture."

I

integration: A social plan in the United States to involve African Americans as equals in white society, especially in areas where the races were formerly separated or segregated.

L

liberalism: A political ideology based on the concept of a federal government that protects individual's freedoms by maintaining domestic order, providing for national defense, and administering justice, but also protects and preserves civil rights of citizens by maintaining programs to aid certain social groups.

LSD (lysergic acid diethylamide): A hallucinogenic drug that disrupts the normal functioning of the nervous system to cause a loss of connection to reality.

P

prejudice: A negative opinion or attitude about a person, race, or group of people that is not based on fact or one's experiences with such people or groups. Instead, such opinions are based on unfounded ideas about how that person, race, or group might be or act.

protest: An organized public demonstration of discontent with the governance of or social circumstances within a society.

psychedelic: Often used as a descriptor relating to a drug that causes hallucinogenic effects, such as the perception of distorted sounds or images. As an adjective, psychedelic is used to describe music and art associated with the hippie movement.

R

radical: Someone who supports an extreme political cause.

riot: A violent, public disturbance by a disorderly group of people.

S

segregation: The separation of social groups based on racial differences. Segregation was legally mandated in some southern states and culturally practiced in some northern states. Segregation was practiced on buses and trains as well as in schools, concert halls, restaurants, and other areas. In some places, bathrooms and water fountains were designated "whites only" or "coloreds only."

sexual revolution: A period in which sexual practices, sexual orientation, and sexual issues—such as public displays of nudity, unmarried couples living together, homosexuality, and abortion—became more openly discussed and accepted.

Space Race: A competition between the United States and the Soviet Union to build space programs that launched rockets and men outside the Earth's orbit. One of the chief objectives of the Space Race was to land a man on the Moon.

U

Uncle Tom: A derogatory term used to refer to a black person who acts in submissive ways toward whites.

V

Vietcong: Guerilla forces in South Vietnam who allied themselves with the North Vietnamese Army in an effort to unify the country under communist rule. The Vietcong fought the U.S. forces that came to aid South Vietnam in its quest to remain independent. Guerilla forces are those involved in unconventional warfare practices, including sabotage and terrorist activities.

W

War on Poverty: The central program of President Lyndon B. Johnson's "Great Society," this effort tried to end poverty by providing poor Americans with education, job training, food, housing, and money.

welfare: Government aid to the needy in the form of money or other necessities, such as foodstuffs or housing.

The Sixties in America

Biographies

Muhammad Ali

Born January 17, 1942
Louisville, Kentucky

Boxer

Muhammad Ali was one of the best athletes of the twentieth century. On three occasions he won the world heavyweight boxing championship. But he is as equally renowned for two controversial decisions that transcend sports. First, in 1964, just after he earned his first boxing title, he announced that he had left the Christian faith to join the Nation of Islam. Three years later, as American involvement in the Vietnam War (1954–75) was rapidly increasing, he refused induction into the U.S. military, citing his religious beliefs. Although Ali was first and foremost a boxer, his commitment to seeking out a meaningful religious identification and engaging in political protest helped make him a symbol for the changes that swept American society in the 1960s.

"[Muhammad] Ali had brought beauty and grace to the most uncompromising of sports.... [T]hrough the wonderful excesses of skill and character, he had become the most famous athlete, indeed, the best-known personage in the world."

—*George Plimpton, quoted in* Time, *June 14, 1999.*

Birth of a boxer

Muhammad Ali was born Cassius Marcellus Clay Jr. on January 17, 1942, in Louisville, Kentucky. His attraction to boxing was sparked when he was twelve years old. Learning that his bicycle had been stolen, he angrily announced that he

Muhammad Ali. *AP/Wide World Photos. Reproduced by permission.*

An Olympic Champ Encounters Racism

Returning to Louisville after representing the United States at the 1960 Olympic Games in Rome, Cassius Clay proudly wore his gold medal for all to see. At the time, segregation—separation of people according to race—still ruled the American South. African Americans were forced to use substandard facilities in all aspects of public life, from restaurants to restrooms. Despite the honor he had brought his country, the young boxer remained a second-class citizen solely because of the color of his skin.

One evening, the young Olympic champion entered a downtown Louisville five-and-dime store to purchase a hamburger and soda. As he attempted to place his order, he was told by the waitress that the store did not "serve coloreds." Clay was shocked and saddened. He walked to a nearby bridge, ripped off the medal that he wore around his neck, and tossed it into the Ohio River.

Cassius Clay (on platform one) receives a gold medal at the 1960 Olympics in Rome, Italy. Among those competing were Z. Pietrzykowski of Poland (right), Tony Madigan of Australia (left), and Giulio Saraudi of Italy (far left). *AP/Wide World Photos. Reproduced by permission.*

would catch and fight the thief. In order to do so, he would first have to learn how to fight. The youngster immediately began doing just that, working out with Joe Martin, a Louisville police officer. He also became skilled in the art and science of boxing under the expertise of Fred Stoner, a trainer. Shortly thereafter, Clay fought and won his first amateur bout.

Throughout his youth, Clay did little more than train, box, and dream about launching a professional career and winning a world championship. During this period he fought 116 amateur bouts and was the winner in 108 of them. His natural athletic ability coupled with his rigid training earned him two Amateur Athletic Union championships, six state Golden Gloves titles, and two national Golden Gloves titles.

When he was eighteen, Clay won a gold medal at the 1960 Olympic Games, which were held in Rome, Italy. Then he turned professional. He won his first pro fight a month later, defeating Tunney Hunsaker in his hometown.

The Louisville Sponsoring Group, which then managed Clay, linked him up with Angelo Dundee (1921–), an experienced and respected trainer. Under Dundee's guidance, Clay, who stood 6 feet 3 inches tall and weighed 190 pounds, further developed as a fighter. The veteran trainer taught the young boxer to use his speed and powerful lower body to his best advantage. He remained in the boxer's corner for the next twenty-one years.

Early in his career, Clay chose not to throw punches to his opponent's body while in the ring. He wanted to avoid getting too close to the other boxer. Instead, he used his legs to glide around the ring, daring an opponent to go on the offensive. Then, at the most opportune moment, when his opponent was unprotected, Clay delivered his own punches. He also developed a foot movement that came to be known as the "Ali Shuffle." Here, the boxer rapidly moved his feet and rose off the ground, making him an even more hard-to-hit target. While on the move, he even occasionally threw a punch.

Another factor separated Clay from other boxers: he was as much a showman as an athlete. Plus, he possessed a gift for grabbing headlines by cleverly taunting his opponents. His mouth was constantly in motion as he teased his rivals, and he often predicted the round in which he would knock them out. "I'm so fast that last night I turned off the light switch in my hotel room and was in bed before the room was dark," he once bragged, as quoted in Walter Dean Myers's *The Greatest*. On another occasion he quipped, "If you even dream of beating me you'd better wake up and apologize." He dubbed himself "The Greatest" and fearlessly mocked opponents by name. He declared that "[Joe] Frazier is so ugly he should donate his face to the U.S. Bureau of Wild Life." He once said: "Now you see me, now you don't. George [Foreman] thinks he will, but I know he won't!" Many of his quips rhymed. One of his most celebrated was: "Float like a butterfly. Sting like a bee. Your hands can't hit what your eyes can't see."

The new heavyweight champ

Cassius Clay, as he still was called, came to the forefront of boxing in the early 1960s when interest in the sport was declining. His talents in the ring, combined with his flair for self-promotion, helped revive the sport. Of his taunts, he noted that he was not boasting if he could prove what he said was true. The boxer did make good on his predictions by piling victory upon victory. In February 1964, he became World Heavyweight Champion by upsetting a tough opponent, Sonny Liston (c. 1932–1970), in Miami, Florida. Before the bout, many boxing journalists rejected Clay, the underdog, as little more than a braggart. He responded to them, after defeating Liston, telling them to "eat" their words because he was the greatest.

The day after his victory, the brash young champ further shocked boxing and non-boxing fans with an announcement. He revealed that he had joined the Nation of Islam, a black militant and separatist movement loosely based on the Islamic religion. After that, he no longer wanted to be called Cassius Clay. Instead, his new name would be Cassius X. The "X" represented the long-forgotten African name that slave owners had stripped from his ancestors centuries earlier. Soon afterward he changed his name again, this time to Muhammad Ali. "Cassius Clay is a slave name," he declared, according to Ali's autobiography, *The Greatest: My Own Story*. "I didn't choose it, and I didn't want it. I am Muhammad Ali, a free name—it means beloved of God—and I insist people use it when speaking to me and of me."

The response to Ali's decision was swift and negative. His popularity plunged. Ali's reaction was equally forceful. "I am America," Ali announced, as noted in his autobiography. "I am the part you won't recognize, but get used to me. Black, confident, cocky—my name, not yours. My religion, not yours. My goals, my own. Get used to me." Many chose not to get used to him and insisted on referring to Ali by his birth name. One was Ernie Terrell, a boxer who challenged Ali in the ring. "What's my name, fool? What's my name?" Ali shouted at Terrell while beating him in a 1967 bout.

A controversial refusal

Controversy aside, Ali kept fighting during the mid-1960s, successfully defending his title. He beat Liston in a

1965 rematch, scoring a first-round knockout. Later that year, he pummeled Floyd Patterson (1935–), another ex-heavyweight champ. Then in 1967, as President **Lyndon B. Johnson** (1908–1973; served 1963–69) escalated the war in Vietnam, Ali was drafted into the U.S. military. Ali decided to refuse induction, based on the fact that he was a practicing Muslim minister. He was also a conscientious objector, someone who refuses military service on moral or religious grounds. That April, Ali appeared at a Houston, Texas, military induction center. He was told to step forward three times. On each occasion, he declined. He was informed that his refusal was a felony, carrying a maximum punishment of five years in prison and a $10,000 fine. Still, he refused induction.

Ali added fuel to the hullabaloo with his much-publicized declaration that he had "no quarrel" with the Vietcong. The Vietcong were allies of the North Vietnamese army, which the U.S. military was fighting overseas. The resulting controversy led just about every municipality in the United States to revoke Ali's boxing license. In May 1967 a federal grand jury indicted him for draft evasion. He stood trial the following month. After discussing the case for just twenty-one minutes, the jury declared him guilty and the judge imposed the maximum penalty. Ali petitioned that the verdict be reversed, but a court of appeals supported his conviction. His March 1967 fight against Zora Folley was Ali's last for three-and-a-half years. His title as World Champion was taken from him, as was his passport; he was sentenced to five years in jail, though he was soon released as his case was appealed.

By 1970, however, the temper of America had radically changed. More and more citizens had begun to oppose the war in Vietnam. Public support for Ali strongly increased, and he was allowed to mount a comeback. He returned to the ring in October 1970, fighting and beating Jerry Quarry in Georgia, which had no state boxing commission. After defeating Oscar Bonavena, he battled Joe Frazier (1944–), an imposing adversary, in March 1971 at New York's Madison Square Garden. Both were undefeated heavyweights, and both received a then-record $2.5 million. Ali's long absence from boxing became a factor on that occasion, as he no longer could dance effectively around the ring. He was floored by a Frazier punch in the fifteenth round and lost the fight. It was his first professional defeat, after thirty-one victories. But Ali soon won a more significant battle. Three months after his defeat by Frazier, the U.S. Supreme Court tossed aside his conviction for draft evasion.

Inside the ropes again

Following the Supreme Court decision, Ali could concentrate solely on revitalizing his boxing career. Between July 1971 and January 1974, he won thirteen bouts (including a rematch with Frazier); his only loss came against Ken Norton. Then he was pitted against George Foreman (1948–), the reigning heavyweight champion. Their October 1974 bout came to be known as "The Rumble in the Jungle," after its location in the tropical jungle of Kinshasa, Zaire, Africa. Foreman already had easily beaten Norton and Frazier and surely would be a tough opponent.

While in training, Ali came up with a secret weapon, called "The Rope-a-Dope." It was a tactic in which Ali leaned on the ropes and covered his body while allowing Foreman to throw punches until he wore himself out. Then, at just the right moment, Ali would go on the offensive. After seven rounds of endlessly pounding Ali, Foreman was exhausted. In the eighth round, Ali knocked Foreman out. He had regained the heavyweight title.

Ali fought Frazier a third time in October 1975 in Manila, the Philippines, in what was billed as the "Thrilla in Manila." Ali emerged the winner. Boxing historians consider this one of the greatest bouts in boxing history. After six more victories, Ali lost his title in February 1978 in an upset against 1976 Olympic Gold Medal winner Leon Spinks, but he won it back in a rematch later that year. This victory made Ali the first boxer in history to become heavyweight champion on three different occasions.

Soon afterward, Ali announced his retirement. But the lure of earning additional millions caused him to return to boxing after a two-year layoff. After two more fights, both defeats (to Larry Holmes in 1980 and Trevor Berbick in 1981), Ali retired permanently with a record of fifty-six wins and five losses. Thirty-seven of his victories came by knockout.

A beloved figure

By the 1980s, the public perception of Ali had completely reversed. Back in the 1960s, he had been called a trai-

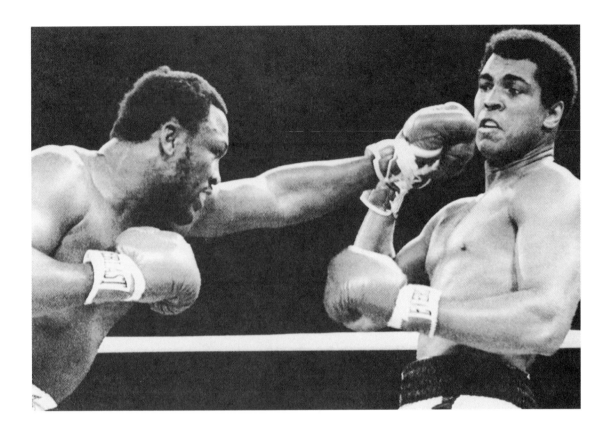

tor to his country and was seen by many as a dangerous symbol of black rage. In the 1980s, however, he was a heroic figure, universally loved and admired.

In retirement, Ali faced serious health issues. In 1982 he was treated for Parkinson's disease, a neurological disorder that severely hampered his ability to talk and move. More specifically, the affliction was diagnosed as Pugilistic Parkinsonism, a condition brought about by continuous trauma to the head. While this once-vibrant man was debilitated by illness, he still remained in the public eye, appearing at sports events and fundraisers. He was again in the international limelight during the 1996 Summer Olympics in Atlanta, Georgia, when he lit the torch that signaled the beginning of the games.

Once famed for spouting quotations in which he brashly and cleverly mocked opponents, Ali also has offered thoughts that are philosophical and humanistic. He has commented on such diverse subjects as poverty, spirituality, and

In the first round of their legendary bout in 1975, Joe Frazier throws a left punch at Ali, who later knocked him out in the fourteenth round to remain champion.
© Bettmann/Corbis.
Reproduced by permission.

racism. Of poverty, he stated: "Wars of nations are fought to change maps. But wars of poverty are fought to map change." His comments on spirituality include: "We have one life. It soon will be past. What we do for God is all that will last." He has also noted: "Rivers, ponds, lakes and streams—they all have different names, but they all contain water. Just as religions do—they all contain truths." And on racism, Ali observed: "Hating people because of their color is wrong. And it doesn't matter which color does the hating. It's just plain wrong." Ali's quotes appear on many Web sites, including *10KTruth*.

For More Information

Books

Ali, Muhammad, with Richard Durham. *The Greatest: My Own Story.* New York: Random House, 1975.

Brunt, Stephen. *Facing Ali.* Guilford, CT: Lyons Press, 2003.

Dennis, Felix, and Don Atyeo. *Muhammad Ali: The Glory Years.* New York: Miramax Books, 2003.

Myers, Walter Dean. *The Greatest: Muhammad Ali.* New York: Scholastic Press, 2001.

Schulman, Arlene. *Muhammad Ali.* Minneapolis, MN: Lerner, 2000.

Tessitore, John. *Muhammad Ali: The World's Champion.* New York: F. Watts, 1998.

Web Sites

Muhammad Ali. http://www.ali.com (accessed August 2004).

"Muhammad Ali: The Making of a Champ." *Courier-Journal.com.* http://www.courier-journal.com/ali (accessed August 2004).

Plimpton, George. "TIME 100: Muhammad Ali." *Time.com.* http://www.time.com/time/time100/heroes/profile/ali01.html (accessed August 2004).

"Quotes by Muhammad Ali." *10KTruth.* http://www.10ktruth.com/the_quotes/ali.htm (accessed August 2004).

Mary Kay Ash

Born May 12, c. 1917
Hot Wells, Texas

Died November 22, 2001
Dallas, Texas

Entrepreneur

Mary Kay Ash created a business empire in the 1960s when many women were just beginning to seek possibilities beyond that of being a wife and mother. In 1963 Betty Friedan's groundbreaking book *The Feminine Mystique* was published announcing women's discontent with only being homemakers. That same year, Ash started her company. Her mission was to enrich women's lives. Ash never lived the life of a suburban homemaker, but instead she worked from a very young age. She was a hard worker and fiercely competitive. Throughout her career, Ash was disappointed that her male co-workers made more money than she did for the same work. She was also concerned that her gender kept her from advancing at some companies. Just months after retiring from her twenty-five-year sales career in 1963, Ash launched a company that offered unlimited job opportunities to women. Mary Kay Cosmetics addressed the concerns of women who wanted to work from home and outside it. The company offered women familiar with the workplace a chance to become as successful as they wanted to be. For wives and mothers, Mary Kay Cosmetics offered the chance to balance family duties with the satisfaction of earning money.

"I wanted to provide an open-ended opportunity to women, to help them achieve anything they were smart enough to do. I didn't think it was fair for women to earn less than a man doing the same work. And I was tired of people telling me that I thought like a woman."

—*Mary Kay Ash.*

Mary Kay Ash. *AP/Wide World Photos. Reproduced by permission.*

Hard work from a young age

It is certain that Mary Kay Wagner was born on May 12 to Edward Alexander and Lula Vember Wagner in Hot Wells, Texas. But as Mary Kay gained celebrity, she closely guarded the year of her birth. She followed the popular convention of the time that "a lady never reveals her age." Various sources speculate that her birth year was as early as 1916 or as late as 1918.

As a young girl, Ash worked hard. While her mother spent fourteen-hour days managing a restaurant, Ash, at age six, was left to go to school, clean the house, cook dinner, and tend to her sick father. Her dad had contracted tuberculosis and was an invalid. Ash's mother offered her daughter constant encouragement. Even though some days Ash's only contact with her mother was over the telephone, she hung on her mother's words. "You can do it!" her mother would say. Ash believed her and found she was right. "Her words became the theme of my childhood," Ash remembered in *Female Firsts in Their Fields: Business and Industry.* "They stayed with me all my life." Ash found her mother so inspiring that she made her mother's saying the motto of Mary Kay Cosmetics.

Ash excelled in school, earning straight A's and winning competitions in debate, public speaking, and typing. She graduated from high school one year early with hopes of becoming a doctor. However, her family could not afford the college tuition. Unable to further her studies, Ash married instead. With her first husband, J. Ben Rogers, she eventually had three children.

Not content to be a stay-at-home mom

As a young wife and mother, Ash was not content to stay at home. She began part-time work in sales, first selling books door-to-door in the late 1930s. In 1939 she became a sales representative for Stanley Home Products. The company was a direct sales business that offered brooms, toothbrushes, and assorted home products. Her choice was unusual at a time when American culture placed a great deal of value on the family. Many women stayed at home after marriage to support their husbands even before children were born. Ash's husband soon joined the military as the United States became involved in World War II (1939–45). When Rogers returned from war duty in 1943, the couple divorced. Ash was left to raise her three children alone at a time when divorce and single motherhood were quite rare.

Though Ash had enrolled in some classes at the University of Houston in 1942, she dropped out within a year to pursue selling full-time. To learn more about selling, Ash attended a Stanley Home Products sales convention. There she saw the top sales representative crowned "Queen of Sales" and awarded an alligator purse. Ash determined that she would win the following year's prize. She started writing weekly goals for herself in soap on her bathroom mirror and scheduling three or more home demonstrations each day. She was honored as Stanley Home Products' top salesperson the next year but was disappointed to find her prize was a fisherman's underwater flashlight. Nevertheless, Ash continued to sell well for Stanley Home Products and became a manager.

By 1952 Ash took a job with World Gift Company, a supplier of home decorations. She was soon promoted to manager of the company's Houston operations and then to national training director. Ash married her second husband in 1960, but she continued to work. Throughout her career, Ash disliked making less than her male co-workers and having her ideas dismissed because of her gender. By 1963 she had grown tired of the unjust practices based on gender. That year she was transferred to a less important position, and a man she had trained was promoted above her at twice her salary. Frustrated, she quit World Gift supposedly to retire.

Started her own company

To Ash, retirement did not mean rest and relaxation. With twenty-five years of sales and management experience, Ash decided to write a book to help women navigate the business world. As she outlined her book ideas, she realized that she had a plan for a different kind of business. A deeply religious person, Ash had based her "dream" company on the Golden Rule from Matthew 7:12 of the Bible: "Do unto others as you would have them do unto you." The more she wrote, the more she realized that she could actually start such a company. She just needed a product to sell, preferably something that could be used up and reordered.

Years earlier, when Ash worked with Stanley Home Products, Ash had met Ova Heath Spoonemore, the daughter of a leather tanner. Noticing that her father's hands were very smooth and soft, Spoonemore experimented with leather tanning solutions to concoct a facial cream. Impressed with the cream, Ash had used it herself for years and bought the recipe. The cream became the base of her new company. She invested her life savings of $5,000 in setting up a Dallas storefront and a small manufacturing plant.

One month before Ash was set to launch her new company called Beauty by Mary Kay, her husband died suddenly of a heart attack. Both her lawyer and her accountant advised her to cancel her business plans. She ignored them and turned to her twenty-year-old son Richard Rogers for help. The two opened Beauty by Mary Kay on September 13, 1963, with nine of Ash's friends employed as "beauty consultants."

Ash's plan outlined a truly new kind of company. It was not the first company to sell goods door-to-door. Indeed, Ash had spent much of her career selling products in people's homes. Nor was it the first beauty products company—Elizabeth Arden, Helena Rubenstein, and Madame C. J. Walker had preceded her with similar products. But it was the first to provide women with unlimited opportunity for advancement. Ash hired "beauty consultants," not salespeople, to offer "classes" in clients' homes. These classes would be held for small groups of five or six people. This was unlike the large home "parties" of twenty-five or more people at which Ash had sold Stanley Home products. Ash reasoned that women would feel more comfortable learning about skin care at home with a small, intimate group of friends. The goal for each consultant was to instruct clients on how to cleanse their skin properly and how to apply makeup in order to flatter their appearance. By the end of the first year, Beauty by Mary Kay reported $198,000 in wholesale revenue.

The nine beauty consultants' enthusiasm for the business persuaded others to join. All a person needed to become a beauty consultant was $100 for a refundable start-up kit and a drive to succeed. Beauty consultants were their own bosses, setting their own goals and hours. The next year company wholesale figures reached $800,000, the number of beauty consultants jumped to 3,000, and the company was renamed Mary Kay Cosmetics.

Cinderella gifts as incentives to succeed

Ash truly wanted her employees to succeed. Unlike other companies, Mary Kay Cosmetics did not establish sales territories. Most of the beauty consultants worked part-time, averaging about nine hours per week, so many beauty consultants could work in the same area. With no sales territories, Mary Kay's consultants could continue to sell their products even if they moved or traveled on vacations.

To motivate her sales force, Ash placed no limit on what they could earn. Consultants bought Mary Kay cosmetics at wholesale prices and set their own retail prices; some sold products at twice the wholesale rate. Ash felt strongly that her best salespeople should be publicly recognized. She rewarded consultants with extravagant conventions during which she awarded prizes that she called "Cinderella Gifts." Ash made sure that the prizes she gave were worth the effort, unlike the underwater flashlight Stanley Home Products offered her years earlier. Beauty consultants won fur coats, diamond jewelry, tropical vacations, and pink Cadillacs.

Over the years, the two most recognized prizes Mary Kay offered were bumblebee-shaped diamond brooches and pink Cadillacs. For Ash the bumblebee symbolized the ultimate in success. The bumblebee's "wings are too weak and its body too heavy for flight," she explained in her autobiography, *Mary Kay.* "Everything seems to tell the bumblebee, 'You'll never get off the ground.' But I like to think that maybe—just maybe—our Divine Creator whispered, 'You can do it!,' so it did!" To inspire employees, Ash promoted such positive thinking and provided personal encouragement to

Mary Kay Ash shows off her pink Cadillac, which became symbolic of Mary Kay Cosmetics. *© Ed Lallo/Getty Images. Reproduced by permission.*

every employee, and to top performers she awarded bumble-bee pins.

Ash's idea for distinctive pink Cadillacs came from an entirely different source. Driving her black car, Ash was often cut off in traffic. Frustrated one day, she drove into her Cadillac dealer and ordered a pink Cadillac. She wanted it the same light pink color as her company's pink lipsticks and eye shadows. When she drove the distinctively colored car, she did not get cut off in traffic anymore. Her sales staff asked how to get one. Ash decided to offer the cars as awards to top sellers. In 1969, the first "Mary Kay pink" Cadillacs were awarded at the company's annual convention.

Built an empire while embracing her femininity

Mary Kay Cosmetics made Ash and many of her beauty consultants wealthy, powerful businesswomen by the time the feminist movement gained momentum in the mid-1960s. Ash shared the feminist view that men and women should be treated equally in the workplace. However, she disagreed with how the feminist movement was trying to gain such equality. "[W]hen I was starting the company, I didn't like the way the feminist movement was taking women—women cutting their hair short and wearing men's style clothing, trying to be men. I think that's nonsense. I think women should look feminine, and should try to look good," Ash noted in an interview quoted by *American Enterprise*. Ash devoted herself to building the confidence and business power of women while at the same time celebrating female beauty. Ash herself wore her dyed blonde hair styled to frame her face. She wore a variety of makeup products to highlight her facial features. She wore shapely business suits with large jeweled earrings and necklaces to work and long flowing gowns at gala events. At the Mary Kay annual conventions, beauty consultants wore different colored suits to indicate their status in the company. Pink suits, of course, were reserved for only the top sellers.

In 1966, Ash married her third husband, Melville Jerome Ash. She took her husband's surname but had already become known nationally as "Mary Kay." The success of Mary Kay Cosmetics continued. In 1968 the company became pub-

Makeup and the Feminist Movement

Before the 1960s, fashion standards for women were quite different than for men. During World War II (1939–45), women struggled to maintain a feminine look with limited supplies. Rationing during the war limited the amount of fabric available to make dresses. Silk hose were scarce because the fabric was needed for parachutes. After the war, French designer Christian Dior introduced the New Look in 1947, which established a very feminine standard for beauty. Women gleefully squeezed their waists with corsets to give themselves an hourglass figure. The tiny corseted waists contrasted dramatically with the flowing skirts of the New Look. With their flowing skirts and tailored tops, women wore stiff hairstyles, heavy makeup, pantyhose, and high-heeled shoes. Mary Kay Ash embraced this feminine standard herself and delighted in the decorative aspects of such styles. She never considered putting on makeup, styling her hair, or walking in high heels as obstacles to being a powerful, confident woman. In fact, she delighted in all the decoration.

In the 1960s, the modern feminist movement organized to push for equal rights for women. As the movement gained momentum, women began to question contemporary standards of femininity. Some feminist activists argued that the feminine ideal of beauty set in the previous decade harmed women, keeping them from being treated as equals of men. They said that factors such as makeup, shaved legs, plucked eyebrows, coiffed hair, high-heels, and hosiery announced women's lesser position in society by making women objects of desire for men. These feminists shunned standard conventions of feminine beauty in favor of clean faces, shorter or looser hairstyles, and more masculine clothes, such as pants and simple shirts.

The opposing views about the "correct" look for women still continue. However, the debate opened the door for women to decide on a look that suited them. By the end of the 1960s, standards of female beauty had become very diverse and based on individual preference. It was as acceptable for women to wear heavy makeup, frilly clothes, and carefully styled hair, as it was for them to wear no makeup, jeans, and a T-shirt. In addition, fashion designers introduced unisex styles that could be worn by men or women, a trend that continued into the early 2000s.

lic, offering stock on the New York Stock Exchange. Stock prices soared 670 percent between the 1970s and 1980s, making Mary Kay the largest direct-sales cosmetics company in the United States. In 1979 the first Mary Kay beauty consultant exceeded $1 million in commissions. Interest in her company and unique management style grew after her autobiography, published in 1981, and her second book, *Mary Kay on People Management,* published in 1984, became bestsellers.

As more and more job opportunities opened to women during the 1970s and 1980s, sales of Mary Kay leveled off. To refocus the company on growth, Ash and her family re-purchased the company for $450 million in 1985. The family succeeded in transforming the company into an international empire. Ash was succeeded by her son in 1987 but remained active in the company until her death on November 22, 2001. By 2003, Mary Kay Cosmetics had more than one million consultants selling more than two hundred different products in thirty countries around the world. The company had achieved wholesale figures of $1.8 billion. More than two hundred beauty consultants had surpassed $1 million in commissions. Ash told *Sales and Marketing Management* in 1994 that "the biggest legacy we are going to leave … is a whole community of children who believe that they can do anything in this world because they watched their mamas do it."

For More Information

Books

Ash, Mary Kay. *Mary Kay.* New York: Harper and Row, 1981; revised, 1986.

Lutz, Norma Jean. *Female Firsts in Their Fields: Business and Industry.* Philadelphia, PA: Chelsea House, 1999.

Pile, Robert B. *Women Business Leaders.* Minneapolis, MN: Oliver Press, 1995.

Periodicals

Lopez, Kathryn Jean. "Strong Women Wear Lipstick." *American Enterprise* (January-February 2002): p. 10.

Sales and Marketing Management (November 1994): p. 41.

Web Sites

"Mary Kay Ash." *Contemporary Authors Online: Biography Resource Center.* www.galenet.com/servlet/BioRC (accessed August 2004).

Mary Kay Inc. www.marykay.com (accessed August 2004).

Rachel Carson

Born May 27, 1907
Springdale, Pennsylvania

Died April 14, 1964
Silver Spring, Maryland

Naturalist, marine biologist, writer, environmental activist

R achel Carson was as much a political activist as a biologist, naturalist, and writer. She spent her lifetime appreciating, exploring, and writing about nature and emphasizing the importance of the natural world in everyday life. In 1962, Carson's book *Silent Spring* was published. In the work, she reported on the manner in which the poisons found in pesticides—chemical mixtures used to wipe out insects that thrive on plants and animals—were destroying Earth and its atmosphere. The publicity her book generated helped give birth to the modern-day environmental movement.

An early love of nature

Rachel Louise Carson was born on May 27, 1907 in Springdale, a rural community located along the Allegheny River in southwestern Pennsylvania. She grew up in a five-room farmhouse, where she was surrounded by nature. Spurred on by her mother, Maria McLean Carson, young Rachel developed an appreciation for the natural world. In particular, she became fascinated by life as it existed in and

"The more I learned about the use of pesticides, the more appalled I became.... I realized that here was the material for a book. What I discovered was that everything which meant most to me as a naturalist was being threatened, and that nothing I could do would be more important."

—*Rachel Carson.*

Rachel Carson. *AP/Wide World Photos. Reproduced by permission.*

around waterways. She also displayed a gift for writing. In fourth grade, she published her first work, a story titled "A Battle in the Clouds," in *St. Nicholas*, a children's magazine.

Carson wished to pursue a writing career. She started out as an English major at the Pennsylvania College for Women (later known as Chatham College), which she attended during the late 1920s. Upon taking a biology course taught by an inspiring professor, May Scott Skinker, Carson changed her major to zoology during her junior year. She graduated with academic honors in 1929 and won a full scholarship to perform graduate work at Johns Hopkins University in Baltimore, Maryland.

Three years later, Carson earned a master's degree in marine zoology, a life sciences discipline that focuses on sea organisms. During this period, she continued her education by spending summers at the Marine Biological Laboratories in Woods Hole, Massachusetts. She also taught zoology at the University of Maryland and summer-school classes at Johns Hopkins.

Early career

For most of her early professional life, Carson worked for the U.S. Bureau of Fisheries. (In 1940 the bureau was combined with the Biological Survey unit and renamed the Fish and Wildlife Service.) Carson first worked on a part-time basis, writing scripts for bureau-sponsored radio programs in 1935. The following year, she accepted a full-time position with the bureau as a biologist-researcher and writer-editor. The information-oriented government pamphlets that she wrote included such titles as *Food from the Sea: Fish and Shellfish of New England* (1943), *Food from Home Waters: Fishes of the Middle West* (1943), and *Fish and Shellfish of the Middle Atlantic Coast* (1945).

Carson also wrote articles about natural history for the *Baltimore Sun*. In 1937 she penned a well-received piece titled "Undersea," published in the *Atlantic Monthly*. In 1949 she was appointed editor in chief of all Fish and Wildlife Service publications.

Books on the environment

Carson's books express her intense interest in nature, particularly the sea, and in environmental protection. Her first three books explore the manner in which living things are interconnected. The first, *Under the Sea-Wind,* published in 1941, was an expansion of Carson's *Atlantic Monthly* article, and "Chesapeake Eels Seek the Sargasso Sea," one of her *Baltimore Sun* pieces. *Under the Sea-Wind* offered a view of life as it exists near waterways and underwater, spotlighting the fierce battle for survival among the creatures living in these environments. Although Carson's later books earned her greater fame, *Under the Sea-Wind* remained her personal favorite.

The Sea Around Us was published in 1951 after being serialized as "A Profile of the Sea" in *New Yorker* magazine. In the book, Carson examined how the oceans, Earth, and Moon came into existence. Unlike *Under the Sea-Wind,* which sold poorly, *The Sea Around Us* became a runaway success. It sold more than 200,000 copies and became a Book-of-the-Month Club alternate selection. It earned Carson the National Book Award for nonfiction and brought her international fame. The work was adapted as a documentary film, which won an Academy Award in 1952.

The financial success of *The Sea Around Us* gave Carson the means to quit her job with the Fish and Wildlife Service. While maintaining a residence in the Washington, D.C. area, she then began spending her summers in a cottage by Sheepscot Bay along the Maine shoreline. From her summer cottage, Carson completed much of the research for her follow-up book, 1955's *The Edge of the Sea.* In the work, she discussed the various forms of life that are found in and by the sea. It also became a bestseller.

Carson's niece Marjorie, with whom she was very close, died in 1957. Carson adopted Marjorie's son Roger. Their relationship—as well as her affection for all young people—served as inspiration for her book, *The Sense of Wonder* (published after her death in 1965). Here, Carson stressed the need for parents to encourage their children's natural curiosity about the world and their environment. The ideas put forth in *The Sense of Wonder* first appeared in a 1956 *Woman's Home Companion* magazine piece titled "Help Your Child to Wonder."

As Carson took on the role of parent, her devotion to her environmental work remained constant. Carson wrote about nature, about the importance of humankind living in harmony with nature, and about the wonder of childhood.

Silent Spring **and Not-So-Silent Protest**

Before *Silent Spring,* the everyday use of pesticides and other chemicals seemed harmless, and their destructive impact on the environment was not considered.

For example, in 1939, Paul Muller, a researcher at Geigy Pharmaceutical in Switzerland, determined that dichlorodiphenyltrichloroethane (DDT) could be effectively used as an insecticide. DDT was a colorless, odorless chemical that was inexpensive to produce. In 1948, he even won the Nobel Prize in medicine and physiology for this finding. After World War II (1939–45), DDT usage increased across the globe. However, it also was discovered that the chemical had a toxic effect on the environment. It destroyed the reproductive cycles of birds and fish, and polluted waterways. Also, because of its chemical makeup, the presence of DDT was not immediately apparent. It slowly built up, often taking up to fifteen years to be detected.

In 1962, the year in which *Silent Spring* was published, efforts to ban DDT began. By 1973, the United States had outlawed DDT's use as a pesticide, but it remained in use in other parts of the world.

She also recognized that America's natural resources were being dangerously mistreated by big business. In 1957 *Holiday* magazine published her article, "Our Ever-Changing Shore." In the piece, she petitioned for the preservation of America's shorelines that were quickly disappearing due to erosion and industrial development.

The culmination of a life's work: *Silent Spring*

Back in 1945 Carson had first become concerned about federal plans to use certain insecticides in pest-control programs. She was worried that the government had not considered the potentially negative, long-term impact of such chemicals on the environment. Her concern increased during the 1950s, when many American companies used these pesticides. This awareness led to the book that was her crowning achievement, *Silent Spring,* published in 1962.

In *Silent Spring,* Carson presents evidence to show how overuse of pesticides threatens to destroy Earth and its atmos-

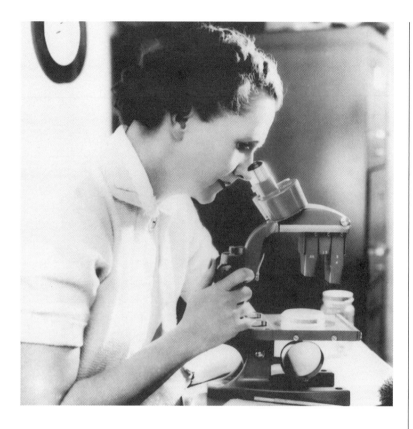

Rachel Carson studies specimens as she researches the effects of pesticides on the environment.
© Bettmann/Corbis.
Reproduced by permission.

phere. She alerted the public to the dire environmental consequences if the usage remained unchecked. She cautioned that the poisons found in pesticides were killing off animals, birds, and fish and even might affect food consumed by human beings. She emphasized that all human beings are responsible for keeping Earth and its atmosphere free from contamination.

Attacks and acclaim

Silent Spring triggered much controversy. The leaders of the chemical and farming industries, whose profits depended on the production and use of pesticides, attacked Carson. She was labeled an alarmist. Her credentials were questioned. Her findings were disputed. She was threatened with lawsuits. Some critics went so far as to question Carson's sanity.

However, Carson had supporters too. For example, her findings were upheld in a report issued by the Science Advisory Committee, which had just been appointed by President **John F. Kennedy** (1917–1963; served 1961–63; see entry). Immediately *Silent Spring* became a bestseller and further added to Carson's international fame. In 1963, she testified before the U.S. Congress about the importance of passing legislation to protect the environment. In a letter to the editor published that year in the *Washington Post,* she declared that "the way is being cleared for a raid upon our natural resources that is without parallel within the present century."

After the publication of *Silent Spring,* Carson was showered with honors, including induction into the American Academy of Arts and Letters. At the same time, she was suffering from breast cancer. She learned that she had cancer while researching the book. After waging a long battle with the disease, she died in 1964.

Rachel Carson's legacy is long-standing and far-reaching. The publication of *Silent Spring* marked the beginning of the environmental movement. It sparked awareness among the general public of the potential dangers of environmental pollution. The work spoke out about humankind's responsibilities toward nature. In March 1999, Carson appeared on the cover of *Time* with Jonas Salk (1914–1995) and Albert Einstein (1879–1955). Each was cited as being among the most significant scientist-theorists of the twentieth century.

For More Information

Books

Archer, Jules. *To Save the Earth: The American Environmental Movement.* New York: Viking Press, 1998.

Carson, Rachel L. *The Edge of the Sea.* Boston: Houghton Mifflin Company, 1955.

Carson, Rachel L. *The Sea Around Us.* New York: Oxford University Press, 1951.

Carson, Rachel L. *The Sense of Wonder.* New York: Harper & Row, 1965.

Carson, Rachel L. *Silent Spring.* Boston: Houghton Mifflin Company, 1962.

Carson, Rachel L. *Under the Sea-Wind.* New York: Oxford University Press, 1941.

Lear, Linda, ed. *Lost Woods: The Discovered Writing of Rachel Carson.* Boston: Beacon Press, 1998.

Lear, Linda. *Rachel Carson: Witness for Nature.* New York: Henry Holt, 1997.

Web Sites

Rachel Carson Council, Inc. http://members.aol.com/rccouncil/ourpage/ (accessed August 2004).

Rachel Carson.org. http://www.rachelcarson.org/ (accessed August 2004).

"TIME 100: Rachel Carson" *Time.com.* http://www.time.com/time/time 100/scientist/profile/carson.html (accessed August 2004).

Walter Cronkite

Born November, 4, 1916
St. Joseph, Missouri

Journalist, television newsperson

"[T]here was a sacred covenant between newspaper people and their readers. We journalists had to be right and we had to be fair."

—*Walter Cronkite.*

Walter Cronkite.
© *Bettmann/Corbis.*
Reproduced by permission.

Walter Cronkite worked in television news from its beginnings in the early 1950s. He played a large role in creating the format of television news programs. From 1962 to 1981, Cronkite anchored the *CBS Evening News* program, not only reporting, but also summing up and analyzing the news. His calm, authoritative manner and his careful, hardworking approach to journalism earned him the trust of his viewers. More than other television personalities, Cronkite became a national figure. His news summaries were watched in millions of households. His nightly sign-off, "And that's the way it is," was familiar and reassuring to many viewers.

A nose for news

Walter Leland Cronkite Jr. was born on November 4, 1916, in St. Joseph, Missouri. His father, Walter Leland Cronkite Sr., was a dentist. When Walter Jr. was young, his family moved to Kansas City, Missouri. There, they lived a comfortable, though not wealthy, middle-class lifestyle. At age seven, Walter took a job selling a weekly magazine called

Liberty, earning a penny for each copy he sold. By the age of nine, he had progressed to selling copies of the Kansas City newspaper, the *Star.*

When Walter was ten, his family moved to Houston, Texas, where he lived for the rest of his childhood. They moved because Walter's father had an offer of a better job. However, the change in location was hard on the family in many ways. The racism and conservatism of the tight southern community shocked the liberal Cronkites. The pressure of the move caused his father to become distant and angry. Walter Sr. became an alcoholic and grew more and more separate from his family. The Cronkites divorced when Walter Jr. was in high school.

Young Walter also had some problems adjusting to life in the South. He was criticized by neighbors for playing with black children. Also, he was punished by a teacher for not saying "ma'am" and "sir" to his elders. However, he was a flexible and cheerful youth, who participated in sports, joined the Boy Scouts, took piano lessons, and got a job delivering purchases for a local drugstore to customers' homes.

Cronkite's early interest in the news was stirred when he entered San Janice High School. There he met Fred Birney, a former newspaper reporter who had begun teaching high school journalism. Inspired by Birney, Cronkite began to write and helped to start a school newspaper. Always a hard worker, he also got a job at the Houston *Post,* where his first on-the-job reporting experience was covering small social events.

Foreign correspondent

Cronkite continued working in the news business after he entered the University of Texas at Austin in 1933. He was fascinated by the exciting medium of radio, which was still in its infancy. He persuaded KNOW, a local radio station, to let him cover sports. He spent much of his leisure time at the state capitol, observing the workings of government. He met journalists there who helped him get a job as a reporter, writing for the International News Service (INS). A news reporting service, the INS was owned by legendary newspaper publisher William Randolph Hearst (1863–1951). Cronkite's position led to a job offer from the Houston newspaper, the *Press*. By 1935, Cronkite had left college to go to work full-time for the Houston *Press*. Between 1935 and 1942, Cronkite worked on various papers and did news shows on radio as well. In 1939, he got a job with United Press (UP), a news service that collected and wrote news for a wide variety of newspapers.

World War II (1939–45) erupted in Europe in 1939. When the United States entered the conflict in 1941, Cronkite soon followed the U.S. troops to Europe as a war correspondent for the United Press. The war journalists of World War II were courageous reporters who often saw the same action that soldiers did, but they carried pens and cameras rather than weapons. Cronkite participated in the "D-day" invasion of Normandy, France, in 1944, which is considered a major turning point in the war. Allied forces stormed the beaches at Normandy and began a major push to defeat the Germans. He followed American soldiers as they fought, reporting on the war for those back home. His work sometimes put him in danger. He flew along on bombing missions and even parachuted out of planes, all in an effort to see and report on the events.

After the war ended in 1945, Cronkite covered the historic trials in the German city of Nuremberg. There, Nazi officers faced charges for crimes committed during the war, such as illegal medical experiments and the extermination of Jews in concentration camps. Far from a hardened reporter, Cronkite was moved many times by the suffering and bravery he witnessed during the war and its aftermath. He communicated these emotions in the reports he sent back to the United States.

After the Nuremberg trials ended in October 1946, Cronkite continued to work in the UP foreign offices for several more years. In 1940, he married his long-time sweetheart "Betsy," Mary Elizabeth Maxwell. Between 1946 and 1949, the couple lived in Amsterdam, The Netherlands, Brussels, Belgium, and Moscow, USSR, while Cronkite worked in these European capitals' news bureaus. In 1950 he returned home to the birth of a new communication and entertainment medium, television.

Television and the news

A respected journalist for his work during World War II, Walter Cronkite was offered a new kind of job when he re-

The Nuremberg Trials

On November 30, 1945, just after the end of World War II, a series of groundbreaking trials began in the southeastern German city of Nuremberg. Twenty-four officials of the Nazi government of Germany were brought individually before a panel of judges from the Allied countries to face charges of violating accepted practices of war. They were accused of many crimes, including starting and waging an offensive war; torturing and murdering civilians (including millions of Jewish citizens); abusing prisoners of war; and using slave labor. Along with the twenty-four high officers, many lesser officials of the government and military were also placed on trial.

The Nuremberg trials represented one of the first times that individuals were held responsible and tried in court for the actions of their government during wartime. Some thought that the trials were just a way of getting revenge for what happened during the war. Others believed that the governments of Europe had agreed on basic rules of warfare and that the German government had violated many of these rules. They argued that individual citizens have a responsibility to refuse if their government asks them to do things which break these international laws.

The world followed the trials with great interest, reading the reports sent back by correspondents such as Walter Cronkite and Janet Flanner. When the trials ended on October 1, 1946, 26 people were sentenced to be hanged, 128 were given prison sentences, and 35 were acquitted.

The effects of the Nuremberg trials were still felt in the early 2000s. The trials increased the reach of international law, a system of laws that crosses national borders. They strengthened the idea that individuals are responsible for what they do, even if they are "following orders." The trials also gave birth to the international human rights movement. Supporters of the movement believe that individuals in every country have basic rights and that everyone has a responsibility to protect those rights, regardless of nationality.

turned home. It would be in the brand new field of television news. The Columbia Broadcasting System (CBS) television network hired Cronkite as a news reporter. Some of his early jobs on television were not the serious newscasting that he was used to doing. Still, Cronkite remained flexible and good humored. He hosted an early history program called *You Are There,* which aired from 1953 through 1957. The show featured re-enactments of historical events, such as Revolutionary War battles or the trial of Joan of Arc. Real news reporters, such as Cronkite, would interview the historical participants

After taking a break from the anchor desk to travel to Vietnam, Walter Cronkite (center) talks to a group of U.S. Marines about their experiences fighting the war. *Photo courtesy of the U.S. Marine Corps.*

being played by actors. The reporters then would give a history lesson, sometimes pointing out a connection between history and modern times.

Another early Cronkite news/entertainment program was *The Morning Show,* which first aired in 1954. There, the experienced reporter shared a news desk with a puppet named Charlemagne the Lion. However, the network saw and valued Cronkite's skill as a reporter, along with his deep voice and mature looks. In 1952, he gained praise for his balanced and accurate coverage of the first televised nominating conventions of the Democratic and Republican parties.

By 1962, Cronkite was a respected television newsperson. CBS decided to give him the lead role on a new program, *CBS Evening News,* creating a new position for Cronkite. Since he would be the solid foundation of the newscast, they called him the "news anchor." He would be the person to coordinate stories from other reporters, comment on them, and analyze the news. In an era when there were only three television networks delivering news, viewers depended on anchors such as Cronkite to sift through the news and bring them the most important facts. Cronkite's distinguished looks and kindly manner caused viewers to have confidence in him. However, Cronkite never became merely a television star. He remained a serious reporter, researching and writing most of his own material throughout his career.

Along with his work on the *Evening News,* Cronkite was a prominent figure in many other television programs. Between 1957 and 1970, he hosted a documentary series called *Twentieth Century* (the name changed to *Twenty-First Century* in 1967). From 1961 to 1979, he did in-depth reporting about current events on *CBS Reports*. From 1980 to 1982, he hosted *Universe,* a news/science magazine show. In addition, he filmed many special programs, including *Vietnam: A War That Is Finished* in 1975, *Our Happiest Birthday* in 1977, and *Dinosaur!* in 1991.

Cronkite continued to anchor the *CBS Evening News* until 1981. Then he exchanged the job for the less demanding one of "special correspondent." This position only required that he issue occasional reports on specific news stories. After leaving his nightly news job, Cronkite continued to be active in both his work and private life. He was often called on to give his opinion about current events. Cronkite did not hesitate to speak out when he saw unfairness or bad government policies. He hosted and narrated numerous television specials, including *Children of Apartheid* in 1987. In 1993, he started his own production company to make documentary films. Three years later, his company produced an eight-hour series called *Cronkite Remembers,* which was shown on both CBS and the Discovery Channel.

In spite of his dignified image as a newscaster, Cronkite also spent his life as an athlete and adventure-seeker. His life-long love of racecar driving led him to become part of a team that drove a twelve-hour race in Sebring, Florida, in 1959. He also loved sailing and spent many hours on his boat with his family. Cronkite wrote several books, including an autobiography called *A Reporter's Life.*

For More Information

Books

Cronkite, Walter. *A Reporter's Life*. New York: Alfred A. Knopf, 1996.

James, Doug. *Walter Cronkite: His Life and Times*. Brentwood, TN: J.M. Press, 1991.

Periodicals

"The Great Anchorman Off Camera." *Life* (November 1980): pp. 132–39.

Miller, Mark Crispin. "Walter Cronkite: And That's the Way It Seems." *Current* (May 1981): pp. 20–38.

Bob Dylan

Born May 24, 1941
Duluth, Minnesota

Singer, songwriter

One of the most influential songwriters of the twentieth century, Bob Dylan is a unique blend of musician, poet, rebel, and social critic. He rose to fame during the 1960s, when his music was favored by college students and those involved in the anti-war movement. With his scruffy looks, his raspy nasal voice, and the stinging political edge of his lyrics, he became an important figurehead for these social movements. He came to represent their attitude of rebellion. However, Dylan resisted the role of star and remained a very private and independent artist. He frustrated his fans over and over by refusing to stick with any one musical style or personal philosophy. However, he continued to win respect and praise again and again. In the early twenty-first century, Dylan continued to create and perform his sharp, perceptive songs to audiences that included several generations.

"It's not me. It's the songs. I'm just the postman. I deliver the songs."

—*Bob Dylan.*

Growing up in the north country

On May 24, 1941, Bob Dylan was born Robert Allen Zimmerman. His middle-class Jewish family lived in the Lake

Bob Dylan. *AP/Wide World Photos. Reproduced by permission.*

Superior port city of Duluth, Minnesota. His grandparents, Jews from Russia and Lithuania, had left their homes to escape anti-Jewish violence. They settled in Minnesota, where Dylan's parents, Abe Zimmerman and Beatrice (Stone) Zimmerman, were born, grew up, and married. In 1946, Abe contracted polio, a disabling disease. The family decided to move closer to relatives in the small town of Hibbing, in the northern Iron Mountain region of Minnesota. Abe worked with other family members there, running an electrical supply store.

The Zimmermans both came from musical families. Abe played violin and Beatrice played piano; family entertainments were common. Young Bobby was only four or five when he first sang at a family gathering. By the age of ten, he began to teach himself to play piano and, soon after, the guitar, autoharp, and harmonica. He was impatient with traditional ways of learning music, such as private lessons or music classes. As a result, he developed his own ways of playing without learning to read music.

Bobby Zimmerman also began to listen to the radio and heard the music that would influence him for the rest of his life. He loved simple, emotional country music best, like the sad songs of Hank Williams Sr. (1923–1953). As Bobby grew older, he began to listen to a new kind of music called rock and roll. He began to imitate early rockers such as Little Richard (1932–) and Elvis Presley (1935–1977). Rock and roll was a rebellious music with roots in African American jazz and blues. Northern Minnesota, a conservative area, had few Jews or blacks. As Bobby Zimmerman grew to be a teenager there, he found much to rebel against. In imitation of his rock heroes, he grew his hair long and combed it back in a high wave called a pompadour. He rode a motorcycle and played in several bands. Once, during a high school talent show, the principal was so angered by the loud performance of Bobby's band that he pulled the plug on their instruments.

A little college and a lot of education

While playing music with bands in high school, Bobby Zimmerman began to use the name Bob Dylan. He preferred not to say exactly why he chose the name. However, he seemed to have first picked Dillon as his stage name, at least partly because he admired Matt Dillon, the tough but sympathetic sheriff on the popular 1950s television western *Gunsmoke*. Always a lover of poetry, Bob Dylan may have changed the spelling as a tribute to the twentieth-century Welsh poet Dylan Thomas.

In 1959, Dylan left Hibbing to attend college at the University of Minnesota in Minneapolis. He did not really like school and thus did not stay in college long. Yet he did continue his musical education in Minneapolis. He became part of a community of young poets, artists, and musicians called "Beatniks." They rejected the views, values, and behaviors of the majority. In addition, they were interested in the revival of folk music.

Folk music had been around for a long time. In fact, folk music was the name given to the traditional songs that had been sung for decades or even centuries in rural North America and Britain. During the late 1950s and early 1960s, however, some rebellious intellectuals had become interested in folk music. They considered it to be more authentic and honest than the popular music of the 1950s, which they thought was bland and artificial. To Dylan and his circle, folk music seemed fresh and meaningful. Dylan was especially drawn to the simple arrangements and heart-felt sentiments of singer/songwriters such as Woody Guthrie (1912–1967). An American folksinger, Guthrie had traveled around the country as a hobo during the Great Depression (1929–41). Guthrie's uncomplicated musical style reminded Dylan of the down-to-earth qualities he had loved in the music of Hank Williams Sr. and the young Elvis Presley. Moreover, Guthrie was a poet of the people because he told the stories of hard lives and pointed out the unfair treatment that poor people often received. Dylan started to see himself as a social rebel like Hank Williams, a rambling poet who would sing the truth.

Dylan began to perform in Minneapolis coffeehouses, singing his own variations of traditional folk songs as well as songs he wrote. He had transformed himself from the pompadoured rocker to the vagabond poet. Soon he left on travels of his own, heading for the center of Beatnik culture, New York City. He might have seen himself as a poet of the people,

Greenwich Village: A Community of Rebels

When Bob Dylan left the Midwest to seek other musicians in New York City, he went to a section of the city famous for its community of artists and free thinkers. Located at the southern end of Manhattan Island, the neighborhood of Greenwich (pronounced Gren'ich) Village has been associated with creative and offbeat intellectuals for most of the twentieth century.

Greenwich Village became known as an artistic and unconventional neighborhood during the early 1900s. As New York City grew outward from its beginnings at the southern tip of Manhattan Island, the wealthy citizens who had populated the Village of Greenwich moved farther north. This left many apartments and houses empty. Rents dropped and these low rents attracted both poor immigrants and poor artists. Painters, writers, musicians, opera singers, and dancers all moved into the inexpensive apartments of Greenwich Village. These artists were usually independent, creative people who did not live by the traditional rules of society. Soon the Village got the reputation of being a tolerant and creative community.

During the late 1950s and early 1960s, many young people began to rebel against a society that they found artificial and repressive. Many of these young rebels embraced the "Beat" lifestyle. It was an untraditional way of living that valued art, poetry, and the hip rhythms of jazz music more than the traditions of marriage, family, and the conventional work career. Greenwich Village became home to many of the "Beatniks."

Many Beats were also drawn to the true stories and deep emotions they found in traditional folk music. During the early 1960s, the Village became a gathering place for such influential folksingers as Pete Seeger, Phil Ochs, Tom Paxton, and the group Peter, Paul, and Mary. Many young "folkies," such as Bob Dylan, arrived in New York looking for kindred spirits. The newcomers could go to clubs such as the Gaslight, the Blue Angel, and Folk City, where they could hear folk music and jam with some of the best folk musicians in the world.

but Bob Dylan also wanted to be famous. New York was the place for an artist who wanted to be discovered.

Dylan was nineteen years old when he arrived in New York at the end of 1960. He headed for the artistic center of the city, Greenwich Village, where he met many other folk musicians. He began to perform in local coffeehouses such as Gerde's Folk City and the Gaslight. Greenwich Village was home to many young folk musicians during the early 1960s. The folk music scene was exploding with excitement. Bob Dylan's songs, with their driving guitar and harshly poetic words, fit right in.

The rise and fall of the folksinger

It did not take long for record company executives to recognize Dylan's talent. During the first year he was in New York, he was offered a five-year record contract with Columbia Records. His first album, *Bob Dylan* (1962), contained traditional folk songs. By the second, *The Freewheelin' Bob Dylan* (1963), all of the songs were original. He wrote about love ("Girl of the North Country"), and he wrote about his heroes ("Song for Woody"). But his most famous and powerful songs were his protest songs, such as "Blowin' in the Wind." An anti-war, anti-racism song, "Blowin' in the Wind" became an anthem for the American 1960s civil rights movement. Other songs, such as "The Times They Are a'Changing," captured the rebellious spirit of the decade. As a result, Dylan seemed to be the spokesperson for those who felt that they were living in a time of great cultural change.

Dylan was a productive songwriter. Many popular singers, such as singer/songwriter Joan Baez (1941–) as well as the folk group Peter, Paul, and Mary sang his songs. Many people preferred to hear others sing Dylan songs because they considered his voice grating, whiny, and unpleasant. However, Dylan fans found his singing both emotional and authentic, especially in his long storytelling songs such as "The Death of Emmett Till" and "The Lonesome Death of Hattie Carroll." Both songs are about African Americans killed by racist whites.

The popular folksinger Joan Baez helped push Dylan into the public eye. She and Dylan were just beginning a two-year romantic relationship when she invited him on stage to sing with her at the 1963 Newport Folk Festival in Newport, Rhode Island. Although the crowd showed little interest in the skinny, unkempt newcomer, Baez's introduction convinced them to listen. Dylan's popularity began to rise.

By the mid-1960s, Bob Dylan had become a star. His songs were popular and his albums were successful. He was performing at festivals and in famous concert halls around the world. Never one to get too comfortable with his success, Dylan began to change his music. In the summer of 1965, he played at the Newport Folk Festival again, this time as a major performer. At a time when most folk musicians believed in keeping the music pure by using only traditional instruments, Dylan put together an all-electric band for the concert. He played the electric guitar. Although some of the audience was thrilled by the new sound, most fans and other folk musicians were horrified as Dylan and his amplified band pounded out several songs. Some were upset because of the loud, electric sound, which they did not consider as folk. Others were angered because the songs Dylan played were personal, and they wanted to hear political protest songs.

Newport was the first of a series of concerts in which Dylan seemed to be almost mocking the fans who had loved his early music. He continued to use electric instruments and acted strangely on stage. He treated many of his old folksinger friends unkindly, including snubbing his old friend Joan Baez. Audiences began to boo him at his concerts.

Retreats, comebacks, and rebirths

In 1966, Dylan had a motorcycle accident and retired from public life for several years. There were stories that he

 **Joan Baez**

For many, singer Joan Baez was the perfect symbol of 1960s folk music. With her long dark hair, bare feet, and clear soprano voice, Baez seemed as simple and authentic as the traditional folk ballads she sang. Some of her fans were delighted and others felt betrayed when Baez later mixed political protest songs with her folk music. Yet she always delivered her music with a direct and heartfelt sincerity that earned the respect of both audiences and critics.

Baez began her career singing in the coffeehouses of Boston, Massachusetts, and Greenwich Village. She was only eighteen when she drew national attention at the 1959 Newport Folk Festival in Newport, Rhode Island. A year later, she released her first album, a collection of enduring folk classics, including "House of the Rising Sun," "John Riley," and "Silver Dagger."

In 1963, Baez began a relationship with Bob Dylan, who was just starting his musical career. Already a respected folksinger, Baez shared her fame with Dylan by inviting him to share the stage with her. They performed together first at the 1963 Newport Folk Festival, then on her concert tour. Though their relationship was over by 1965, it was an important one for both of them. Baez immortalized it in one of her best-known songs, "Diamonds and Rust" (1975). She continued to sing and record Dylan's music into the 2000s.

Joan Baez was never content with being simply a singer who sang pretty songs. Early in her career, she began to use the stage as a place from which to speak out about social issues. She frequently sang at political events to support particular causes of the 1960s and 1970s, including the civil rights movement, the anti-Vietnam War movement, and immigration and prison reform. She promoted boycotts in support of farmworkers, did not pay taxes that would go to support war, and often donated money from her concerts to activist organizations. In 1965, she founded the Institute for the Study of Nonviolence to explore alternatives to war.

had broken his neck and nearly died. However, much evidence suggests that his injuries were slight and that the accident merely became his excuse for getting away from criticism of his music in order to rethink his career. Dylan had married Sara Lownds in 1965, and he spent the next several years living a quiet domestic life.

In 1969 Dylan released an album which, while it contained a major hit, also marked another big change in musical style. *Nashville Skyline* left behind the hard-driving music of Dylan's rock period and headed in the direction of country music. The best-known track from the album, "Lay, Lady, Lay," was a Top 40 hit for eleven weeks. However, Dylan did not revive his former popularity. His next album, *Self Portrait* (1970), was so unpopular and so musically strange that many thought it had been made as a joke. During this period, Dylan expanded his writing and published two books, an autobiography, *Bob Dylan, Self-Portrait* (1970), and a novel, *Tarantula* (1971).

In 1975, Dylan made still another comeback. He separated from his wife and turned the pain of that troubled relationship into a new album. *Blood on the Tracks* was well received by critics and fans alike. Many thought the songs were among the best Dylan had ever written. Songs such as "Shelter from the Storm," "Idiot Wind," and "Tangled Up in Blue" clearly expressed the deep loss and anger at the end of a marriage.

In 1979, Dylan renounced his Judaism and became a born-again Christian. By this time, fans had become used to his extreme changes of direction. Few took much notice of his Christian album *Saved* (1980). By 1983, Dylan had returned to Judaism. He continued to write, perform, and record. In 1989 he was inducted into the Rock and Roll Hall of Fame. His 1998 album *Time Out of Mind* won the Grammy award for Album of the Year. In 1986 Dylan married again, though he kept his marriage to Carol Dennis a secret for many years. They divorced in 1992. He had five children from his first marriage and one from his second. One of his sons, Jakob, followed his father into a successful career in popular music with the band, The Wallflowers.

For More Information

Books

Horn, Geoffrey M. *Bob Dylan*. Milwaukee, WI: World Almanac Library, 2002.

Richardson, Susan. *Bob Dylan*. New York: Chelsea House, 1995.

Scaduto, Anthony. *Bob Dylan: An Intimate Biography*. New York: Signet, 1979.

Schuman, Michael. *Bob Dylan: The Life and Times of an American Icon*. Berkley Heights, NJ: Enslow, 2003.

Shelton, Robert. *No Direction Home: The Life and Music of Bob Dylan*. New York: William Morrow, 1986.

Sounes, Howard. *Down the Highway: The Life of Bob Dylan.* New York: Grove Press, 2001.

Web Sites

Bobdylan.com. http://www.bobdylan.com (accessed August 2004).

Betty Friedan

Born February 4, 1921
Peoria, Illinois

Writer, women's rights activist

"The problem lay buried, unspoken, for many years…. As [each suburban wife] made the beds, shopped for groceries, matched slipcover material, … chauffeured Cub Scouts and Brownies, lay beside her husband at night—she was afraid to ask even of herself the silent question—'Is this all?'"

—Betty Friedan

Betty Friedan. *AP/Wide World Photos. Reproduced by permission.*

The feminist movement began sweeping American society in the late 1960s and early 1970s. It consisted of people who believed in equal rights for both sexes. It might have come about without Betty Friedan, but her presence within and her impact on the movement were vast. Friedan's book *The Feminine Mystique* (1963) clearly defined many issues concerning women's rights. Such ideas were central to what came to be known as the Women's Liberation Movement.

Early education and work

Betty Friedan was born Betty (possibly Bettye) Naomi Goldstein in Peoria, Illinois, on February 4, 1921. Her birth was less than one year after the passage of the Nineteenth Amendment to the U.S. Constitution, which allowed women across the United States the right to vote. Her father, Harry, was a jeweler. Miriam (Horowitz), her mother, had quit her job as the women's page editor of a local newspaper upon her marriage and became a homemaker. Miriam Goldstein missed her former job and encouraged Betty to attend college and become a journalist.

Friedan majored in psychology at Smith College in Northampton, Massachusetts. She graduated summa cum laude, which is Latin for "with the highest praise," in 1942. At Smith, she established a literary magazine, edited the school newspaper, and became preoccupied with social justice issues and the plight of American workers. She started graduate work in psychology at the University of California at Berkeley. Friedan won a research scholarship that would have fully funded her studies, but after one year she quit graduate school and moved to New York City. Her first job there was reporting on labor-related issues for a small newspaper. Despite her good work, Friedan was forced to relinquish the job to a returning soldier at the end of World War II (1939–45).

The war had a major effect on women in terms of working outside the home as well as the types of jobs they could do. When men went off to fight the war, women were needed to assume many of the jobs left open by men. Some women worked in war munitions or bomber factories, others became reporters, accountants, farmers, and even baseball players. When the war ended and the soldiers returned home, many women were expected or forced to give up their jobs to them. Some women found other work, while others returned to life as homemakers. For many, the accomplishments they felt as working women stayed with them forever. Such feelings prompted some women to seek careers in addition to having families.

Work and family

In 1947, Betty married Carl Friedan, a theater producer and advertising executive. For a time, she worked for a labor union paper. When she became pregnant, she went on maternity leave and came back to her job after giving birth. Upon learning that she was pregnant with her second child in 1949, Friedan asked for another maternity leave. Instead of granting her request, the paper laid her off. Her union refused to come to her assistance, even though her contract allowed for the maternity leave. Friedan settled into a life as a homemaker, mother, and occasional freelance writer for women's magazines. Carl and Betty Friedan eventually moved to the suburbs of New York. They had a third child together, but their marriage did not last. They divorced in 1969.

Friedan's married life was like that of many people who were married in the 1940s through the 1960s. In the 1940s, husbands provided most of the money for the family, and, upon marrying, women were expected to stay home to tend to household chores and raise children. In the 1940s and 1950s, some women attended university not to prepare for a career, but rather to find a "college man" to wed. Such women were looking for a man whose education would enable him to secure a high-paying job that would adequately support a family and a suburban-American lifestyle. Some women did enter the workforce briefly, but many, like Friedan, eventually left their jobs to take care of their growing families.

Evolution of a book

Being a homemaker and mother left Friedan feeling unfulfilled. She viewed her choices and those of other women as very limited. To see if others felt the same way, Friedan wrote a questionnaire and distributed it to her former college classmates in 1957. She discovered that many shared her frustration. She then sent out more detailed surveys and carried out interviews. Friedan discussed her findings with psychologists and behavioral experts, people who specialize in analyzing human behavior. Her findings, plus her own ideas and experiences, formed the basis for her first book, *The Feminine Mystique* (1963). Her book immediately sparked controversy. It became a bestseller, with more than three million copies in circulation. The work was translated into thirteen languages. More importantly, it helped spark the women's liberation movement of the late 1960s and early 1970s.

The Feminine Mystique was read and taken to heart by a generation of women who agreed with Friedan's point of view. At the same time, other readers with more conservative and traditional views opposed Friedan's work. They claimed that her ideas would upset the framework of American society. As of the early 2000s, the ideas in *The Feminine Mystique* continued to be approved by some and criticized by others. But over the years since its publication, the long-lasting and far-reaching impact of the book has been significant. *The Feminine Mystique* is looked upon as one of the most significant books published in the United States during the twentieth century.

"The Problem That Has No Name"

In *The Feminine Mystique,* Friedan explored how women fit into American society in the fifteen years following the end of World War II. She argued that women were oppressed by what she called the "mystique of feminine fulfillment." This was the false notion that personal satisfaction came only through what she believed was a false femininity. According to traditional values, women were expected to be good wives and mothers and have pride in the accomplishments of their husbands and children. In this regard, they could only experience fulfilling lives if they married and became mothers. Women as a group also were discriminated against socially and in the job market. They were stereotyped in popular culture and were depicted in television shows and commercials as happy homemakers who were forever baking cookies for their children or mindlessly smiling as they ironed clothes or washed floors. In *The Feminine Mystique,* Friedan labeled this dilemma "the problem that has no name."

Devotion to "The Movement"

In 1966, Friedan was one of the co-founders of the National Organization for Women (NOW). A political action group, NOW formed to win equal rights for women. As the group's first president, Friedan set out to integrate women into the economic and political mainstream of America. She organized drives to elect more women to political office, establish child-care facilities for working mothers, and halt the publication of job notices that specified gender. At the time, abortion was illegal. In 1969, Friedan also co-founded the National Abortion and Reproductive Rights Action League (NARAL).

Friedan remained in the top position at NOW until 1970, when she left to help coordinate the Women's Strike for Equality, a national women's rights protest. It was held on August 26, 1970, marking the fiftieth anniversary of the passage of the Nineteenth Amendment. Friedan also became one of the more high-profile supporters for passage of the Equal Rights Amendment. The proposed constitutional amendment would make all individuals equal before the law regardless of gender. In 1971, she became a founding member of the National Women's Political Caucus. The group's goal was to increase women's involvement in American politics and to support women interested in gender equality in their efforts to

Betty Friedan marches with other women in the fight for gender equality in 1970. The occasion marks the fiftieth anniversary of the Nineteenth Amendment, which gave women full voting rights. © *JP Laffont/Sygma/Corbis. Reproduced by permission.*

win public office. Two years later, she was named director of the First Women's Bank and Trust Company, founded and operated by women. At the time, nearly all commercial banks showed prejudice against women who attempted to borrow money or secure mortgages. Her activism on behalf of her gender extended beyond the borders of the United States. She lobbied the United Nations to proclaim 1975 as the "International Year of Women." In 1989, she co-founded *Women,*

Men, and Media, a yearly analysis of the manner in which women are reported on in newspapers, television, radio, and other media.

On occasion Friedan's ideas have conflicted with those of other women's movement leaders. She has maintained that the women's movement should focus on basic issues affecting all women, such as equal pay for equal work. Her vision was that women and men should cooperate with each other. In the early 1970s, she became distressed by the more radical feminists who pitted women against men in an attempt to gain equality. Nevertheless, Friedan has continued to work toward her own ideals.

More books written and awards won

Although *The Feminine Mystique* was Friedan's most notable book, it was not her only one. *It Changed My Life: Writings on the Women's Movement,* describing her involvement in the movement, was published in 1976. *The Second Stage,* published in 1981, reported on the significance of the movement to that date. *The Fountain of Age,* published in 1993 when Friedan was in her early seventies, explored what it means to enter one's "golden years" in a culture that reveres the young and sees no value in growing older. *Beyond Gender: The New Politics of Work and Family* (1997) explored and questioned the effect of the women's movement on relations between the sexes. In 2002, Friedan wrote a memoir, *Life So Far.* It was written in part as a response to two biographies—Judith Hennessee's *Betty Friedan, Her Life* and Daniel Horowitz's *Betty Friedan and the Making of "The Feminine Mystique."* Friedan felt these books portrayed her in an unflattering light.

Friedan also has written on the subject of feminism for dozens of publications. For example, between 1970 and 1973, she wrote a column for the woman's magazine *McCall's.* Titled "Betty Friedan's Notebook," it described her efforts to publicize the women's movement across the world. She lectured extensively around the world and held visiting university professorships. She taught at New York University, the University of Southern California, and other institutions of higher learning. She was a Chubb Fellow at Yale University and Adjunct Scholar at the Wilson International Center for

Scholars at the Smithsonian Institution. Her many awards include the Wilhelmina Drucker Prize for contribution to the emancipation of men and women (1971); the Humanist of the Year award (1975); and the Eleanor Roosevelt Leadership Award (1989). In 1994, Columbia University granted her an honorary doctorate.

For More Information

Books

Archer, Jules. *Breaking Barriers: The Feminist Revolution from Susan B. Anthony to Margaret Sanger to Betty Friedan.* New York: Viking, 1991.

Friedan, Betty. *Beyond Gender: The New Politics of Work and Family.* Washington, DC: Woodrow Wilson Center Press, 1997.

Friedan, Betty. *The Feminine Mystique.* New York: Norton, 1963.

Friedan, Betty. *The Fountain of Age.* New York: Simon & Schuster, 1993.

Friedan, Betty. *It Changed My Life: Writings on the Women's Movement.* New York: Random House, 1976.

Friedan, Betty. *Life So Far.* New York: Simon & Schuster, 2000.

Friedan, Betty. *The Second Stage.* New York: Summit Books, 1981.

Hennessee, Judith. *Betty Friedan, Her Life.* New York: Random House, 1999.

Horowitz, Daniel. *Betty Friedan and the Making of "The Feminine Mystique."* Amherst, MA: University of Massachusetts Press, 1998.

Sherman, Janann, ed. *Interviews with Betty Friedan.* Jackson, MS: University of Mississippi Press, 2002.

Periodicals

Wolfe, Alan. "The Mystique of Betty Friedan." *Atlantic Monthly* (September 1999): pp. 98-105.

Barry Goldwater

Born January 1, 1909
Phoenix, Arizona

Died May 29, 1998
Paradise Valley, Arizona

Republican politician and
presidential candidate

B arry Goldwater's campaign for the presidency in 1964 represented an important change in American politics. Goldwater drew national attention to a debate over the role of the federal government. In basic terms, the debate was over the extent to which the federal government should involve itself in solving social problems such as poverty and racism. Although Goldwater lost the presidential election to **Lyndon B. Johnson** (1908–1973; served 1963–69; see entry), his candidacy marked the beginning of the conservative movement in America. The movement rallied people behind political ideals that went by the labels "individual freedom," "self-reliance," and "decentralized government." Nicknamed "Mr. Conservative" for his leading role in the conservative movement, Goldwater had a fiery personality and striking good looks. He was able to use his presidential campaign to rally people to reduce the size of the federal government. Although Goldwater's ideas frightened some during the 1960s, within twenty years of his campaign some of his ideas formed the bedrock of the Republican Party's political platform. Voters showed their support for these conservative ideas with the election of

"I would remind you that extremism in the defense of liberty is no vice. And let me remind you that moderation in the pursuit of justice is no virtue."

—*Barry Goldwater.*

Barry Goldwater. *Photo courtesy of The Library of Congress.*

47

Republican president Ronald Reagan in 1980 and the election of a Republican majority in Congress in 1994.

Building the family business

Barry Morris Goldwater was born on January 1, 1909, in Phoenix, Arizona. He was the son of Baron and Josephine (Williams) Goldwater. His father ran a successful department store, which offered young Barry a wealthy upbringing. A year after graduating at the top of his class from Staunton Military Academy in 1928, Barry entered the University of Arizona. After his father died, Barry left his studies at the University of Arizona to start working in the family business as a junior clerk. He became general manager of the Phoenix store at age twenty-seven. His skill in running the family business fueled his rise to the presidency of Goldwater Inc. by 1937.

As Goldwater rose in his career, he started a family. Goldwater married Margaret Johnson on September 22, 1934, and the couple soon had four children: Joanne, Barry Morris Jr., Michael Prescott, and Margaret.

He managed Goldwater Inc. with innovative ideas. He offered employees health benefits, organized a flying club, instituted a five-day workweek, and was the first to hire black sales clerks in Phoenix. Having made Goldwater Inc. the most prestigious store in Arizona, he developed a national reputation for it by advertising in such magazines as the *New Yorker* and introducing new product lines.

Beginning in 1930, Goldwater started taking flying lessons. By the outbreak of World War II (1939–45), he was a licensed pilot and serving in the U.S. Army Air Force Reserve. Goldwater took leave of his business to support the United States during the war. Unable to secure a combat flying position, he flew supplies across both the Pacific and Atlantic Oceans for the U.S. Army Air Force. His missions mostly involved flying between the United States and India. At war's end, Goldwater organized the Arizona National Guard, culminating his career in the military as brigadier general in the Air Force Reserve.

Although his life seemed to be running smoothly, Goldwater suffered personally from two nervous breakdowns and from trouble with alcohol. Although these problems did not stop him, they were matters of discussion by others as he began to pursue a career in politics.

Becoming "Mr. Conservative"

Back in Phoenix after the war, Goldwater continued his innovative managerial style at Goldwater Inc. He also began to show an interest in his city government. In 1949 he was recognized as Phoenix's "Man of the Year." He won a nonpartisan seat on the Phoenix City Council by a landslide. Within three years, Goldwater had outgrown local politics and set his sights on a seat in the U.S. Senate. In 1952, Goldwater won the election as a Republican. Over the next decade, Goldwater emerged as a strong conservative leader within the Republican Party. He supported cutting back the federal government's programs and spending. He became chairperson of the Republican Senatorial Campaign Committee in 1960 and traveled to every state to meet with conservative Republicans. He fostered his growing dominance in the party by publishing a newspaper column three times a week. In 1960, he issued a book titled *The Conscience of a Conservative,* which outlined his approach to politics.

His book defined the political beliefs of many conservatives. A telling quotation from his book sums up his approach: "I have little interest in streamlining government or in making it more efficient, for I mean to reduce its size. I do not undertake to promote welfare, for I propose to extend freedom. My aim is not to pass laws, but to repeal them. It is not to inaugurate new programs, but to cancel old ones that do violence to the Constitution, or that have failed in their purpose, or that impose on the people an unwarranted financial burden." He added: "I will not attempt to discover whether legislation is 'needed' before I have first determined whether it is constitutionally permissible. And if I should later be attacked for neglecting my constituents 'interests,' I shall reply that I was informed their main interest is liberty and that in that cause, I am doing the very best I can."

Goldwater's plan was to reduce the size of the federal government by cutting existing federal programs. He sought to repeal existing laws that placed social rules and financial obligations on citizens. These ideas thrilled people who believed that only state governments had the authority to regulate individual's lives. But for some, Goldwater's plan was frightening. Blacks living in states with racially discriminatory laws worried that they would never obtain equal rights if Goldwater won the election.

Changing the Republican Party

By 1964 Goldwater had won the Republican presidential nomination. He had begun his history-making campaign against Lyndon B. Johnson, who had assumed the presidential office after the 1963 assassination of **John F. Kennedy** (1917–1963; served 1961–63; see entry). As a presidential candidate, Goldwater became the spokesperson for the conservative wing of the Republican Party. He was much more conservative than previous Republican nominees. As such, his candidacy for the nation's top office threatened to split the Republican Party. He opposed federal programs and laws that took what he considered to be constitutionally protected freedoms away from Americans and private businesses. Goldwater believed individuals were responsible for themselves, and states ought to be free to design their own laws regarding their residents. Goldwater disagreed with the civil rights movement, the equal rights movement, and government aid for the poor. These movements urged the federal government to write laws in these areas of American lives. As senator he voted against the 1964 Civil Rights Act.

But Goldwater did not oppose all government power. He considered the threat of communism real and worth funding. Goldwater sought to expand the American military in order to aggressively control the threat of communism. During the presidential campaign he warned that Johnson was losing the Vietnam War (1954–75) to the communists. He called for the use of atomic bombs against the enemy.

Goldwater's views were embraced by those who feared the changes that some people were demanding in the 1960s. Some supporters of Goldwater feared that civil rights, feminism, and protests against the war would erode traditional morals and values that they associated with American life. Moreover, supporters of Goldwater worried that these

Grassroots Efforts for Goldwater

As Goldwater's 1964 presidential campaign got more intense, his supporters banded together to promote their candidate. Goldwater rallied conservatives by telling them in a campaign speech that Republicans were not losing elections because more people were voting for the Democrats. Instead, he claimed that conservatives were just not getting out to vote.

Youth groups sprang up around the country, attracting thousands of conservative students as Goldwater supporters. One group of Peabody College students assembled a folk band, calling themselves the Goldwaters. They recorded an album, the cover of which featured a picture of the quartet in red sweaters and khaki pants with the words "The Goldwaters Sing Folk Songs to Bug the Liberals." The Goldwaters cut their album in Nashville, Tennessee, and distributed it in 1964 to Republican groups around the country. Soon the Goldwaters were asked to perform live at functions for Goldwater groups and Republican organizations.

Earlier, the Youth for Goldwater group, which developed into the Young Americans for Freedom (YAF), organized 2,700 members across 115 college campuses and published a directory of 97 conservative clubs on campuses in 25 states. Three thousand supporters attended the YAF's first rally in New York in 1961. Another three thousand were turned away. The YAF campaigned strongly for Goldwater. They hoped through grassroots (local, popularly based) efforts to land a conservative president in the White House and take control of the Republication Party. For the California primary, nearly eight thousand activists from the Young Republicans, Young Americans for Freedom, and the John Birch Society combed through California precincts to turn out every vote for Goldwater.

When Goldwater lost the election, many conservative youth groups dissolved. But their efforts paved the way for those who, in the coming years, would again champion a conservative vision of government. The conservatives had developed efficient organizing efforts at the grassroots level of the Republican Party that would enable them to take control of the party in the coming years.

changes would raise their taxes and that they might give some groups of Americans an unfair advantage over others.

Speaking candidly, and often without a prepared speech, Goldwater never softened his opinions, no matter to whom he was speaking. During a 1961 news conference, the *Chicago Tribune* recorded Goldwater saying, "sometimes I think this country would be better off if we could just saw off the Eastern Seaboard and let it float out to sea," as quoted in

Barry Goldwater greets his enthusiastic supporters in Indianapolis, Indiana, during the 1964 presidential campaign. *AP/Wide World Photos. Reproduced by permission.*

The Goldwater Caper. On the campaign trail in Tennessee, where the government controlled America's largest public power company, Goldwater suggested that government-owned property be sold to private investors. He criticized farm subsidies in front of a crowd of North Dakotan farmers. In South Carolina, where blacks and whites lived segregated lives, Goldwater reminded voters that he had voted against the Civil Rights Act of 1964. He declared that the reasons poor people might need government aid stemmed from laziness or stupidity.

Goldwater triggered national fear of nuclear war when he discussed the idea of using atomic weapons in Vietnam in 1963. Goldwater acknowledged that he sometimes spoke without considering the consequences first. He stated that "There are words of mine floating around in the air that I would like to reach up and eat," according to the *Washington Post.* His statements so upset his aides that they would ask reporters to "write what he means, not what he says," noted the *Washington Post.*

The press published several attacks on Goldwater's mental fitness for the presidency. The *Saturday Evening Post* called him a "wild man, a stray." The paper wrote: "For the good of the Republican Party, which his candidacy disgraces, we hope that Goldwater is crushingly defeated." During Goldwater's campaign, his psychological fitness was questioned. *Fact* magazine published a sixty-four-page survey of professional psychologists that suggested Goldwater was mentally unfit to become president. Goldwater's campaign slogan, "In Your Heart, You Know He's Right," was turned against him with rhymes that reflected the fear he stirred. His opponents said: "In Your Heart, You Know He Might [use nuclear weapons]" and "In your guts, you know he's nuts."

Goldwater recognized that the press found him a troubling candidate. He recalled in his memoirs, *With No Apologies: The Personal and Political Memoirs of United States Senator Barry M. Goldwater,* being labeled during the campaign as "a fascist, a racist, trigger-happy warmonger, a nuclear madman, and the candidate who couldn't win." The *Washington Post* related that "he would have voted against himself in 1964 if he believed everything that had been written or said on radio and television about him."

Johnson defeated Goldwater by a huge margin in the 1964 presidential election. Goldwater remembered the race for presidency as like "trying to stand up in a hammock," according to *With No Apologies.* Even though Goldwater lost, his candidacy spurred a rightward movement in American political thought and marked the first time the majority of voters in the South voted for a Republican candidate.

Goldwater did not run for his senatorial seat at the same time he ran for president. As a result, he spent four years out of political office. In 1968 Goldwater won reelection to his senatorial seat, and he remained a conservative leader in the Senate until he retired in 1987. His last major act as a senator was to help pass the Defense Department Reorganization Act of 1986, which restructured the military command at the Pentagon. Goldwater remembered it as "the only goddamn thing I ever did in the Senate that was worth a damn." He went on to say that he could now "go home happy, sit up on my hill and shoot the jackrabbits," according to the *Arizona Republic*.

Goldwater's wife, Margaret, died in 1985. He married health care executive Susan Schaffer Wechsler in 1992. Even after his retirement, Goldwater continued to speak out about political issues. Always someone who spoke his mind, even when it conflicted with the general Republican platform, Goldwater was pro-choice in the abortion debate and was in favor of allowing gays to serve in the military. He died in 1998.

For More Information

Books

Edwards, Lee. *Goldwater: The Man Who Made a Revolution.* Washington, DC: Regnery, 1995.

Goldberg, Robert Alan. *Barry Goldwater.* New Haven, CT: Yale University Press, 1995.

Goldwater, Barry M. *The Conscience of a Conservative.* Shepherdsville, KY: Victor Publishing Company, 1960.

Goldwater, Barry M. *With No Apologies: The Personal and Political Memoirs of United States Senator Barry M. Goldwater,* New York: William Morrow, 1979.

Perlstein, Rick. *Before the Storm: Barry Goldwater and the Unmaking of the American Consensus.* New York: Hill and Wang, 2001.

Rovere, Richard H. *The Goldwater Caper.* New York: Harcourt, Brace, and World, 1964.

Periodicals

Barnes, Bart. "Barry Goldwater, GOP Hero, Dies." *Washington Post* (May 30, 1998): p. A1.

Buckley, William F., Jr. "Barry Goldwater, RIP." *National Review* 50 (June 22, 1998): pp. 20-23.

Cooper, Matthew. "The Founding Father." *Newsweek* 131 (June 8, 1998): p. 35.

Edwards, Lee. "He Ran Up the Conservative Flag and a Rising Generation Saluted." *Insight on the News* 14 (June 29, 1998): pp. 30-31.

Poole, Robert W., Jr. "In Memoriam: Barry Goldwater." *Reason* 30 (August-September 1998): p. 11.

Web Sites

"Goldwater Biographical Info." *Arizona Republic.* http://www.azcentral.com/specials/special25/articles/0602GoldwaterFacts01-ON.html (accessed August 2004).

Berry Gordy Jr.

Born November 28, 1929
Detroit, Michigan

Music industry business manager;
founder of Motown Records

Berry Gordy Jr. AP/Wide World Photos. Reproduced by permission.

In 1959, thirty-year-old Berry Gordy Jr. was a former professional boxer, failed record-store owner, ex-automobile plant assembly line worker, and moderately successful songwriter. That year he started his own company, which came to be known as The Motown Record Corporation. The company began releasing singles and record albums featuring African American artists. The following year, the Motown single "Shop Around" by The Miracles gave Gordy his first gold record, selling five hundred thousand copies. Many more gold records were to follow. During the 1960s, Motown became one of the leading independent record companies in the United States. It was also the country's biggest and most successful black-owned entertainment-industry business. Its distinctive "Motown Sound" appealed to people of all races and was among the most popular music of the 1960s.

Prizefighter/jazz-lover

Berry Gordy Jr. was born on November 28, 1929, in Detroit, Michigan. He was the son of Berry Sr. and Bertha

Gordy. Unlike many other African Americans of the period, his family was solidly middle-class. The Gordy family operated a successful painting and construction company. His father owned a grocery store, and his mother was one of the founders of a life insurance company.

Young Berry was not interested in following his parents into business, however. He left high school during his junior year to become a professional prizefighter. He served in the U.S. Army between 1951 and 1953. Upon returning to Detroit, he opened a record store that specialized in jazz records. Because of his fondness for this type of music and his desire to promote it commercially, Berry refused to sell the rhythm-and-blues recordings that were more popular in the African American community. In 1955 Gordy's store went out of business.

By the mid-1950s, Gordy had married and fathered three children. To support his family, he took a job working as an upholstery trimmer on an assembly line at a Lincoln-Mercury automobile manufacturing plant. But Gordy remained consumed by his fascination with music. He was convinced that he could build a career in the entertainment industry. He soon left the plant to seek his destiny as a songwriter.

First success

In the mid-1950s, the Flame Show Bar was a popular Detroit nightspot that presented many of America's top black entertainers. Al Green, the bar's owner, also managed a number of these performers. Gordy began composing songs for them. His initial success came in 1957 with "Reet Petite," written with Tyran Carlo, who also worked under the name Roquel "Billy" Davis. The tune was sung by Jackie Wilson, who was celebrated for his striking tenor voice. With his sister, Gwen, and Billy Davis, Gordy wrote additional hits for Wilson. The trio composed the rhythmic classic "Lonely Teardrops" and a ballad, "To Be Loved," both of which became hits in 1958. They also wrote the bouncy "That's Why (I Love You So)" and "I'll Be Satisfied." In the late 1950s Gordy also began producing some of the songs he composed.

One day, Gordy saw the singing group The Matadors audition for Jackie Wilson's manager. The manager was unimpressed, but Gordy felt the group had talent. Gordy began managing the group, which changed its name to The Miracles. In 1958 the group produced its first record, "Got a Job," a musical response to "Get a Job," a hit by The Silhouettes. "Got a Job" disappeared after gaining brief radio airplay. But in the process Gordy formed a close friendship with The Miracles' lead singer, Smokey Robinson.

At this point, Gordy's songs were recorded and released by different record labels. He had no influence on how they were marketed or on their ultimate success. For this reason, he decided to borrow $800 from his family and form his own record label. In January of 1959 the Tamla Record Company opened for business. "Tamla" was a variation of *Tammy,* a popular movie of the era starring Debbie Reynolds, who had scored a hit with the title song. Tamla's first release—"Come to Me" by Marv Johnson—was issued only regionally because Gordy lacked the resources to market it nationally. As it rose on the charts, he licensed it to United Artists Records. "Come to Me" eventually became a Top-30 hit. Later in 1959 Tamla enjoyed success with "Money," by Barrett Strong, which was distributed nationally by Anna Records and also broke into the Top 30.

"Hitsville U.S.A."

In 1960, Gordy renamed his company The Motown Record Corporation. He established offices in a two-story house located at 2648 West Grand Boulevard in Detroit (now home to the Motown Historical Museum). He transformed the basement into a recording studio and placed a "Hitsville U.S.A." sign out front. Motown's first release, in June 1960, was "Sugar Daddy," by The Satintones. It was not a chartbuster. Around this time, Gordy also established his own music publishing company—named Jobete in honor of his three children, Hazel Joy, Berry, and Terry. He also started a management agency, International Talent Management.

The year 1961 was a banner year for Gordy and Motown. In January, "Shop Around" by The Miracles rose to number one on the national rhythm-and-blues charts and to number two on the pop Top 100. At a time when civil rights demonstrations were increasing racial tensions across the

United States, the record's rating was an extraordinary accomplishment. The across-the-board success of "Shop Around," not to mention Motown's future hits, was proof that Gordy's music transcended racial barriers. That June, Gordy issued his first full-length record albums on the Tamla label: *Hi! We're The Miracles* and *The Soulful Moods of Marvin Gaye.* Gordy signed such future star acts as The Supremes (who started out as backup vocalists), The Temptations, and Steveland Morris. Steveland was a sweet-voiced pre-teen who had been blind since birth and who was billed as Little Stevie Wonder. Finally in December, "Please Mr. Postman" by The Marvelettes— Motown's first girl group—became Motown's first number one pop hit. The singers first met Gordy through one of their high school teachers.

In 1962 Gordy helped assemble the songwriting-production team of Brian Holland, Lamont Dozier, and Eddie Holland, soon to become legendary as Holland-Dozier-Holland. The team's first Top-30 hit, Martha and The Vandellas' "Come and Get These Memories," came the following year. That group's lead singer, Martha Reeves, came to Motown as a secretary. She and The Vandellas began recording for Gordy as backup singers. One of their later hits, "Dancing in the Streets," became an urban American anthem for celebration and good times. The Contours' "Do You Love Me" was another important Gordy hit of this period, as was Mary Wells' melodic "You Beat Me to the Punch." The latter became the first Motown single to be nominated for a Grammy Award, the music industry's top honor. The year 1962 climaxed with a national road tour of top Motown performers, which ended in a ten-day appearance at the Apollo Theater in Harlem, New York. The participating acts included The Miracles, Martha and The Vandellas, The Marvelettes, The Contours, The Supremes, Marvin Gaye, Mary Wells, Marv Johnson, and Singin' Sammy Ward.

At Motown, the hits rolled in and the company rapidly developed into a hit-producing factory. The Supremes' first recordings were unsuccessful, but under the supervision of Holland-Dozier-Holland, the group became a star act. The group enjoyed a dazzling succession of number one singles, starting with "Where Did Our Love Go" in 1964. Between 1964 and 1967, The Supremes were the world's top female singing act. Two contrasting classics, Mary Wells's "My Guy"

and The Temptations' "My Girl," both topped the charts. Marvin Gaye and the group Gladys Knight and The Pips each scored with different renditions of the same song, "I Heard It Through the Grapevine." Motown releases regularly crashed the charts, often hitting number one. In 1966, an astounding 75 percent of all Motown singles made the Top 100.

Grooming for stardom

Many Motown performers came to Gordy as raw, unpolished talents who were still in, or barely out of, their teens. He guided them, hiring top professionals to teach them how to talk, dress, and move onstage. Then he marketed them, arranging for appearances on the era's top TV variety shows, such as *American Bandstand* and the *Ed Sullivan Show.* However, not all Motown acts were entertainment

The Supremes (from left, Florence Ballard, Diana Ross, and Mary Wilson) sing one of their hit songs in 1965.
© Bettmann/Corbis.
Reproduced by permission.

industry novices. In 1963 Gordy signed The Four Tops, a group of singers who had been performing together for a decade. Under Gordy they enjoyed their greatest success with such smash hits as "Baby I Need Your Loving," "I Can't Help Myself (Sugar Pie, Honey Bunch)," "Reach Out I'll Be There," and "Standing in the Shadows of Love." In 1969 The Temptations' "Cloud Nine" became the first Motown release to win a Grammy. The following year, five siblings called The Jackson 5, featuring lead vocals by twelve-year-old Michael Jackson, enjoyed their first Motown chart-topper: "I Want You Back."

By the end of the 1960s, Berry Gordy had built an entertainment industry empire. He owned numerous record labels, in addition to his management and publishing companies, and had earned millions. Motown had become the biggest and most profitable black-owned entertainment industry corporation in the United States and one of the most prosperous black-operated businesses of any type. The success of Motown also helped carve a spot in the record industry for younger, up-and-coming black producers and executives.

Despite its successes, however, Motown's foundation was jolted by discontent among its performers and production team. In 1967 Gordy fired Florence Ballard, one of The Supremes, who was becoming increasingly jealous of the popularity of lead singer Diana Ross. The next year, he dismissed The Temptations' David Ruffin. Finally, Holland-Dozier-Holland left the company in a dispute over royalties and filed a $20-million lawsuit against Motown.

During the 1970s Gordy focused on the careers of such emerging acts as The Jackson 5 and Diana Ross, who had left The Supremes and gone solo. He relocated to Hollywood, founded Motown Industries, and became involved in the production of motion pictures, television shows, and Broadway musicals. Although many of its original acts left the company and signed with other record labels, Motown remained a significant power in the industry. Diana Ross stayed with the label, as did Stevie Wonder, Marvin Gaye, and The Commodores. Unlike the good-time feeling that characterized previous releases, a few Motown records dealt with topical political and social issues. "War" (1970) by Edwin Starr mirrored the era's anti-Vietnam sentiment. Marvin Gaye's spiritual album, *What's Going On* (1971), generated three hit singles: "Mercy Mercy Me (The Ecology)," "Inner City Blues (Make Me Wanna Holler)," and the title song.

The Motown of the 1980s resembled the original company even less, with additional performers leaving it. But in 1983 Gordy mounted a triumphant twenty-fifth-anniversary commemoration, featuring many original Tamla/Motown

 ## The "Motown Sound"

At a time when crossover between African American and white culture in America was rare, the infectious gospel-inspired sound of Motown appealed to teenagers of all races and backgrounds. The classic mid-1960s Motown recordings followed a winning formula. They were danceable and soulfully romantic. Their beats were crisp and lively. They were characterized by the pounding, finger-snapping rhythms provided by The Funk Brothers, Motown's in-house band.

Motown lyrics centered on such youthful concerns as falling in or out of love, devotion to or yearning for one's boyfriend or girlfriend, and dancing and having fun. Motown recordings avoided traditional black blues, with its obvious references to sexuality, drug and alcohol use, and gloomy, tragic love affairs. This distinctive formula defined what came to be known as the "Motown Sound." It was publicized by Gordy as "The Sound of Young America."

artists, that was broadcast on ABC-TV. At the same time, former employees, including various Marvelettes and Vandellas, sued Gordy, claiming that they had not been paid royalties.

In 1988, Gordy sold his Motown empire to MCA and Boston Ventures for $61 million. He was elected to the Rock and Roll Hall of Fame in 1990. Four years later, he published his autobiography, *To Be Loved: The Music, the Magic, the Memories of Motown.*

For More Information

Books

Dahl, Bill. *Motown: The Golden Years.* Iola, WI: Krause, 2001.

George, Nelson. *Where Did Our Love Go? The Rise and Fall of the Motown Sound.* New York: St. Martin's Press, 1985.

Gordy, Berry, Jr. *To Be Loved: The Music, the Magic, the Memories of Motown.* New York: Warner Books, 1994.

Periodicals

Whitall, Susan. "Berry Gordy Jr." *Detroit News* (April 8, 2001).

Web Sites

"Berry Gordy Jr." *Rock & Roll Hall of Fame and Museum.* http://www.rockhall.com/hof/inductee.asp?id=111 (accessed August 2004).

Classic Motown. http://www.motown.com/classicmotown (accessed August 2004).

Edwards, David, and Mike Callahan. *The Motown Story and Album Discography.* http://www.bsnpubs.com/gordystory.html (accessed August 2004).

Virgil "Gus" Grissom

Born April 3, 1926
Mitchell, Indiana

Died January 27, 1967
Kennedy Space Center,
Cape Canaveral, Florida

American astronaut

Frustrated that the Soviet Union had launched the first manmade object into orbit in 1957, the United States stepped up its efforts to be the first to put a human into space. To win the space race, the U.S. Congress created the National Aeronautics and Space Administration (NASA) in 1958. Among the first to respond to his country's call to pioneer space travel was Virgil "Gus" Grissom. From among five hundred military pilots who met the standards NASA set for its first astronauts, Grissom passed weeks of testing to be named one of America's first astronauts for the Mercury 7 project launch on April 9, 1959. Grissom's work over the next eight years helped create a strong foundation for the future of the U.S. space program.

> "If we die, we want people to accept it. We're in a risky business, and we hope if anything happens to us, it will not delay the program. The conquest of space is worth the risk of life."
>
> —*Gus Grissom, several weeks before his death.*

For the love of flying

Born Virgil Ivan Grissom on April 3, 1926, in Mitchell, Indiana, "Gus" Grissom grew up in a loving family. His father, Dennis, a Baltimore and Ohio Railroad employee, and his mother, Cecile, raised Gus with his two younger

Gus Grissom.
© Bettmann/Corbis.
Reproduced by permission.

brothers and sister. As a child, Gus assembled balsa wood airplane models, learned to hunt and fish, and became a Boy Scout. He earned spending money delivering newspapers twice a day. In the summer, he picked peaches and cherries in the orchards near town.

The United States was involved in World War II (1939-45) as Grissom finished high school. During his senior year, he enlisted as an aviation cadet. After graduation he immediately reported to the Army Air Corps, which later became the U.S. Air Force, to learn to become a pilot. The war had ended by the time he had finished training. Grissom was discharged in November 1945.

Grissom married his high school sweetheart, Betty Moore, on July 6, 1945. The couple settled in Mitchell. Grissom worked at a bus manufacturer in Mitchell to earn money but knew he did not want to install doors on school buses forever. He decided to study mechanical engineering at Purdue University in West Lafayette, Indiana. Betty worked as a long distance telephone operator, and Gus flipped hamburgers at a local diner to pay for his education. He graduated with a bachelor's degree in 1950.

Earns his wings

With his degree in hand, Grissom set a new goal for himself. He sought to become a military test pilot and rejoined the U.S. Air Force. By 1951 he had earned the rank of lieutenant and his pilot's wings. His first assignment was to fly an F-86 fighter jet during the Korean War (1950–53). Unlike other pilots who named their planes after their wives or girlfriends, Grissom chose the name "Scotty" for his plane, in honor of his newborn son. He flew one hundred combat missions, earning a Distinguished Flying Cross and two Air Medals by war's end.

In 1953, Grissom became an Air Force flight instructor and the father of a second son, Mark. Over the next few years, Grissom's good work earned him the rank of captain and a coveted spot in the test-pilot school at Edwards Air Force Base in California. Grissom had just become a test pilot when in 1957 the Soviet Union launched *Sputnik 1,* the first

manmade object to go into orbit. When the U.S. Congress established NASA to seek and train astronauts to man the first rockets into space, Grissom met all the requirements. He was younger than 40; less than 5 feet 11 inches tall; had more than 1,500 hours of flying time; and had graduated from test-pilot school.

Grissom did not just sign up to become an astronaut, he was given an invitation. One day he received a message classified as "Top Secret" instructing him to report in civilian (non-military) clothes to an address in Washington, D.C., on a particular date. Grissom said, "in the Air Force you get some weird orders, but you obey them, no matter what…. I was convinced that somehow or other I had wandered right into the middle of a James Bond novel," according to his memoir, *Gemini.* At his appointment, Grissom learned that he was among the 110 candidates selected to go through extensive medical and psychological testing. The tests would determine who among them would be the first American astronauts.

The first men chosen for the U.S. space program hold model spacecraft (from left: Walter M. Schirra, Alan B. Shepard, Gus Grissom, Donald K. Slayton, John H. Glenn, M. Scott Carpenter, and L. Gordon Cooper).
© Bettmann/Corbis. Reproduced by permission.

Those selected went through weeks of testing. This included challenges such as being locked in a completely darkened room, enduring high frequency noises while being shaken by a vibrating machine, and activating buttons and switches at an increasingly quick pace. Grissom was nearly disqualified. He was allergic to ragweed pollen, and this fact worried Air Force officials. But Grissom convinced the Air Force to let him continue. According to Betty Grissom and Henry Still in *Starfall,* Gus argued that "there won't be any ragweed pollen in space." On April 9, 1959, Grissom and six others were named America's first astronauts. The group was nicknamed the Mercury 7 after the rocket that would hurl them into space. Mercury 7 included Grissom, Navy Lieutenant M. Scott Carpenter, Air Force Captain L. Gordon Cooper Jr., Marine Lieutenant Colonel John H. Glenn Jr., Navy Lieutenant Commander Walter M. Schirra Jr., Navy Lieutenant Commander Alan B. Shepard Jr., and Air Force Captain Donald K. Slayton. These seven would man the flights of Project Mercury, NASA's attempts to orbit Earth in the early 1960s. Upon accepting his new position, Grissom moved his young family to the Langley Air Force Base in Virginia so he could live near the training program.

Learning to be the "man in the can"

When Grissom and his fellow astronauts began training to fly into space, no one really knew what to expect. No one had ever done such a thing. Scientists gauged what space might feel like to humans by using mathematical calculations and sophisticated guesses. NASA technicians created simulators, testing devices that created the forces that astronauts might experience when the rocket blasted off and reentered Earth's atmosphere. Astronauts were strapped in a huge centrifuge, a device that simulates the effects of differing forces of gravity. The device spun at dizzying speeds that imitated the pressure of blast off and reentry. NASA technicians also figured out how to imitate the weightlessness, called zero gravity, that they expected to exist in space. Astronauts experienced zero gravity inside the cargo hold of a transport plane. The plane gained altitude and then quickly dove steeply, tossing the astronauts into a moment of weightlessness, and often each other. Even though these astronauts

Why Did America Care about Beating the Soviets to the Moon?

The U.S. space program was established to demonstrate the technological and economic superiority of the United States. It became an important strategic tool in 1961 to help the United States show its strength during the Cold War (1945–91). The Cold War was the long-simmering political conflict between the United States and the Soviet Union. U.S. president John F. Kennedy felt pressure to establish the United States as a leader of rival nations. The nation had just bungled an invasion of Soviet-aided Cuba at the Bay of Pigs. The United States also endured the rise to worldwide fame of Soviet cosmonaut Yuri A. Gagarin (1934–1968) after the Russian became the first to orbit Earth in 1961. Kennedy conceived of Project Apollo as a tool to put America on top in the political conflict. He believed that having American feet be the first on the Moon would prove to the world that the United States was the most powerful nation.

The program took economic power as well as technological knowledge. Project Apollo was the second most expensive non-military technological expenditure in U.S. history at the time, costing $25.4 billion. It was second only to the building of the Panama Canal. When the monitors in the control center in Houston flashed the words "TASK ACCOMPLISHED, July 1969," announcing the successful Apollo trip to the Moon, the United States had proven itself to be a world leader.

were accomplished pilots and spent hours studying rocket and flight operations, they were not expected to actually fly a rocket. The astronauts joked that they were just the "man in the can"; the only control they learned was how to abort the flight in an emergency.

At the same time Americans were preparing to orbit Earth, the Soviets were making similar preparations. One month before Alan Shepard (1923–1998) manned the first U.S. rocket flight on May 5, 1961, the Soviets successfully sent a cosmonaut (the Russian term for astronaut) once around Earth. Shepard's fifteen-minute flight in *Freedom 7* reached an altitude of 116 miles (186.6 kilometers) above Earth and raced at a speed of 5,146 miles per hour (8,279.9 kilometers per hour) but did not go into orbit. The Soviets had beat the Americans again. Rather than admitting defeat, President **John F. Kennedy** (1917–1963; served 1961–63; see entry) saw the Soviets' accomplishment as proof that a new goal should be set for the space race. He proposed that the United States commit itself to sending a man to the Moon by the end of the 1960s.

Grissom's first flight

Kennedy's challenge inspired Congress to fund NASA with huge amounts of money to continue its efforts to orbit a man around Earth and to prepare for a successful trip to the Moon. On July 21, 1961, Grissom manned the second U.S. space flight in *Liberty Bell 7*. Grissom's fifteen-minute, thirty-seven-second flight did not go into orbit, but Grissom did perform some maneuvers with his spacecraft, becoming the first astronaut to be more than just a "man in the can."

Liberty Bell 7 splashed into the Atlantic Ocean as planned. Grissom began checking his instruments while helicopters flew to retrieve him. "I was sitting there minding my own business when, *POW* ... I saw blue sky," Grissom later said, according to *Starfall*. The capsule hatch cover had blown off and water started pouring into *Liberty Bell 7*. Grissom threw off his helmet and swam out into the ocean, but the downdraft from the helicopters hovering overhead pushed him underwater. After three attempts, Grissom was finally able to grab the rope that pulled him to safety. In the meantime, the *Liberty Bell 7* sank to the ocean floor.

In all, Project Mercury included six preparatory flights that helped develop a space program to fly a man to the Moon. John Glenn (1921–) followed Grissom's flight to become the first American to orbit Earth. During the next three flights, NASA increased the number of orbits. On May 15, 1963, Gordon Cooper (1927–) completed Project Mercury by successfully orbiting Earth twenty-two times. NASA was now ready to start Project Gemini, the program that would put a man on the Moon.

The unsinkable Molly Brown

Rather than one astronaut, the capsules of the next program, called Gemini, held two. Unlike the earlier flights, the twelve missions planned for Project Gemini required astronauts to fly the spacecraft, dock with other capsules, and even perform repairs while "walking" in space. Work on Project Gemini was done in Houston, Texas, at NASA's new Manned Space Center, which opened in 1964. The Grissom family moved into a new house near the space center the same year. This allowed Gus, who spent ten to twelve hours training each day, to be able to spend more of his free time with his wife and two sons.

On March 23, 1965, Grissom became the first person to fly into space twice. He flew with John Young in the first Gemini mission. Nicknaming the capsule *Molly Brown* after the popular Broadway play *The Unsinkable Molly Brown,* Grissom hoped his second flight might not have such a disastrous ending as his first. The flight, which orbited Earth three times, lasted five hours. During the flight Grissom performed a series of maneuvers that altered the rocket's orbit. At the same time, Young prepared the first food in space. As Grissom flew, Young asked him if he wanted to eat. Instead of offering the typical mushy space food, Young pulled a corned beef sandwich out of his spacesuit. Grissom took a bite but quickly stashed it away as bread crumbs scattered and began floating all around the cabin.

The flight soon ended with a splash in the Atlantic Ocean. Grissom and Young waited patiently for the rescue ship to arrive before opening the hatch. The heat building in the capsule prompted the astronauts to strip down to their long underwear to keep from overheating in their space suits. Bobbing around in the ocean made Grissom and Young sick to their stomachs, and both were happy when the helicopter hoisted them onto the rescue ship filled with cheering sailors.

Reaching for the Moon

In all, Project Gemini's twelve flights gave NASA the information it needed to surpass the Soviet space program. It led to Project Apollo, the program that would land a man on the Moon. Grissom, Edward White, and Roger Chaffee were selected to fly abroad the first Apollo mission. In preparation for their first Apollo flight, the three astronauts spent hundreds of hours learning emergency procedures.

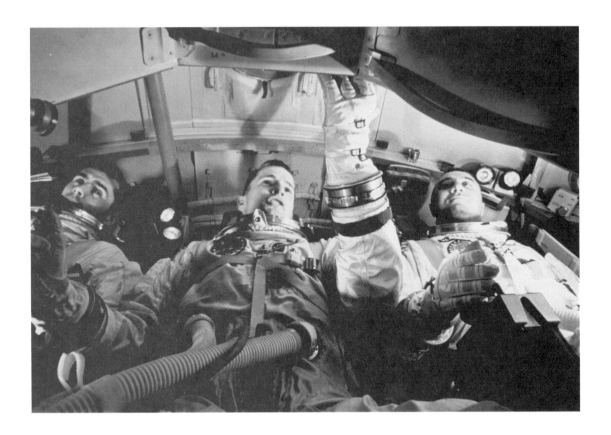

The Apollo 1 crew—Roger Chaffee (left), Ed White (center), and Gus Grissom (right)—take part in a practice test in January 1967. *AP/Wide World Photos. Reproduced by permission.*

As they practiced, the poor design of the spacecraft became apparent. Parts leaked and some engineering changes had not been completed. On January 22, 1967, Grissom stopped at home before going to the final preflight tests at Cape Canaveral. Upset with all the problems the crew had been having with the spacecraft, Grissom pulled a large lemon off a tree in his backyard. He told Betty as he kissed her goodbye: "I'm going to hang it on that spacecraft," she remembered in *Starfall.*

On January 27, 1967, the *Apollo 1* rocket sat on launch pad 34 at Cape Canaveral, Florida, the official blast-off location. Grissom and his crew ate lunch and dressed in their full gear for a practice countdown. The actual departure was scheduled for the next month. The astronauts climbed into the cabin and took their seats in the capsule. The three reclining crew seats were located near hundreds of dials and switches, connected by 15 miles (24 kilometers) of wiring. The capsule hatch was sealed from the outside. The seal was designed to fit very tightly and would require ninety seconds to reopen from the inside. Once sealed, the cabin was filled with pure oxygen and pressurized, as was planned for the final launch.

At 1:00 P.M. the test began. For hours the crew checked the workings of the rocket. Clearly the rocket needed more work. Several times the transmissions between the capsule and the control center were disrupted by static. Grissom complained, "If I can't talk with you only five miles away, how can we talk to you from the Moon?" according to the *Houston Chronicle.* Frustrated by the huge number of problems found in the first five hours of testing, one NASA engineer suggested quitting for the day. Nevertheless, the test conductor began another practice countdown.

With ten minutes left in the countdown, White noticed a fire. Grissom confirmed, "I've got a fire in the cockpit!" according to Dick Lattimer in *All We Did Was Fly to the Moon.* Images of the cabin catching fire flashed on the control center monitors. The pad crew rushed to pry open the hatch, but an explosion inside the capsule poured out smoke and fire that kept them back for six minutes. "You wouldn't want a description of what we found in there," was all one worker could say after prying the hatch open, according to Lattimer.

The astronauts lay in a heap on the capsule floor near the hatch. They had been trying to get out. Their spacesuits had protected their bodies from the flames, but the capsule's pressurized, pure oxygen environment had burned quickly and with great intensity. The astronauts had suffocated. NASA studied the burned area for seven hours before moving the bodies. NASA's later study of the blast found that a spark from a wire that short-circuited near Grissom's seat was the likely cause of the fire. The cabin had become a deadly environment within twenty-four seconds after the fire started.

Grissom was buried at Arlington National Cemetery, near Washington, D.C., with full military honors on February 10, 1967. Chaffee was buried next to Grissom later the same day. White's funeral took place at the U.S. Military Academy in New York.

These tragic deaths were taken seriously. NASA redesigned the capsule hatch to open within seconds from the inside. Plus, the rocket cabin was filled with a mixture of gases that would not feed fire as well as pure oxygen does. The next three *Apollo* missions were flown unmanned to perfect the rocket before risking more lives. And on July 20, 1969, NASA succeeded in landing a man on the Moon with *Apollo 11.*

For More Information

Books

Barbour, John. *Footprints on the Moon.* New York: Associated Press, 1969.

Bredeson, Carmen. *Gus Grissom: A Space Biography.* Springfield, NJ: Enslow, 1998.

Grissom, Betty, and Henry Still. *Starfall.* New York: Thomas Y. Crowell, 1974.

Grissom, Virgil. *Gemini: A Personal Account of Man's Venture into Space.* New York: Macmillan, 1968.

Lattimer, Dick. *All We Did Was Fly to the Moon.* Gainesville, FL: Whispering Eagle Press, 1985.

Shepard, Alan, and Deke Slayton. *Moon Shot.* Atlanta, GA: Turner, 1994.

Periodicals

Rossiter, Al, Jr. "Apollo Astronauts Meet Death Sealed in Blazing Space Capsule." *Houston Chronicle* (January 28, 1967): p. A1.

"Saga of *Liberty Bell.*" *Time* (July 28, 1961): p. 34.

Web Sites

Kennedy Space Center. http://www.ksc.nasa.gov (accessed August 2004).

Tom Hayden

Born December 11, 1939
Royal Oak, Michigan

**Political activist, organizer and reformer,
politician, writer**

T om Hayden came of age as a controversial, well-known
political activist and organizer during the 1960s. He was a
leader in what came to be known as the New Left. The movement was made up of students and young adults who
emerged from America's middle class and were discouraged
by the majority's tolerance for the continuation of poverty
despite the presence of wealth. During the decade, Hayden
first committed himself to the struggle for civil rights, then in
community organizing, and finally in the growing movement
against U.S. involvement in the Vietnam War (1954–75). Unlike many other political radicals from the 1960s, Hayden remained active in politics, most prominently as a member of
the California legislature.

Student activist

Tom Hayden was born in Royal Oak, Michigan, on
December 11, 1939. His interest in political activism developed during the late 1950s and early 1960s when he was attending the University of Michigan in Ann Arbor. He wrote

"We are people of this
generation, bred in at
least modest comfort,
housed now in
universities, looking
uncomfortably to the
world we inherit.... If we
appear to seek the
unattainable ... then let it
be known that we do so
to avoid the
unimaginable."

—*Excerpt from the Port Huron
Statement, 1962.*

Tom Hayden. *AP/Wide World
Photos. Reproduced by
permission.*

for and edited the *Michigan Daily,* the school newspaper. While with the paper he visited the South and reported on the rapidly expanding civil rights movement. He assisted in the formation of VOICE, a student political party that was unaffiliated with any established campus organization. VOICE soon evolved into a chapter of the politically radical group called Students for a Democratic Society (SDS), of which Hayden was a founding member.

Hayden became an SDS field secretary. In this capacity he worked with the Student Non-Violent Coordinating Committee (SNCC), a student activist organization. He participated in the group's attempt to end segregation, the separation of the races in public facilities, that existed in the American South. He also worked with the SNCC to assist Southern blacks in registering to vote. Hayden, who is white, and his fellow civil rights workers, some white and some black, were beaten by segregationists in McComb, Mississippi, while attempting to register black voters. He and ten SNCC members were detained by police as they tried to integrate an Albany, Georgia, train depot by having black SNCC members use facilities designated for whites, and vice-versa. In 1961 he wrote a booklet, *Revolution in Mississippi,* in which he outlined voter registration strategies.

Manifesto for the New Left

In 1962, Hayden wrote the first draft of the Port Huron Statement, a proposal which summarized the ideas and goals of the SDS. In the statement, Hayden pushed for America's emerging younger generation to reject a U.S. power structure that was dominated by major corporate interests, the military, and greedy politicians. He encouraged young people to contribute to the U.S. democracy by becoming political activists and working on a grassroots level for civil rights and fairness in government and big business. Grassroots efforts involve ordinary people working to effect change. He also urged the American working class to become more actively involved in their government. The ideas Hayden put forth in the Port Huron Statement served as the basis for what came to be known as the New Left.

The New Left movement wanted to distinguish itself from the so-called Old Left of the 1930s. The Old Left was

The Port Huron Statement

The Port Huron Statement, the first draft of which was written by Tom Hayden in 1962, expressed the concerns of young Americans who were made uneasy by the injustices in their country and the world.

In his introduction, titled "Agenda for a Generation," Hayden wrote: "We are people of this generation, bred in at least modest comfort, housed now in universities, looking uncomfortably to the world we inherit."

He went on to say: "When we were kids the United States was the wealthiest and strongest country in the world.... As we grew, however, our comfort was penetrated by events too troubling to dismiss. First, the permeating and victimizing fact of human degradation, symbolized by the Southern struggle against racial bigotry, compelled most of us from silence to activism. Second, the enclosing fact of the Cold War, symbolized by the presence of the Bomb, brought awareness that we ourselves, and our friends, and millions of abstract 'others' we knew more directly because of our common peril, might die at any time." Hayden added: "We might deliberately ignore, or avoid, or fail to feel all other human problems, but not these two, for these were too immediate and crushing in their impact, too challenging in the demand that we as individuals take the responsibility for encounter and resolution."

The Port Huron Statement went on to express in some detail the values and goals of the members of the Students for a Democratic Society, or SDS. It was one of the most important political statements of the entire decade.

known for being sympathetic toward communism, like that practiced in the Soviet Union. After World War II (1939–45), many in the United States grew greatly concerned about the spread of communism. This fear was increased as the United States and the Soviet Union entered into the Cold War (1945–91). During the Cold War, both nations began stockpiling nuclear weapons. Each was prepared to use its bombs if the other country began acting in an aggressive or threatening way. The threat of nuclear war was one of the points that Hayden commented on in the Port Huron Statement.

In June 1962, the Port Huron Statement became the official SDS manifesto, a statement that explains the group's intentions. Hayden became the organization's president, serving from 1962 to 1963. As president he helped design the Economic Research and Action Project (ERAP), a strategy for community organizing in poverty-stricken northern U.S. ghettos. In the fall of 1963, he settled in Newark, New Jersey, where he established a thriving ERAP operation. Under his guidance, ERAP set up the Newark Community Union Project. The group lobbied government officials to take action with regard to issues and problems facing the city's poor. The Project remained in existence until the summer of 1967, when the city was devastated by race riots.

Anti-war activism

In 1965, President **Lyndon B. Johnson** (1908–1973; served 1963–69; see entry) greatly increased U.S. participation in the Vietnam War (1954–75). At the time, most Americans supported the president. Hayden was not one of them, however, and he became actively involved in the anti-war movement.

During the first years of the Vietnam War, many Americans believed that the conflict was a reasonable attempt to limit the spread of communism in Asia. As the war went on, American losses mounted, and it gradually became apparent that the United States was on the losing side of a very bloody civil war in Vietnam. More and more Americans began questioning their country's involvement in the war. In 1965, however, Hayden's vocal anti-war stance was, to many, nothing less than treason. That year, and again in 1967, he journeyed to communist North Vietnam, his country's battlefield opponent. He stated that his visits were intended to allow him to know America's "enemies" as human beings. In 1967, the North Vietnamese released into Hayden's custody three American prisoners of war. It was an action meant to display North Vietnamese solidarity with American anti-war protestors.

A presidential election took place in 1968. That summer, the Democratic Party was scheduled to hold its national convention in Chicago, during which time its delegates would select the party's presidential nominee. Hayden and Rennie Davis, both former SDS activists, were asked by David Dellinger, leader of the National Mobilization Committee to End the War in Vietnam, to help coordinate a massive anti-war protest in the Chicago streets during the convention. The actual protest was broadcast live on television, and it garnered international attention when the Chicago police force was shown attacking and beating demonstrators.

Hayden, Davis, Dellinger, and five others were indicted by the U.S. Justice Department for their involvement in organizing the protest. Originally, the media dubbed the defendants the "Chicago Eight." However, the group became the "Chicago Seven" when Bobby Seale, national chairperson of the radical Black Panther Party, was separated from the other defendants. While the jury was debating the case, Julius Hoffman, the judge who oversaw the trial, sentenced the seven to jail terms for contempt of court. The jury agreed on a verdict in February of 1970, finding five of the seven, including Hayden, guilty of plotting to cross state lines with the intention of provoking a riot. The contempt sentences and guilty verdicts were appealed and then reversed by the U.S. Court of Appeals. The court ruled that Judge Hoffman had acted inappropriately by purposefully provoking the defense. The entire trial received much publicity. It became a symbol of the growing political power of the anti-war movement, even when it directly challenged the government.

Members of the Chicago Seven talk to the press (from left, back row: John Froines, Lee Weiner, David Dellinger, Rennie Davis, and Tom Hayden; Jerry Rubin is seated in the front next to his girlfriend, who was not on trial). *AP/Wide World Photos. Reproduced by permission.*

In the early 1970s, Hayden helped set up a commune in Berkeley, California. Communes are shared living spaces for a group of like-minded people. Hayden traveled the country attending and speaking at anti-war demonstrations and protest events. One such rally, on May 16, 1971, was held in Berkeley's People's Park, a small area, owned by the University of California, that students and community residents had made into a park. Two years earlier, at the urging of California governor Ronald Reagan (1911–2004), the university had reclaimed the land. Since then, it had been a rallying point for anti-war protesters. On this occasion, a student was shot to death by California state troopers. Afterward, Hayden was arrested, but no charges were filed against him.

Also in 1971, Hayden became acquainted with actor and political activist Jane Fonda (1937–) at an anti-war demonstration in Ann Arbor. The two began attending similar rallies together and campaigned for George McGovern (1922–), the 1972 Democratic Party presidential nominee. Additionally, they established the Indochina Peace Campaign, a touring anti-war show that featured Fonda; Hayden; actor Donald Sutherland; folksinger Holly Near; Scott Camil, a decorated U.S. Marine and leader of the Vietnam Veterans Against the War; and George Smith, an ex-prisoner of war who had been held in North Vietnam for two years. In 1973 Fonda became Hayden's second wife, but the two eventually divorced.

Enters mainstream politics

Hayden's support of McGovern reflected the beginnings of his transformation from radical dissident, one who disagrees strongly with the majority, to active participant in the established political process. In 1976 he failed in a bid to be elected California's U.S. senator, losing in the Democratic Party primary to incumbent John V. Tunney. Despite the loss, Hayden earned 40 percent of the vote, a remarkable total given his negative reputation. The following year, he established the Campaign for Economic Democracy (which later became Campaign California), an organization that supported jobs for all able workers, rent control, public management of corporations, and a change in the country's tax laws. In 1982 he won election to the California State Assembly, and he earned a state senate seat in 1992.

As a state politician, Hayden was a steadfast liberal. He authored and supported legislation that affirmed the rights of women, African Americans, Latinos, and Holocaust survivors. His political agenda covered a range of issues from the protection of endangered species to the use of solar energy as a replacement for nuclear energy. He also supported halting tuition increases at state universities.

In 1994, Hayden attempted to win the Democratic Party nomination for governor of California but came in third place in the primary election. He retired from California State government in 2000. He also wrote dozens of articles and books examining the issues to which he devoted his career, first as a political activist and then as an elected official.

For More Information

Books

Bunzel, John H. *New Force on the Left: Tom Hayden and the Campaign against Corporate America.* Stanford, CA: Hoover Institution Press, 1983.

Hayden, Tom. *The Lost Gospel of the Earth: A Call for Renewing Nature, Spirit, and Politics.* San Francisco, CA: Sierra Club Books, 1996.

Hayden, Tom. *Rebel: A Personal History of the 1960s.* Los Angeles, CA: Red Hen Press, 2002.

Hayden, Tom. *Reunion: A Memoir.* New York: Random House, 1988.

Web Sites

"The Port Huron Statement." *The Sixties Project.* http://lists.village.virginia.edu/sixties/HTML_docs/Resources/Primary/Manifestos/SDS_Port_Huron.html (accessed August 2004).

Tom Hayden. http://www.tomhayden.com (accessed August 2004).

"Tom Hayden." *The Nation.* http://www.thenation.com/directory/bios/bio.mhtml?id=92 (accessed August 2004).

Abbie Hoffman

Born November 30, 1936
Worcester, Massachusetts

Died early April, 1989
Bucks County, Pennsylvania

Political activist and writer

"Revolution is not something fixed in ideology, nor is it something fashioned to a particular decade. It is a perpetual process embedded in the human spirit."

—*Abbie Hoffman.*

Abbie Hoffman. *AP/Wide World Photos. Reproduced by permission.*

During the troubled 1960s and into the 1970s, few people challenged authority more defiantly or urged radical social change more strongly than activist Abbie Hoffman. A dedicated political organizer, Hoffman was also a prankster who knew how to use the media to bring his causes to national attention. He was arrested fifty-three times during his days as an activist. Hoffman used his comic personality and outrageous antics to lighten up serious political discussion. He used his sharp political intelligence to encourage social awareness in rebellious youth. Conservatives and less extreme radicals were often irritated by Hoffman's outrageous behavior and thought he was being disrespectful. However, he viewed himself as a "cultural revolutionary." Throughout his life, he worked in his own way to create what he believed would be a better society.

A small town boy

Hoffman was born Abbott Howard Hoffman on November 30, 1936, in the town of Worcester, Massachusetts.

His father, John, had come to the United States as a baby when his parents emigrated from Russia. Settling in Massachusetts, John's father worked as a street peddler, selling fruit and vegetables from a truck. When John grew up he married Florence Shanberg, who also came from a poor working-class family. Her father was a junk dealer, while her mother sewed clothes in a sweatshop, a factory where workers were paid slight wages for long, hard hours of work.

By the time young Abbie was born, the family had climbed to the middle class. John ran a medical supply company. Florence no longer worked outside the home because John did not want her to do so. Both the Hoffmans and the Shanbergs were close, and Abbie grew up surrounded by a large, extended family.

The Hoffmans were Jewish. Growing up during the 1940s in a town with a small Jewish community, Abbie learned what it was like to be on the receiving end of prejudice. His experiences with anti-Jewish attitudes influenced his later decision to fight prejudice and other forms of oppression. During his childhood, Abbie and his brother Jack often got into fistfights with Catholic boys in the neighborhood who taunted or attacked them.

Abbie showed signs of mischief and rebellion from early childhood. He fought constantly with his strict father and frequently got into trouble for neighborhood pranks. He was an excellent athlete and became a championship tennis player. Yet, he also delighted in playing poker and pool with the neighborhood kids, enjoying the role of the tough rebel. Hoffman was loud, charming, and conceited. He had a knack for making people laugh.

In school, Hoffman was a quick and intelligent student. However, he seldom worked hard and was frequently in trouble for talking back to teachers. He read a lot and was fond of bringing up controversial subjects in class. He was expelled from high school when he hit a teacher who objected to a paper he wrote defending atheism, the belief that there is no God.

Introduction to radical politics

In his dramatic way, Hoffman made the most of being kicked out of high school. However, after a short time of hanging out in the neighborhood, he quietly finished his high school years at a private boarding school. In 1955, he went on to college at Brandeis University in Waltham, Massachusetts. Even in the repressive anti-communist climate of the 1950s, Brandeis had many politically radical professors. Hoffman began to learn about social and political activism.

He also began to study a new type of psychology, called "humanistic psychology." Humanistic psychologists, like Hoffman's teacher Abraham Maslow (1908–1970), were beginning to change their view of the individual's place in society. Rather than assuming that a healthy individual should work to fit into society, they said that sometimes society might be wrong or unjust and that rebelling against that injustice could be a healthy activity. These new ideas were exciting to Hoffman and influenced him to choose psychology as his major.

As he studied these new ideas, Hoffman was also introduced to a new lifestyle. It was a rebellious style that many people called "Beatnik" or "bohemian." The bohemians wore black clothes, listened to jazz and folk music, and urged a relaxed, open lifestyle, free from society's rules. The rebellious, bohemian way of life appealed to many college students, and Hoffman was among them.

After he graduated from Brandeis in 1959, Hoffman continued his education, in both psychology and in radical politics. He attended graduate school at the University of California at Berkeley. Although he never received his master's degree, he did participate in several stimulating political actions there. One of these actions was a large protest against the House Un-American Activities Committee, a Congressional committee that investigated people who were alleged to have communist connections. In 1960 he returned to Worcester to take a job in a state mental hospital. He also married Sheila Karklin, his college sweetheart.

New battlegrounds: Vietnam and the American South

Hoffman's personality was characterized by a seemingly endless supply of energy. While working two jobs in

Worcester, one as a psychologist and one selling medical supplies for his father, he found time to involve himself in most of the radical political groups in town. He became involved in two major movements: the effort to stop U.S. participation in the Vietnam War (1954–75) and the attempt to improve the status of African Americans.

Southern blacks were involved in a struggle to end racial segregation, the practice of designating separate facilities for whites and for blacks. Many sympathetic northern whites worked to support them. Hoffman worked with Worcester groups that supported African American activists by raising money and publicizing their cause. In the summer of 1965, Hoffman took his father's company car and headed south to Mississippi to work in a more direct way for civil rights. There, he joined voter registration drives to increase black participation in elections. Racist southern whites were threatened by the civil rights movement and especially hated the northern supporters. Hoffman was harassed and even beaten, but these experiences only increased his commitment to political work.

By 1967 many black radicals no longer wanted to work with white activists. Hoffman felt hurt by their decision, especially when the Student Non-Violent Coordinating Committee (SNCC) asked white members, including Hoffman, to leave. However, he still had plenty of energy for political work, and he turned it to the anti-Vietnam War movement. Around this time, Hoffman published his first book of political philosophy, *Revolution for the Hell of It*. He and Sheila divorced in 1966, and he married fellow activist Anita Kushner in 1967.

From hippies to Yippies

Always dramatic by nature, Hoffman added an element of theater to the many anti-war demonstrations he helped plan. For example, Hoffman and others formed a "Flower Brigade" and joined a New York City veterans' parade carrying peace signs. For this behavior, they suffered verbal abuse and beatings. Another demonstration involved standing in the visitors' gallery above the New York Stock Exchange and throwing dollar bills down on the trading floor—an action that sent stockbrokers scrambling for the bills. The

Displaying his comic side, Abbie Hoffman does a somersault in front of reporters and photographers as he heads to court on charges of conspiring with others to cause a riot during the 1968 Democratic national convention.
© Bettmann/Corbis. Reproduced by permission.

act was intended to show that stockbrokers were consumed by their desire for money. The action that brought Hoffman into the national spotlight was a playful addition to a large anti-war demonstration at the Pentagon, the central military headquarters in Washington, D.C. Hoffman arranged for a group of witches to attend the demonstration to attempt to use psychic power to lift the building off the ground.

Perhaps Hoffman's best-known political prank occurred during the 1968 Democratic presidential nominating convention in Chicago. Hoffman and friend and political ally Jerry Rubin (1938–1994) planned a Festival of Life to take place in the streets of Chicago during the convention. A new political party, the Youth International Party (YIP), would sponsor the festival. Members of the party would be called Yippies, a variation on the term "Hippies" that was used to refer to rebellious youth in the 1960s. The Yippies would nominate their own candidate, a pig named Pigasus, for president.

Several thousand anti-war demonstrators showed up in Chicago for the Yippies' Festival of Life. The Chicago police, angered by the demonstrators' aggressive and disrespect-ful attitudes, responded with violence. Demonstrators were chased and beaten by the hundreds. The demonstrations went on for several days, and the police response continued to be aggressive and brutal. By the end, eight of the organiz-ers were arrested and charged with working together to cause a riot. Abbie Hoffman was among them.

The trial of the Chicago Eight, as they were soon called, began in March of 1969. The group became known as the Chicago Seven when one of the defendants was tried sep-arately. Hoffman treated the trial like any other demonstra-tion, turning it into political theater by teasing the judge and playing jokes in the courtroom. In the end, all of the defen-dants were acquitted. Hoffman had become such a well-known troublemaker that eleven states made laws specifically forbidding him from entering their states. In 1969, he pub-lished his second book, *The Woodstock Nation: A Talk-Rock Album*. This publication was followed in 1971 by *Steal This Book*, a sort of survival handbook for revolutionaries.

In 1974, Hoffman's public activism was brought to a sudden halt when he was arrested for selling a large amount of cocaine to an undercover police officer. Facing a sentence of fifteen years to life, Hoffman skipped bail and lived in hiding from the law for the next six years. He used his time in hiding to write his autobiography, *Soon to Be a Major Motion Picture* (1980). He began to work again as an activist for environmen-tal causes, using the assumed name Barry Freed. In 1980, tired of life as a fugitive, Hoffman turned himself in and bargained to have his sentence reduced to eleven months.

After his release from prison, Hoffman tried to con-tinue his activist work. By the 1980s, however, the political atmosphere had changed dramatically. Drug use and revolu-tionary politics were no longer as popular among young people as they had been in the late 1960s and early 1970s. Hoffman felt that young people of the time had become more self-centered and less concerned about changing soci-ety. From 1984 to 1986 Hoffman staged a series of comic de-bates with former activist Jerry Rubin titled "Yippie versus Yuppie." "Yuppie" was short for "young urban professional." Hoffman was arrested at a few demonstrations, but the fire seemed to have gone out of him. During the 1980s he was

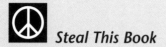

Steal This Book

The book most closely identified with the outrageous politics of Abbie Hoffman is a funny and brash collection of tips, recipes, and advice for those living outside the law. The book combines instructions for how to make free long distance telephone calls or construct a bomb with thoughts about Hoffman's revolutionary political philosophy. The moral lessons offered by Hoffman are clear, yet clearly non-traditional. "To steal from a brother or a sister is evil," he writes in the introduction. "To *not* steal from the institutions that are the pillars of the Pig Empire is equally immoral."

Hoffman's political ideas were extremely controversial and offended those who had more conservative beliefs. Even the title of the book was controversial. A book that asked people to steal it was bound to irritate publishers and bookstore owners. In fact, *Steal This Book* was turned down by thirty publishers before Hoffman and a friend decided to publish it themselves. Even then, many bookstores refused to stock the radical work.

Despite these troubles, *Steal This Book* became a bestseller in 1971, the year of its publication. From April through November of that year more than 250,000 copies were sold. Within a few years, however, the book went out of print. In the early 2000s it had become a collector's item, with copies selling for as much as $100. In 1990, the *New York Times Book Review* listed *Steal This Book* as one of the top ten books stolen from bookstores and libraries. In the early 2000s the book could be "stolen" from the World Wide Web, where it can be found at http://www.tenant.net/Community/steal.

diagnosed with manic-depression, a psychological disorder involving intense highs followed by deep depression.

By 1980 he and Anita had divorced, and Hoffman had become romantically involved with Johanna Lawrenson, another left-wing activist. On April 12, 1989, Lawrenson became worried when Hoffman did not answer his phone. She called a friend to check on him. Hoffman was found dead. He had taken an overdose of pills with alcohol. Although most people assumed that he had killed himself, some believed his death was an accident, partly because he left no suicide note.

Abbie Hoffman was one of the most unforgettable characters to emerge from the political turmoil of the 1960s. A believer in the energy and power of youth, he was said to be the author of the phrase, "Never trust anyone over thirty."

He had four children who often complained that it was difficult to rebel in the Hoffman household because their father praised them for each troublemaking activity. Perhaps one of the most revealing insights into Hoffman's philosophy is the name he and Anita gave their first child. They called him America, they said, because he represented the hope they had for their country. Although Hoffman may have killed himself during a time of depression, his legacy was not despair, but an impish childlike hope for a better future.

For More Information

Books

Hoffman, Abbie. *Soon to Be a Major Motion Picture.* New York: Berkley Books, 1980.

Hoffman, Abbie. *Steal This Book.* New York: Pirate Editions, 1971.

Hoffman, Jack, and Daniel Simon. *Run, Run, Run: The Lives of Abbie Hoffman.* New York: Putnam's, 1994.

Jezer, Marty. *Abbie Hoffman: American Rebel.* New Brunswick, NJ: Rutgers University Press, 1992.

Sloman, Larry. *Steal This Dream: Abbie Hoffman and the Countercultural Revolution in America.* New York: Doubleday, 1998.

Periodicals

Kunen, James S. "A Troubled Rebel Chooses a Silent Death." *People Weekly* (May 1, 1989): pp. 100–106.

Web Sites

Steal This Book. http://www.tenant.net/Community/steal (accessed August 2004).

Dolores Huerta

Born April 10, 1930
Dawson, New Mexico

**Union organizer, lobbyist,
and political activist**

"I would like to be remembered as a woman who cares for fellow humans. We must use our lives to make the world a better place to live, not just to acquire things. That is what we are put on the earth for."

—Dolores Huerta.

Dolores Huerta. *AP/Wide World Photos. Reproduced by permission.*

B orn and raised among poor immigrant laborers, Dolores Huerta devoted her life to improving the lives of working people. An energetic and courageous activist, Huerta helped start the first national union for farmworkers. She sought to ensure passage of many laws to protect the lowest paid and least powerful workers. Along with tireless union organizing and raising eleven children, mostly as a single mother, she worked on many other social issues. These included civil rights, women's rights, environmental protection, and support for the poor. Although she was beaten up and arrested for her political activism and fought her way back from serious illness, Huerta continued to devote herself to the fight against injustice. In 2004, she won a $100,000 Creative Citizen Award from the Puffin Foundation. She donated the entire amount to starting a foundation for training young activists in how to continue the work that she and others began during the 1960s.

Growing up among workers and activists

Huerta was born in 1930 in a Mexican American community in a small mining town in New Mexico. Her parents divorced when she was only three years old. Dolores and her mother, Alicia Chávez, moved to the city of Stockton, in the agricultural heart of California. Chávez worked as a waitress until she was able to start her own restaurant and small hotel. Young Dolores learned about both hard work and community service by helping out in the family business. Her mother often provided food and lodging to poor farmworkers for free. Dolores learned about tolerance and appreciation of diversity by growing up in a racially mixed neighborhood, surrounded by many first- and second-generation immigrants.

Huerta also remained close to her father, Juan Fernandez, who worked as a coal miner and farmworker in New Mexico while attending classes to obtain his college degree. She was inspired by her father's commitment to education and by his political career. He was elected to the New Mexico State Legislature in 1938. Fernandez used his position to try to improve the condition of working people, just as his daughter would do two decades later.

Unlike many working-class Chicanas (Mexican American women), Huerta attended college. She graduated with a teaching certificate from the Delta Community College of the University of the Pacific in the early 1950s. She then went to work teaching elementary school in Stockton, California. Before long, however, she was overwhelmed with both sympathy and anger regarding the poverty of her students, many of whom were children of farmworkers. She began to feel that she must help them.

Organizing for the rights of farmworkers

Huerta met a California activist named Fred Ross, who had founded a group called the Community Service Organization (CSO) in 1949. The CSO worked to end segregation, the legalized separation of whites and blacks, and racism against Mexican Americans in California. It was a grassroots organization, which means that it was locally organized by working people who usually volunteered their time. Huerta was interested in Ross's ideas and appreciated his commitment to working in Chicano communities. In 1955 she helped to start a Stockton chapter of the CSO.

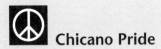

Chicano Pride

During the 1960s, many ethnic and racial minorities began to protest against the discrimination and prejudice they experienced. They began to demand protection of their civil rights. These different minorities inspired and learned from each other, especially from the successful and energetic African American civil rights movement. The Chicano struggle was one of these important progressive movements

The origin of the word *Chicano* is unclear. Some historians believe that it arose during the early 1900s, from the Spanish-language custom of using a "ch" sound to indicate affection or familiarity. Thus, the familiar form of *Mexicano* (Mexican man) became *Mechicano,* which was soon simply shortened to *Chicano.* Although some Mexican Americans disliked the term, which they considered crude, political activists of the 1960s adopted it as a symbol of racial pride.

Many Chicanos had long called the United States home, although not as the United States. Much of the southwestern United States, including California, Texas, New Mexi-co, and Arizona, were once part of Mexico. In these areas lived thousands of Chicano families that had been American for generations. But Mexican Americans of the 1960s often found themselves treated as unwelcome guests in a land that had belonged to their ancestors. They were discriminated against in education, in employment, and in the institutions of government. As English-speaking Americans came to dominate Chicanos' ancestral lands, Chicanos were often expected to give up their language and customs in order to blend with "Anglo" or non-Latino society.

Activists of the 1960s and 1970s began to speak out about these injustices. They worked to change racist laws, organized voter registration drives, and promoted pride in Chicano identity. Leaders such as Reies López Tijerina (1926–), Rodolfo Gonzales (1928–), César Chávez (1927-1993), and Dolores Huerta drew national attention to the Chicano cause. They convinced lawmakers to pass legislation to protect minorities and helped to found Chicano Studies departments in schools and universities.

For the next five years, Huerta worked in the CSO. However, she began to feel that the group was not doing enough to help farmworkers. Such farmworkers are laborers who travel throughout the agricultural regions of the country during harvest season picking fruits, vegetables, and cotton. They work long hours in the hot sun for very little pay. New immigrants and illegal immigrants often work as pickers on farms and in orchards. When Huerta began her work, farmworkers often labored under very bad conditions and had no legal protection of their rights as workers. They often had to live in bare shacks with no electricity or water. Those who owned the farms and orchards sometimes cheated workers by refusing to pay them. Huerta began to think that farmworkers needed a union that could help improve their working conditions.

While working in the CSO, Huerta had met a young farmworker named César Chávez (1927–1993) who was also interested in organizing a union. When the CSO refused to help form a union, Huerta and Chávez left the organization in 1960 and formed the Agricultural Workers Association. It soon became the United Farm Workers of America (UFW). With Chávez as president, Huerta as vice president, and a staff of five people, the union began to reach out to those who picked the crops. They encouraged workers to join the union and fight for their rights. Although many people later associated only the name of César Chávez with the farmworkers' union, he and Dolores Huerta worked side by side in the union for many years, becoming as close as brother and sister.

Following in the footsteps of her politically involved father, Huerta spent much of her time over the next several years at the California state legislature. She worked to get legal protection for farmworkers. She became a very successful lobbyist, someone who talks to legislators to try to convince them to vote for certain laws. Between 1960 and 1962, Huerta successfully lobbied for the passage of fifteen bills of law. Among them were laws that granted public assistance money and retirement benefits to non-citizens who work in California. She also worked for laws that required voting and driver's license tests be given in Spanish as well as English. In addition, Huerta urged for laws that extended disability insurance to farmworkers.

UFW goes national: boycotts and pickets

Though the UFW had been very active in recruiting members and lobbying the legislature, no grower had yet signed a labor contract with the union. This situation changed in 1965. When Filipino grape pickers went on strike for better wages in Delano, California, the UFW joined the effort. On September 16, 1965, five thousand farmworkers went

Dolores Huerta (center), wearing a sweater with the UFW symbol, encourages other workers to fight for their rights. *AP/Wide World Photos. Reproduced by permission.*

out on strike in Delano. The strike lasted five years. Striking workers marched in front of the vineyard where grapes were grown and the stores where they were sold, carrying union signs asking workers not to pick the grapes and shoppers not to buy them. Huerta became director of these picket lines because of her skill in encouraging workers to leave their jobs and join the strike. According to Barbara L. Baer in *Progressive*, Huerta would call, "Don't be a marshmallow," to those who passed her picket line. "Walk the street with us into history. Get off the sidewalk. Stop being vegetables. Work for justice. Viva the boycott!"

In 1968, as the strike continued, the UFW decided to try a new tactic. The group called for a national boycott of non-union grapes. The farmworkers' union would ask people all over the country not to eat grapes until the owners of the vineyards agreed to pay the farmworkers a decent wage. Huerta directed the national grape boycott, which became the largest and most successful boycott in U.S. union history.

After two years of the boycott, the California grape growers signed a contract with the UFW, the first time an agricultural business had accepted a labor union of its workers.

Changes in the federal law and continuing protest

The farmworkers' union membership soared. By the late 1970s, membership had reached seventy thousand, and four hundred staffers worked in UFW offices. During the mid-1970s, Huerta led two more successful national boycotts, one of head lettuce and one of Gallo Wine. As more growers signed contracts with union workers, Huerta continued to lobby the legislature on such issues as toxic chemicals used in the fields and amnesty for illegal immigrants who had worked in the United States for many years. In response to Huerta's work, the U.S. Congress passed the Agricultural Labor Relations Act of 1975, which officially gave farmworkers the right to unionize. Congress also approved the Immigration Act of 1985, which allowed many longtime illegal immigrants to apply for legal status.

During the 1980s, as U.S. government policies became more conservative, the UFW experienced a decline in membership. However, Huerta continued to work with Chávez and other union leaders for "*la causa,*" the cause of the farmworkers. In 1984 she was honored with the California Outstanding Labor Leader award. However, Huerta's constant challenges to those in power were not always appreciated. She was arrested twenty-two times for her union activities. In 1988 she was badly beaten by a San Francisco police officer when she attended a rally for presidential candidate George H. W. Bush to protest the use of pesticides.

Even into her seventies, Huerta continued to work for civil rights and justice. Although her primary cause was the rights of farmworkers, Huerta also worked throughout her life for many other causes. As a Mexican American woman, she has fought strongly against racism and sexism. In 1993, she was inducted into the National Women's Hall of Fame.

Huerta's courage and dedication were rewarded with many other awards, including the American Civil Liberties Union Roger Baldwin Medal of Liberty in 1993 and the *Ms.*

Magazine Woman of the Year in 1998. She was awarded honorary doctorate degrees from three universities and served on many state and federal commissions. In 2002, the Dolores Huerta Center for Workers' Rights was established in Las Vegas, Nevada, to provide help and information to poor working people.

For More Information

Books

De Ruiz, Dana Catharine, and Richard Larios. *La Causa: The Migrant Farmworkers' Story.* Austin, TX: Raintree Steck-Vaughn, 1992.

Dunne, John Gregory. *Delano: The Story of the California Grape Strike.* New York: Farrar, 1976.

Griswold del Castillo, Richard, and Richard A. Garcia. *César Chávez: A Triumph of Spirit.* Norman, OK: University of Oklahoma Press, 1995.

Perez, Frank. *Dolores Huerta.* Austin, TX: Raintree Steck-Vaughn, 1996.

Periodicals

Baer, Barbara L. "Stopping Traffic: One Woman's Cause." *Progressive* (September 1975).

Web Sites

"Dolores Huerta: Biography." *United Farm Workers.* http://www.ufw.org/dh.htm (accessed August 2004).

"Dolores Huerta: The UFW's Grand Lady of Steel." *LaRed Latina.* http://www.lared-latina.com/huerta.html (accessed August 2004).

Lyndon B. Johnson

Born August 27, 1908
Near Stonewall, Texas

Died January 22, 1973
Near Johnson City, Texas

Politician, thirty-sixth
president of the United States

Lyndon B. Johnson was one of the most charismatic and complex leaders in U.S. history. His five-year presidency was marked by accusations of corruption and by the growing nightmare of American military involvement in the Vietnam War (1954–75). But his administration also made reforms that had a dramatic effect in reducing poverty and improving civil rights. Although some remember Johnson as a warmonger, others regard him as a political giant who improved the lives of millions of poor Americans.

Texas childhood

Lyndon Baines Johnson was the eldest of five children. His father was Sam Ealy Johnson, a farmer, local politician, and newspaper owner who served in the Texas state legislature for eighteen years. His mother was Rebekah Baines Johnson, a talented woman who occasionally wrote for local newspapers and produced amateur plays. She also taught neighborhood children elocution, the art of speaking properly. When Johnson was five years old, his mother persuaded

"Almost anything you can say about Johnson had a tinge of truth in it, good or bad. He was vengeful and bullying.... But he was also visionary, energetic, a man whose goal it was to be the greatest American president, doing the greatest amount of good for the American nation."

—*Jack Valenti, in* The Wilson Quarterly.

Lyndon B. Johnson. *AP/Wide World Photos. Reproduced by permission.*

his father to move from their isolated farm to Johnson City, a small town 55 miles (88.5 kilometers) west of Austin.

Johnson was always singled out by his parents as special. Even as a child he was known for his confidence, his willingness to argue, and his ability to bring people around to his point of view. By the age of thirteen he was winning debating competitions against older high school students. The family moved back to the farm in 1918. By 1922, the farm had failed, leaving the family in debt and forcing them to return to Johnson City. Johnson graduated from Johnson City High School in May of 1924, before his sixteenth birthday.

Always a rebel, Johnson ran away to California with some friends after graduating from high school. He worked as a clerk for Tom Martin in his San Bernadino law office but returned to Texas in 1925 when it became clear that Martin's business dealings were questionable. Johnson then began working on a construction crew building a highway between Johnson City and Austin.

The ambitious New Dealer

Johnson attended Southwest Texas State Teachers' College and graduated with a bachelor's degree in 1930. But he had interrupted his studies at the end of his junior year to teach for nine months in Cotulla, a small town in southern Texas. There, he came in contact with the grinding poverty experienced by poor Hispanic children. He also witnessed segregation—the practice of separating the races. Johnson was shocked by the lack of decent housing and food. This memory stayed with him throughout his political career. After a brief spell as a teacher in Houston, Texas, Johnson became congressional secretary to Richard Kleberg in 1931.

On November 17, 1934, Johnson married Claudia Alta Taylor. Known as "Lady Bird," Johnson's wife became a popular figure on the political circuit and one of Johnson's most important advisers. She was also influential in her own right. Money from her business ventures gave Johnson the freedom to pursue his own political career. By 1934 he was already gaining influence in Washington, D.C. In 1935, he became Texas director of the National Youth Administration (NYA), a program designed to provide part-time work to young people. The NYA was part of the New Deal, a set of government programs created by President Franklin D. Roosevelt (1882–1945; served 1933–45) to help America recover from the economic depression of the 1930s. Johnson's ability to persuade and coax people into doing what he wanted made him a great success in his new role. In 1937 he was elected to Congress as a supporter of Roosevelt.

By 1941 Johnson felt ready to run in the Senate race against Texas governor W. Lee O'Daniel. It was a close race, but Johnson lost. The results of the election were questioned; some complaints surfaced that the votes were mishandled. On December 7, 1941, the Japanese bombed the naval base at Pearl Harbor, Hawaii, and the United States entered World War II. Johnson quickly volunteered for active duty with the U.S. Navy and began serving two days later. A lieutenant commander, Johnson was injured slightly when his plane was attacked by the Japanese. He served thereafter in a non-combat role and was also awarded a Silver Star. After leaving the service, Johnson finally won a seat in the U.S. Senate in 1949. During the tough campaign, he became known, humorously, as "Landslide Lyndon." He also gained a reputation for tough dealing and ruthless ambition.

The Kennedy era

Throughout the 1950s Johnson gained influence in Washington. He became Senate Majority Leader in 1955, the second most powerful position in the government. With a Democratic majority in Congress, he was able to influence the Republican president Dwight D. Eisenhower (1890–1969; served 1953–61) to pass legislation on social security, public housing, and the creation of the National Aeronautics and Space Administration (NASA). Most importantly, the Civil Rights Bill of 1957 became a starting point for more significant civil rights legislation in the 1960s. In 1960 Johnson was a leading contender for the Democratic presidential nomination, but in the end he lost out to **John F. Kennedy** (1917–1963; served 1961–63; see entry).

After Kennedy won the presidential nomination, Johnson accepted the vice-presidential slot on the ticket. He worked the southern states, where Kennedy was less popular.

President Lyndon B. Johnson (seated) signs the landmark civil rights bill. *Photo courtesy of the Library of Congress.*

After the Democrats won the election with a margin of less than 1 percent of the vote, Kennedy gave Johnson a powerful role in his administration. Johnson's background made him an ideal figure for pushing forward Kennedy's plan to compete with the Soviet Union in the exploration of space. Johnson was also a committed supporter of the administration's civil rights legislation. The need for civil rights reform grew increasingly urgent as civil unrest became more widespread through 1962 and 1963.

The Kennedy administration was troubled with the Cuban Missile Crisis and the attempted U.S. invasion of Cuba at the Bay of Pigs. These international crises were related to the long-standing political conflict between the United States and the Soviet Union known as the Cold War (1945–91). Kennedy's administration also faced problems while it tried to push legislation through Congress. Yet the combination of Kennedy's youthful charisma and Johnson's tough persuasiveness was an important factor in the administration's successes. When Kennedy was assassinated in Dallas on November 22, 1963, a remarkable political alliance was brought to an end. Johnson was sworn in as president aboard Air Force One the following day, in the presence of Kennedy's widow, Jacqueline. Kennedy's body was also aboard the plane.

The Johnson administration

Many commentators in 1963 did not consider Johnson suitable for the presidency. He was almost the exact opposite of Kennedy, his smooth, glamorous predecessor. But Johnson came to be viewed as one of the most accomplished political minds of his generation. He adapted well to his new role, so well, in fact, that he won a comfortable victory over **Barry Goldwater** (1909–1998; see entry) in the 1964 presidential election that followed.

Many foreign policy problems had been resolved in 1963 with the nuclear test ban treaty with the Soviet Union. Johnson was a strong believer in personal contact with other leaders. He believed that "as long as I could take someone into a room with me, I could make him my friend, and that included anybody, even [Soviet leader] Nikita Khrushchev" (1894–1971), as quoted in Doris Kearns Goodwin's *Lyndon Johnson and the American Dream*. This attitude served him well on domestic policy as well.

Johnson's friendly, confident style won over the American people. It enabled him to persuade Congress to pass bills that might otherwise have failed. These included the Civil Rights Act of 1964, giving civil rights to blacks and women that had previously only applied to white men. There were also numerous smaller pieces of legislation passed under his Great Society program, including reforms of Medicare and Medicaid, extensions in social security benefits, increases in the minimum wage, and programs to improve housing and employment for the poorest of Americans.

All of this work was achieved despite a Congress that was generally opposed to social reform. Despite conservative sentiments in Congress, Johnson was effective in exploiting the popular mood to get his way. For example, when the Reverend **Martin Luther King Jr.** (1929–1968; see entry), was assassinated in Memphis, Tennessee, in April of 1968, Johnson

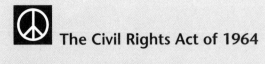

The Civil Rights Act of 1964

In August 1963 almost 250,000 marchers gathered at the Washington Monument to protest the treatment of blacks in the southern states and to rally support for the Civil Rights Bill. Among their leaders were the Reverend Martin Luther King Jr. and A. Philip Randolph (1889–1979). However, the marchers also included Lyndon Johnson and Senator Edward "Ted" Kennedy (1932–), one of the president's brothers. After marching to the Lincoln Memorial, the leaders met with President Kennedy, who expressed his support for their cause.

The bill came before the Senate after President Kennedy's assassination in November of 1963. It fell to Johnson to pass it into law. Seventeen southern senators attempted a filibuster, an effort to continue a debate so that a vote cannot be taken. Johnson's legendary powers of persuasion were tested in his efforts to persuade Republicans to support the bill. While Johnson negotiated behind the scenes, Minnesota senator Hubert Humphrey (1911–1978) worked to bring the debate to an end so voting could take place.

For the first time in history a filibuster over civil rights legislation was defeated. The Civil Rights Act became law in 1964. The act made illegal any discrimination in employment, in public accommodation (such as hotels), in schools, and most other areas of life. In an accident of legislative procedure it was not only blacks that benefited. As part of the effort to defeat the bill, southern Republicans added women to the list of those requiring civil rights protection. Nobody bothered to remove the word "women" from the final draft, so American women were given much-needed civil rights protection only as an unforeseen side effect of African American civil rights campaigns.

used the public mood to push through the Fair Housing Act, banning discrimination in housing.

A war president

Since 1954, American military advisers had been stationed in South Vietnam, where their stated mission was to prevent the communist government in the north from expanding south. Opinion was always divided over whether the United States should have become involved in this conflict. In early 1964 Johnson was against the deployment of more American troops to Vietnam. But his position changed later the same year when an American warship was allegedly attacked by North Vietnamese forces. The Gulf of Tonkin Resolution was quickly pushed through Congress, giving the administration support for increasing American involvement in the war, including sending combat troops.

In the following years, military advisers told Johnson that sending more American troops was the answer to the conflict in Vietnam. This advice proved false. Rather than weakening, the North Vietnamese forces seemed to gather strength. Growing numbers of American troops were killed or wounded. Public support for the war collapsed as TV networks carried vivid images of the fighting. Perhaps the turning point in Johnson's presidency came on January 31, 1968, when North Vietnam launched a series of attacks on American forces known as the Tet Offensive. The city of Saigon, where American forces had their headquarters, was overrun and the American embassy was briefly taken. Despite massive and successful U.S. counter-attacks, many Americans turned strongly against the war—and against Johnson.

The timing of America's failure in Vietnam could not have been worse for Johnson's political career, for 1968 was an election year. He realized that he had little chance of beating challenger Robert Kennedy (1925–1968), brother of the deceased president, in the Democratic primaries. As his health was also declining, Johnson withdrew from the race. In the same televised speech in which he announced his withdrawal, Johnson also spoke about an end to the bombing in Vietnam. After Robert Kennedy was assassinated while campaigning in Los Angeles, Vice President Hubert Humphrey (1911–1978) won the nomination. However, he lost the 1968 election to Richard Nixon (1913–1994; served 1969–74).

Johnson died from a heart attack on his Texas ranch on January 22, 1973. At the time of his death, most Americans associated Johnson with his mistakes in foreign policy, especially in Vietnam. With the passage of time, however, historians have come to acknowledge Johnson as one of the most successful reforming presidents in U.S. history, with real achievements in economic and civil rights reform.

For More Information

Books

Dallek, Robert. *Flawed Giant: Lyndon Johnson and His Times, 1961–1973.* New York: Oxford University Press, 1998.

Dallek, Robert. *Lone Star Rising: Lyndon Johnson and His Times, 1908–1960.* New York: Oxford University Press, 1991.

Eskow, Dennis. *Lyndon Baines Johnson.* New York: F. Watts, 1993.

Goodwin, Doris Kearns. *Lyndon Johnson and the American Dream.* New York: St. Martin's, 1991.

Schuman, Michael A. *Lyndon B. Johnson.* Springfield, NJ: Enslow, 1998.

Periodicals

McPherson, Harry, and Jack Valenti. "Achilles in the White House" (panel discussion). *The Wilson Quarterly,* vol. 24, no. 2 (Spring 2000).

Web Sites

Lyndon Baines Johnson Library and Museum. http://www.lbjlib.utexas.edu/ (accessed August 2004).

Frances Oldham Kelsey

Born July 24, 1914
Vancouver Island,
British Columbia, Canada

Pharmacologist

Dr. Frances Oldham Kelsey made a name for herself as someone committed to protecting public health. She stood steadfast against granting U.S. Food and Drug Administration (FDA) approval to the drug thalidomide. She refused to cave in to pressure from the Richardson-Merrell Company, which wanted to distribute thalidomide in the United States. The drug was already in wide use in Europe and Japan during the 1950s. The company tried to cast doubt on Kelsey's professional abilities and threatened that she would lose her job. Yet she insisted on further testing to clear up questions about thalidomide effects. Soon, reports began surfacing that the drug caused birth defects overseas. Due to Kelsey's refusal to approve the drug in the United States, she single-handedly protected countless unborn American babies from developing birth defects. Ultimately, her work led to stricter laws for regulating the introduction of new drugs.

"They gave [the thalidomide application assignment] to me because they thought it would be an easy one to start on. As it turned out, it wasn't all that easy."

—Dr. Frances Oldham Kelsey.

Early education and career

Frances Kathleen Oldham was born on July 24, 1914, in Cobble Hill on Vancouver Island in British Columbia,

Canada. A bright student, she received a bachelor's degree in science in 1934 and a master's degree in science in 1935 from McGill University in Montreal, Quebec, Canada. She continued her education at the University of Chicago in Illinois, earning a PhD in pharmacology in 1938 and an MD in 1950. As a pharmacologist, she would study drugs and their use in human medicine. She married fellow university faculty member Dr. Fremont Ellis Kelsey in 1943, and they eventually had two daughters. After completing an internship at Sacred Heart Hospital in Yankton, South Dakota, in 1954, Frances Kelsey became an associate professor of pharmacology at the University of South Dakota. The next year, she became a naturalized U.S. citizen. In 1957 Kelsey left her professorship to open her own private practice, which she ran until 1960 when her husband took a position that required the family to move to Washington, D.C.

Early in her career, Kelsey had investigated, with her husband, the effects of drugs on bodies at different stages of life. The couple published the results of their findings in several respected scientific journals, such as the *Journal of Pharmacy and Experimental Therapy.* In one study, the Kelseys discovered that the bodies of adult rabbits, pregnant rabbits, and rabbit embryos all reacted to the drug under investigation in different ways and that it proved deadly to the embryos. This research fueled her continued interest in the effect of drugs on fetuses and the safety issues involved when women take certain drugs during pregnancy.

Not long after moving to Washington, D.C., Frances Kelsey landed a job as a medical officer with the U.S. Department of Health, Education, and Welfare's Food and Drug Administration (FDA). As medical officer, she was to act as a gatekeeper between pharmaceutical companies and the public. In this job, she evaluated applications for marketing new drugs in the United States, checking to see if the new drug was proven to be safe. In September 1960, she started working on her first assignment. This work would soon bring her national attention.

One woman against an entire company

The William S. Merrell Company, a division of Richardson-Merrell of Cincinnati, Ohio, bought the rights to

Thalidomide Still in Use

Kelsey's work to ban the distribution of thalidomide drew great public attention to the dangers of drugs created by pharmaceutical companies. But continued research into the use of thalidomide indicated that the drug did have redeeming qualities as a medication. Thalidomide proved to be beneficial in treating inflammation in leprosy patients in studies conducted in 1965. After that researchers studied thalidomide's effectiveness in treating diseases which cause tissues to swell.

By the late 1990s, thalidomide was known to provide relief to patients who suffered from arthritis, an inflammation of the joints. It also healed mouth and throat sores in people infected with Human Immunodeficiency Virus (HIV), the virus that causes Acquired Immunodeficiency Syndrome (AIDS). Some of the HIV/AIDS sufferers became thin and more vulnerable to infection because their mouth sores made eating extremely painful. In these controlled situations, thalidomide use was carefully administered and monitored. Doctors prescribing it were mindful of the irreversible nerve damage that the drug caused in the fingers and toes. They also carefully monitored women of childbearing age, cautioning them not to become pregnant while using the drug.

sell a drug called thalidomide in the United States. Developed in West Germany in the 1950s, thalidomide was marketed throughout Europe as a sleep aid. According to German manufacturer Chemie Grunenthal, thalidomide was good for aiding sleep and treating morning sickness or nausea in pregnant women. The manufacturer also claimed the drug could be given safely to those at risk of suicide because it did not absorb into the body at toxic or dangerously unhealthy levels. This meant that suicidal people, who might need sleeping pills in order to rest and relax, would not be able to kill themselves by swallowing too many of the pills. The popularity of the drug and the belief in thalidomide's safety led to its availability without prescription in Europe after 1957.

To prepare the U.S. market for the anticipated release of the drug, Richardson-Merrell distributed thalidomide samples to American doctors to give to patients, a practice that was legal in the late 1950s. With its FDA application, Richardson-Merrell provided research that suggested the relative safety of thalidomide. But Kelsey was not persuaded by the research. She wondered why the drug acted differently in animals than similar drugs. She asked for more tests and refused to let Richardson-Merrell market thalidomide until she was satisfied that the drug was safe. Richardson-Merrell submitted more research, but Kelsey rejected it. According to *FDA Consumer,* Kelsey said that: "The clinical reports were more on the nature of testimonials, rather than the results of well-designed, well-executed studies."

Merrell did not take kindly to Kelsey's stubborn search for proof of the drug's safety. The company exerted pressure on her to approve the drug. Representatives from the company repeatedly called and visited. Growing increasingly frustrated with Kelsey's resistance, they complained to her supervisors that she was unnecessarily delaying the release of the drug. But Kelsey took the pressure in stride, recalling to *FDA Consumer*: "I think I always accepted the fact that one was going to get bullied and pressured by industry. It was understandable that the companies were very anxious to get their drugs approved."

Kelsey did not give in. In February of 1961, she read a report in the *British Medical Journal* indicating that thalidomide caused tingling in the limbs. In November of 1961 the proof she had demanded appeared. German scientist Dr. Widukind Lenz published test results that indicated thalidomide use was the source of a German epidemic of phocomelia, a malformation of limbs in newborn babies. Richardson-Merrell asserted this report was false, arguing that the test results were inconclusive. But Kelsey stood fast. By December, the reports could no longer be denied. The German government pulled thalidomide from the market. By early 1962, Merrell withdrew its application. More than 10,000 cases of phocomelia in European children were eventually attributed to the use of thalidomide.

Protected American newborns

Once the FDA officially recognized the dangers of thalidomide, it published news releases warning of the drug's dangers. The agency sent field staff to locate the doctors who had been given thalidomide samples to urge them to contact patients who might have taken the drug. Although

Richardson-Merrell had distributed more than 2.5 million thalidomide tablet samples to more than 1,000 doctors throughout the United States, only seventeen cases of birth defects have been traced to the drug within the United States. Despite the severe side effects of thalidomide use during pregnancy, as of the early 2000s the drug continued to be used to treat some diseases.

Kelsey's diligence saved countless American babies from having deformed arms and legs. In July 1962, the U.S. Senate recognized Kelsey for her "great courage and devotion to the public interest." On August 7, 1962, President **John F. Kennedy** (1917–1963; served 1961–63; see entry) awarded her the President's Award for Distinguished Federal Civilian Service. The award declared, as recorded in an FDA press release: "Her exceptional judgment in evaluating a new drug for safety for human use has prevented a major tragedy of birth deformities in the United States. Through high ability and steadfast confidence in her professional decision she has

Dr. Frances Kelsey, second from left, watches as President John F. Kennedy (center, seated) signs the Kefauver-Harris Amendments into law in 1962. © *Bettmann/Corbis. Reproduced by permission.*

made an outstanding contribution to the protection of the health of the American people."

Kelsey's discovery and the news about how much pressure she had endured to keep the public safe triggered renewed interest in drug safety legislation. The federal Food, Drug, and Cosmetic Act, passed in 1938, required drug manufacturers to prove that their drugs were safe. But the law President Kennedy signed on October 10, 1962—commonly called the Kefauver-Harris Amendments—required drug manufacturers to register proof with the Food and Drug Administration that new drugs were both effective and safe. The new law also provided for more rapid recall of new drugs deemed hazardous. In addition, the law required drug companies to report to the FDA any adverse reactions to a drug.

In 1963, Kelsey became chief of the Investigational Drug Branch of the FDA, the Center for Drug Evaluation and Research (CDER). The center was created to evaluate and observe clinical trials to make sure they meet new drug regulations. Kelsey continued to care for public health, serving as deputy of scientific and medical affairs in CDER's office of compliance well into her eighties. On October 7, 2000, nearly forty years after her cautious review of the thalidomide application, Frances Kelsey was inducted into the National Women's Hall of Fame in Seneca Falls, New York.

For More Information

Books

Hoffman, William, and Jerry Shields. *Doctors on the New Frontier*. New York: Macmillan, 1980.

Shearer, Benjamin F., and Barbara S. Shearer. *Notable Women in the Life Sciences: A Biographical Dictionary*. Westport, CT: Greenwood Press, 1996.

Periodicals

Grigg, W. "The Thalidomide Tragedy–25 Years Ago." *FDA Consumer* (February 1987): pp. 14–17.

Hunter, M. "Stiffer Drug Law Urged by Kennedy." *New York Times* (August 12, 1962): p. 1.

Web Sites

Bren, Linda. "Frances Oldham Kelsey: FDA Medical Reviewer Leaves Her Mark on History." *FDA Consumer* (March-April 2001). http://www.fda.gov/fdac/features/2001/201_kelsey.html (accessed August 2004).

"FDA's Dr. Frances Kelsey to be Inducted into National Women's Hall of Fame." *Food and Drug Administration Press Office.* http://www.fda.gov/bbs/topics/NEWS/NEW00739.html (accessed August 2004).

John F. Kennedy

Born May 29, 1917
Brookline, Massachusetts

Died November 22, 1963
Dallas, Texas

Politician, thirty-fifth president of the United States

John F. Kennedy *Photo courtesy of the Library of Congress.*

ohn F. Kennedy was a war hero, U.S. congressman, and senator before being elected to the presidency in 1960. He is remembered as one of the most appealing and beloved political leaders of the twentieth century. He brought to the U.S. president's Oval Office an abundance of style and wit. However, his presidency and his political agenda were cut short by his assassination on November 22, 1963.

Political roots

John Fitzgerald Kennedy was born on May 29, 1917, in Brookline, Massachusetts, a community just outside Boston. He was one of nine children born to Joseph and Rose Kennedy. His father, a businessman and diplomat, made a fortune in banking and was the U.S. ambassador to England between 1937 and 1940. His maternal grandfather, John Francis Fitzgerald (1863–1950)—nicknamed "Honey Fitz"—was a popular Boston mayor and U.S. congressman.

John Kennedy, called "Jack" by family and friends, was a sickly baby. At age three, he contracted scarlet fever, a potentially fatal disease. Throughout his early years, he was afflicted with many illnesses. Yet, he had an otherwise happy childhood. He enjoyed the company of his siblings as well as the water sports and touch football games they played at the family's summer home. Their summer residence was located on Cape Cod, a Massachusetts peninsula that sticks out into the Atlantic Ocean. A sense of competition was instilled in him and his siblings—particularly the males in the Kennedy clan—by their father. Kennedy's father was an ambitious man who wanted the children to thrive in their careers.

Kennedy attended Choate, a boys' boarding school in Connecticut. There, he excelled in sports but achieved only an average academic record. Upon graduating from Choate in 1936, he entered Harvard University. Again, he actively participated in sports while earning no better than average grades. One day while playing football, he shattered a disk in his spine. At that point, his athletic career was over, and the injury never healed completely. From then on, Kennedy often suffered severe back pain.

The ambassadorship and relocation to England of his father, Joseph Kennedy (1888–1969), sparked within Jack a fascination with European history and current world politics. During the late 1930s, Adolf Hitler (1889–1945) and Benito Mussolini (1883–1945) ruled as dictators of Germany and Italy, respectively. Their policies to take control of other countries led Europe into World War II (1939–41). The conflict began when Germany invaded Poland on September 1, 1939. At that time, Kennedy was a Harvard senior. For his senior thesis, he chose to examine why England was ill-equipped to go to war with Germany. In 1940 the paper was published as a book, titled *Why England Slept.*

Kennedy graduated from Harvard in 1940 and joined the navy. The United States entered World War II after the Japanese attacked the U.S. naval base at Pearl Harbor, Hawaii, on December 7, 1941. Kennedy made his way through the naval ranks. By 1943, he had attained the rank of lieutenant and was in command of a patrol torpedo (PT) boat in the South Pacific. During the night of August 2, 1943, as Kennedy and his twelve-man crew were on patrol, a Japanese destroyer rammed their boat. Two men died instantly. The others jumped into the water. During the confusion that followed,

Kennedy helped one of his badly injured crewmembers to a section of the boat that remained afloat where the other survivors were holding fast. At sunrise, Kennedy directed the men to a small island nearby, from which they eventually were rescued. For his heroism, Kennedy was presented the Navy and Marine Corps Medal.

From war hero to freshman congressman

Joseph Kennedy was determined that one of his sons would grow up to become the first Roman Catholic U.S. president. His first choice was his eldest, Joseph Jr. , an exceptionally handsome young man who was two years older than Jack. Joe Jr. might have fulfilled his father's wish. However, during World War II, as a U.S. Navy flier, he died when his plane burst into flames during a bombing mission in Europe. Younger Jack now became the focus of his father's dream.

World War II ended in 1945. The following year, John F. Kennedy began his political career when he was elected to the U.S. Congress, representing the eleventh congressional district in Massachusetts. A Democrat, Kennedy served three terms as a congressman before winning a U.S. Senate seat in 1952. The following year, at age thirty-six, he married Jacqueline "Jackie" Bouvier, twelve years his junior. She was a former debutante who had worked as an "inquiring photographer" for the *Washington Times-Herald*. While Kennedy was in the Senate, his back problems returned. The pain was so severe that he underwent two operations. While recuperating, he composed a manuscript about American politicians who had endangered their careers by remaining committed to their principles. It was published as *Profiles in Courage,* and it won Kennedy the Pulitzer Prize in 1957. Also that year, the Kennedys became the parents of their first child, Caroline. A son, John Jr.—lovingly nicknamed "John-John"—was born in 1960. An unnamed daughter had been born and died on the same day in 1956. A fourth child, Patrick, was born prematurely in 1963 and died two days later.

During the mid-1950s, Kennedy was a rising star of the Democratic Party. In 1956, he narrowly missed being named the party's vice-presidential nominee. However, the party's candidate, Adlai Stevenson (1900–1965), lost to the Republican in-

The Importance of Looking Good

In the early 2000s, television played a crucial role in the election process. Candidates who were attractive and photogenic and who delivered speeches in a polished manner had an increased chance of winning. The content of their speeches or their stands on issues often was of secondary importance.

The first televised political debates were between John Kennedy and Richard Nixon in 1960. As these men battled for the presidency, the two faced off in four televised debates. All aired live in September and October. Seventy million Americans watched the first debate.

Nixon had just been released from the hospital, where he had been treated for an infection. He was wearing a light-colored suit that did not photograph well. On-camera, he appeared pale and nervous. Kennedy, however, looked healthy and relaxed.

A majority of those who heard the debate on radio felt that Nixon had won, while those who saw it on television believed that Kennedy was the victor. So emerged the premise that the appearance of candidates will have more impact in swaying voters than their policies. American political campaigns were forever changed.

cumbent, Dwight Eisenhower (1890–1969; served 1953–61). Kennedy then determined to strive for his party's nomination in 1960 and began traveling across the country to build support. His efforts were rewarded on the evening of July 13, 1960 when, at the Democratic Party's national convention, he became his party's nominee. For his running mate, he named **Lyndon B. Johnson** (1908–1973; served 1963–69; see entry), who had been one of his rivals for the top spot on the Democratic ticket. Kennedy conducted a vigorous campaign and narrowly defeated his Republican rival, Richard Nixon (1913–1994). Inaugurated at age forty-three, Kennedy became the youngest U.S. president in history, as well as the first Roman Catholic U.S. president and first chief executive born in the twentieth century.

Mr. President

Kennedy officially became the thirty-fifth president on January 20, 1961. Before Kennedy, most chief executives were grandfatherly. Their wives were stately and matronly, and their children were adults. But Jack and Jackie—who was just thirty-one years old when she became first lady—were youthful, energetic, and glamorous. They had two young children whose presence changed the atmosphere of the usually prim and reserved White House. The president adored his children and, despite his hectic schedule, set aside time to spend with Caroline and John-John.

Furthermore, both Kennedys believed that the White House should be a hub for American art, history, and accomplishments. This tone was set when Robert Frost (1874–1963), the celebrated poet, recited one of his poems at Kennedy's inauguration. Throughout Kennedy's presidency, authors, scientists, scholars, athletes, actors, and artists were invited to White House events. Jacqueline Kennedy supervised the redecoration of every White House room, filling the presidential home and office with fine art and high-quality furnishings.

International and national conditions

When he entered the White House, Kennedy—and the nation—faced many serious issues. The most persistent, and definitely the one with the most potentially serious consequences, was the Cold War (1945–91). Since the end of World War II in 1945, the United States and the Soviet Union, representing the democratic and communist ways of life, respectively, had engaged in a bloodless competition. This political standoff, consisting of threats and gamesmanship, was called the Cold War. Both nations stockpiled nuclear weapons that they were prepared to use if the other nation began taking aggressive action against them. People throughout the world were concerned about the threat of a nuclear strike that would result in massive devastation.

During his presidency, Kennedy most famously confronted the Soviet Union in what came to be known as the Cuban Missile Crisis. In October 1962, he forced the Soviet premier Nikita Khrushchev (1894–1971) to remove long-range missiles that the Soviets had placed in Cuba. Arguably, that crisis was the closest the world had ever come to nuclear war at that time.

In the United States itself, Kennedy's biggest dilemma was racial discrimination, prejudice based on race. By the

time Kennedy came to office, the civil rights movement was well under way. Activists were continuing to work to end segregation, the separation of blacks and whites, that was still being practiced in many of the southern states. The civil rights movement had gained some ground since the end of World War II, including the desegregation of the U.S. military. In 1947 Jackie Robinson (1919–1972) had become the first African American to play major league baseball in the twentieth century. In 1954, the U.S. Supreme Court ruled that segregation in public schools was illegal. However, many white Americans, particularly in the South, resisted these efforts for equality. Southern restaurants, movie houses, and buses remained segregated. Beginning about 1960, some black and white Americans began peacefully demonstrating against this inequality. However, their nonviolent protests were often met with violence from police and bystanders.

Initially, the president was not in favor of such public protests. Although he agreed with the protesters' aims, he believed their actions angered many whites and subsequently would make it even harder to pass additional civil rights leg-

U.S. Attorney General Robert F. Kennedy (left) and his brother, President John F. Kennedy, privately discuss the mounting tensions between the United States and the Soviet Union. *AP/Wide World Photos. Reproduced by permission.*

islation. As his presidency evolved, however, he changed his view. In a televised address delivered on June 11, 1963, he announced his intention to convince Congress to pass a civil rights bill. Although a union of northern Republicans and southern Democrats joined ranks to prevent the bill from becoming law during Kennedy's term in office, the legislation passed in Congress after his death.

To maintain the role of the United States as an example of freedom and democracy, President Kennedy was determined that the country should be a leader in education, science, and the arts. He coined the term "New Frontier" to describe his aspirations for the future of the United States. One of Kennedy's earliest actions as president was to establish the Peace Corps. The Corps consisted of volunteers who were sent to developing countries to work as teachers, healthcare workers, educators, and builders. Furthermore, when Kennedy came into office, the United States lagged behind the Soviet Union in the exploration of space. The president requested that Congress set aside $220 billion for programs to send American astronauts to the Moon before the end of the 1960s. When American astronauts Neil Armstrong (1930–) and Edwin "Buzz" Aldrin (1930–) set foot on the Moon on July 20, 1969, they fulfilled President Kennedy's aspirations for a "New Frontier." But Kennedy did not live long enough to see it for himself.

A day that shook the world

In November 1963, John Kennedy was preparing for his reelection campaign. He and Jackie flew to Dallas, Texas, where he was scheduled to deliver a series of speeches. On November 22, the president and first lady waved from the backseat of a convertible to the crowd along a Dallas thoroughfare. Suddenly, the air was pierced by the sound of gunshots. The president was critically wounded and died soon afterward. Later that day, a suspect, Lee Harvey Oswald (1939–1963), was arrested for the crime. Two days later, while in police custody, Oswald himself was gunned down by Jack Ruby (1911–1967), a Dallas nightclub owner. Meanwhile, hundreds of thousands traveled to Washington, D.C., for the murdered president's funeral.

Vice President Johnson, who assumed the presidency shortly after Kennedy's death, established the Warren Commission to investigate the assassination. The seven-member commission issued a report in September 1964 concluding that Oswald was the lone assassin and that neither he nor Ruby was part of a conspiracy. Nevertheless, many disputed the commission's findings and were convinced that others were involved in a plot to kill the president.

After his death, Kennedy was remembered as a chief executive with as much reverence as George Washington (1732–1799; served 1789–97), Abraham Lincoln (1809–1865; served 1861–65), and Franklin Roosevelt (1882–1945; served 1933–45). Schools, streets, airports, and space centers were named for him. However, in actuality, his presidency was characterized perhaps more by unfulfilled hopes than it was by concrete achievements.

For More Information

Books

Dherbier, Yann-Brice, and Pierre-Henri Verlhac. *John F. Kennedy: A Life in Pictures.* New York: Phaidon, 2003.

Kennedy, John F. *Profiles in Courage.* New York: Harper, 1956.

Kennedy, John F. *The Uncommon Wisdom of JFK: A Portrait in His Own Words,* edited by Bill Adler. New York: Rugged Land, 2003.

Maier, Thomas. *The Kennedys: America's Emerald Kings.* New York: Basic Books, 2003.

Semple, Robert B., Jr. *Four Days in November: The Original Coverage of the John F. Kennedy Assassination.* New York: St. Martin's Press, 2003.

Web Sites

John F. Kennedy Library and Museum. http://www.cs.umb.edu/jfklibrary (accessed August 2004).

"John F. Kennedy National Historic Site." *National Park Service.* http://www.nps.gov/jofi (accessed August 2004).

Ken Kesey

Born September 17, 1935
La Junta, Colorado

Died November 10, 2001
Eugene, Oregon

Author and prankster

Ken Kesey was one of the central figures in the "psychedelic sixties," a decade when various people, including many college students, experimented with mind-altering drugs, such as LSD. Kesey was at the forefront of the cultural explosion in the late 1960s that celebrated joyful expressiveness, the rejection of authority, loud rock music, and drug use. As a cultural figure, Kesey is renowned as the leader of the Merry Pranksters, a ragtag group representing the rowdy, fun-loving, anti-authoritarian nature of the psychedelic era. Their epic cross-country bus trip was chronicled by author Tom Wolfe in *The Electric Kool-Aid Acid Test* (1968). As a novelist, Kesey is best known for two works: *One Flew Over the Cuckoo's Nest* (1962) and *Sometimes a Great Notion* (1964). Kesey remained a hero to countercultural rebels—those people who reject the values and behaviors of the majority—until his death in 2001.

All-American youth

Kesey's status as a cultural rebel was in contrast to his wholesome upbringing. He was born Ken Elton Kesey on September 17, 1935, the older of two sons born to Fred and Geneva Kesey. Both of his parents came from farming and ranching families. Kesey spent the first ten years of his life in Colorado. For five of those years, from 1941 to 1945, his father served with the U.S. Navy in World War II (1939–45). When Kesey's father returned, the family packed up and moved to an area near Eugene, Oregon. Fred began working in dairy farming and before too long had become a successful and well-liked leader in the industry. In fact, he started a dairy marketing cooperative, called the Eugene Farmers Cooperative, that eventually marketed its products under the name Darigold.

Kesey's father taught both of his sons how to hunt, fish, and camp in the beautiful surroundings of Oregon's Willamette Valley. Kesey grew up surrounded by family. The family gatherings were characterized by two things that shaped Kesey's attitudes toward life: competition and storytelling. The men in the family loved to compete in all variety of sports. The boys were invited to join the contests from an early age. At the end of the day, the entire family sat around and told stories, carrying on a tradition handed down from the frontier days of the 1800s and 1900s. Kesey also inherited from his father a real love of reading. From an early age he consumed books of all kinds, from Zane Grey westerns to Tarzan stories to comic books.

Strong, full of energy, and with a sparkling intelligence, Kesey was voted "most likely to succeed" when he graduated from high school in Springfield, Oregon. He went on to study speech and communications at the University of Oregon. He also became an outstanding wrestler in the 174-pound class. In 1956 he married his high-school sweetheart, Faye Haxby, and he graduated from college in 1957. During college Kesey had dabbled in writing for television and radio and also in acting. After graduation he and Faye determined that they would head to California to pursue either acting or writing. When he won a Woodrow Wilson Fellowship to attend Stanford University's creative writing program, he embarked on a journey that shaped his future career and the culture of the 1960s.

Experimenting in San Francisco

As Kesey journeyed south to San Francisco, he recognized that he was leaving one way of life behind and was eagerly embracing new experiences. His imagination had been fired while reading *On the Road* (1957), a novel by Jack Kerouac (1922–1969). The book was the literary highpoint for the Beatniks, a group of intellectuals and poets who rebelled against established values in the 1950s. Kesey was excited about Kerouac's ideas on individual expression. However, he did not want to be part of an existing artistic movement like the Beats. He wanted to be part of something new and original. He found a group of people at Stanford who were eager to push the boundaries of both literary expression and personal behavior. Living in a neighborhood called Perry Lane, Kesey began to recreate his life.

The writers and intellectuals teaching or attending school at Stanford or living in Perry Lane were impressive. Kesey's teachers included noted writers Wallace Stegner (1909–1993), Richard Scowcroft (1916–2001), and Frank O'Connor (1903–1966), and influential editor Malcolm Cowley (1898–1989). His classmates Larry McMurtry (1936–), Wendell Berry (1934–), and Robert Stone (1937–) would all go on to write important novels. Together, these writers pushed each other to explore new literary territory. Under this literary influence, Kesey wrote a novel called "Zoo" about Beat life in San Francisco, but the novel was never published.

Kesey's experiments did not end with literary expression. In order to support his pregnant wife, in 1959 Kesey took a job as night attendant at a psychiatric hospital near San Francisco. At the hospital, Kesey volunteered for experiments that doctors were conducting with so-called "psychomimetic," or mind-altering, drugs. These included lysergic acid diethylamide, more commonly called LSD; psilocybin; mescaline; peyote; and other drugs. In the early 1960s Harvard professor **Timothy Leary** (1920–1996; see entry) spoke out in favor of LSD experimentation. Kesey thrilled to the mind-expanding effects of the drugs, which were then legal. The drugs seemed to allow him to see things he had never seen before. He credited them with unlocking his creative potential. He and his friends at Perry Lane experimented regularly with these drugs and with marijuana. In fact, Kesey was working at the hospital under the influence of peyote, a drug that causes hallucinations or delusions, when he saw a vision of an enormous Native

LSD: The Road to Enlightenment and Back

In the early 2000s, lysergic acid diethylamide (LSD) was widely known as an illegal drug that causes the user to see visions that bear little or no relationship to reality. But the drug was not always illegal. In fact, LSD was once considered as a possible treatment for a number of psychological troubles, from schizophrenia to alcoholism.

LSD was first developed in 1938 by Swiss chemist Dr. Albert Hoffman. It was perfected by the U.S. Office of Strategic Services (a forerunner of the Central Intelligence Agency, or CIA) as a possible "truth drug" to be used on captured prisoners to make them confess. After World War II (1939–45), the CIA launched a series of tests of LSD on civilians. These experiments led to the development of powerful forms of LSD that caused lengthy hallucinogenic episodes, nicknamed "trips." For many users, these trips were intense experiences that seemed to reveal new ways of perceiving the world, even new ways of experiencing spirituality or communion with the supernatural.

The growing reputation of LSD as a mind-altering drug created interest among psychiatrists and researchers at universities such as Stanford and Harvard. They began to sponsor widespread studies of the drug, paying college students and others to swallow doses while under observation. LSD became a popular drug among rebellious young intellectuals such as Allen Ginsberg, Ken Kesey, Timothy Leary, and others in the counterculture of the mid-1960s.

This widespread drug use began to alarm various healthcare workers, police officers, politicians, and other citizens. This concern was increased by reports that some users experienced "bad trips," which caused injuries or even death. For example, reports surfaced that LSD made some users feel like they could fly. Some who tried to fly from the tops of buildings fell to their deaths instead. In 1966 the drug was made illegal. Fans of the drug claimed that the authorities made it illegal because they were afraid that if everybody attained the enlightenment made possible by LSD, the government and police would no longer be necessary. Making the drug illegal only increased its popularity among people taking part in the countercultural movement. By the early 1970s, however, interest in the drug subsided. LSD became one of a number of illegal drugs that circulated in music clubs and discos, mostly in urban areas. In the early 2000s, while the drug remained illegal and versions of it available on the street could be very dangerous, chemists were still researching the therapeutic possibilities of LSD-based drugs.

American patient who eluded the control of the nursing establishment. It was this vision that gave the spark to his most-praised novel.

One Flew Over the Cuckoo's Nest

One Flew Over the Cuckoo's Nest was shaped by several forces. These included Kesey's ongoing drug experimentation and the influence of Beat writer Jack Kerouac. The work was also inspired by Kesey's experiences working in a mental hospital at a time when psychiatric inmates were often treated very severely. The work was completed under the guiding wisdom of editor Malcolm Cowley. Large parts of the book were written while Kesey was under the influence of hallucinogenic or mind-altering drugs. This led him to write in a loose, rambling style. Cowley advised Kesey how to contain these drug-inspired episodes in a more tightly structured narrative. The result was a book that became an instant classic. It was later made into a Broadway play and an award-winning movie, starring Jack Nicholson. In the early 2000s the book was still read in high school and college courses, praised for its message of anti-authoritarianism and its unique style.

As the novel opens, a group of confined mental patients are being carefully controlled by hospital staff through a combination of drugs, force, and intimidation. The staff are led by a stern and cruel authority figure, Nurse Ratched. Soon, Randle McMurphy enters the hospital as a patient. Confident and swaggering, he is a "hundred-percent American con man," according to the book. McMurphy has conned his way into the mental hospital to avoid hard work in a state prison. He immediately sets out to disrupt and weaken the power structure at the hospital. He encourages the patients to ignore the rules of the institution and leads them in various outrageous pranks. His rebellious energy only confuses some of the mentally ill patients. However, McMurphy inspires a huge Native American patient named Chief Bromden (who is the book's narrator) to imagine a life outside the institution. Nurse Ratched finally crushes McMurphy's rebellious spirit by forcing him to undergo a lobotomy, a surgical procedure on the brain that decreases mental function. Denying Ratched her victory, Bromden smothers his friend McMurphy and escapes to freedom—and sanity.

One Flew Over the Cuckoo's Nest struck a nerve among a generation of younger Americans. The book sold millions of copies. This generation of Americans had grown suspicious of authority figures and the "establishment," a term used to describe the politicians and corporate leaders who control American society. Kesey and his readers identified with the character of Randle McMurphy, a confident smart aleck who showed no fear of authority figures. The way to deal with abusive and rigid authority, suggests McMurphy, is to mock it, reject it, and go one's separate way. It is a model for individual action that pleased many and was followed most notably by Kesey himself.

In his next book, *Sometimes a Great Notion* (1964), Kesey continued to experiment with style and content. The novel tells the story of a divided Oregon logging family that comes together in defiance of a labor union and the entire local community. Kesey continued to push the boundaries of style. He used unusual techniques, such as remarks in parentheses, to take readers inside the heads of his characters. Although it was not as popular or as critically praised as *Cuckoo's Nest,* the novel saved Kesey from being considered a one-book author.

Merry Pranksters

During the early 1960s when he was writing about strong, confident, anti-authoritarian figures, Kesey continued to push beyond the boundaries of conventional behavior in his own life. Around 1963 a new force came into Kesey's social circle: Neal Cassady (1926–1968). Cassady was the outrageous traveling companion whom Jack Kerouac had made the hero of *On the Road.* Cassady, who resembled the McMurphy character from *Cuckoo's Nest,* and Kesey inspired each other's appetite for mischief. The two became the center of a new social circle that gathered at Kesey's house in the rural town of La Honda, outside San Francisco. Together the pair led a group that called itself the Merry Pranksters.

The Merry Pranksters were committed to experimentation. This included both hallucinogenic drugs (then still legal, but increasingly controversial) and public acts of outrageous behavior. For example, they might interrupt a poetry reading by jumping onto the stage and chasing imaginary rodents with a fly swatter. Or they might hold impromptu parades in the middle of a town. The group brewed big pots of chili laced with LSD and hung out together at the Kesey La Honda farm.

Ken Kesey sits atop the "Acid Bus" of the Merry Pranksters in San Francisco, California, talking to onlookers. © *Ted Streshinsky/ Corbis. Reproduced by permission.*

In 1964 the Merry Pranksters had the wild idea that they should take their activities on the road. They bought a 1939 bus, painted it in psychedelic colors, and took off on a journey across the United States. During that summer, the rowdy Pranksters wandered across the country, taking drugs, staging pranks, and filming their exploits. They stopped to visit some of the figureheads of American rebellion, including Timothy Leary and Jack Kerouac. Their behavior was so excessive that both Leary and Kerouac found them unbearable to be around for long. The best record of the journey remains author Tom Wolfe's *The Electric Kool-Aid Acid Test.*

Getting off the bus

Life with the Merry Pranksters took a toll on Kesey's writing and eventually got him into trouble with the law. In 1965 he was arrested for possession of marijuana. Rather than serve jail time, he fled to Mexico. The thrill of being on the run from the law soon wore thin, however. Kesey turned himself in to the police in California. After he served a six-month jail term, he and his family moved back to Oregon in November of 1967, settling near his relatives in Pleasant Hill.

Following the publication of Wolfe's book in 1968, Kesey became something of a countercultural hero. Young people who were just beginning to experiment with drug use and rebellion looked to him as a sort of guru, or spiritual teacher. Many made visits to his Oregon farm. Yet Kesey no longer felt like a hero, as he recounted in his story *The Day After Superman Died* (1980). He denied any special wisdom or knowledge, especially about the revolutionary politics that were so important to the youth movements of the late 1960s. Kesey wrote: "I know more about my brother's creamery than I do about the revolution."

Kesey's literary output after the mid-1960s was sporadic and, according to most critics, not up to the standards of his early work. A 1973 work, called *Kesey's Garage Sale,* was a loose, comic book-style gathering of Prankster memories and assorted writings. It included a screenplay that revealed Kesey's attitudes about his fast-paced life in the mid-1960s. The character had been "amped out on too much something," according to the book. "I don't know whether it was psychedelics, electronics, or heroics." By the end of the story, the character was looking for some way to "get off the bus."

Kesey did "get off the bus" to live a more normal life with his family on his farm in Oregon. He had two children. He wrote several other works, including two books for children and a well-received novel, *Sailor Song* (1992). Kesey also helped edit a series of miscellaneous collections called *Spit in the Ocean*. He suffered a stroke in 1997 and died of liver cancer in 2001. He is remembered as one of the most brilliant and adventurous writers of the psychedelic era.

For More Information

Books

Carnes, Bruce. *Ken Kesey.* Boise, ID: Boise State University Press, 1974.

Kesey, Ken. *The Day After Superman Died.* Northridge, CA: Lord John Press, 1980.

Kesey, Ken. *Kesey's Garage Sale.* New York: Viking, 1973.

Kesey, Ken. *One Flew Over the Cuckoo's Nest.* New York: Viking, 1962.

Kesey, Ken. *Sometimes a Great Notion.* New York: Viking, 1964.

McClanahan, Ed, ed. *Spit in the Ocean #7: All About Kesey.* New York: Penguin, 2003.

Perry, Paul. *On the Bus: The Complete Guide to the Legendary Trip of Ken Kesey and the Merry Pranksters and the Birth of the Counterculture.* New York: Thunder's Mouth, 1990.

Stevens, Jay. *Storming Heaven: LSD and the American Dream.* New York: Grove Press, 1987.

Tanner, Stephen L. *Ken Kesey.* Boston, MA: Twayne, 1983.

Wolfe, Tom. *The Electric Kool-Aid Acid Test.* New York: Farrar, Straus, & Giroux, 1968.

Martin Luther King Jr.

**Born January 15, 1929
Atlanta, Georgia**

**Died April 4, 1968
Memphis, Tennessee**

Minister and civil rights leader

Martin Luther King Jr. led nonviolent protests during the civil rights movement of the 1960s. He believed that the peaceful coordination of large groups of people could bring about change in society. Before the 1960s, blacks were segregated, separated from whites, especially in the South. Public facilities were divided into those for whites and those for blacks. Segregation applied to schools, bathrooms, neighborhoods, jobs, and even seats on buses and trains. Usually, black facilities were in much worse condition than those available to whites. In some areas, whites verbally and physically attacked blacks because of their ethnicity. During the 1960s, blacks and whites who opposed these practices started to demand an end to segregation and other types of racial discrimination. A strong public speaker, the Rev. Dr. Martin Luther King Jr. became a leader among the protestors and attracted many to the civil rights movement. The demonstrations that King helped to organize gave rise to the Civil Rights Acts and Voting Rights Act that formed a legal basis for the end of segregation and discrimination in the United States.

"I have a dream that my four little children will one day live in a nation where they will not be judged by the color of their skin but by the content of their character."

—*Rev. Martin Luther King Jr.*

Martin Luther King Jr.
*AP/Wide World Photos.
Reproduced by permission.*

The making of a minister

Born Michael Luther King Jr. on January 15, 1929, King was renamed Martin when he was six years old by his parents Alberta Williams and Michael Luther King Sr. His father was a minister who preached at Ebenezer Baptist Church in Atlanta, Georgia. King learned to recite the biblical scriptures before he was five years old and took to reading early, especially the Bible. His parents did their best to protect him from the discrimination against blacks that was widespread in Atlanta during the 1930s. But King was still forced to sit at the back of the bus, attend segregated black schools, and suffer racial prejudice.

When King was six years old he began attending an elementary school for black children. His white friends were sent to a different school. He and his friends were told that they could not be friends anymore because they were of different races. This event upset him so much that his mother was forced to tell him the story of their people's slavery and the subsequent segregation of the United States. But she insisted that he was just as good as anyone else, a belief that never faded from King's mind. King attended Booker T. Washington High School, the only black high school in Atlanta. Despite the poor quality of his school, King excelled academically and was admitted to Morehouse College in 1944 at age fifteen.

King had great respect for Dr. Benjamin E. Mays (c. 1894–1984), president of Morehouse College, who often preached about social justice. He also enjoyed the sermons of Dr. George D. Kelsey, head of the theology (religion) department. Both of these men helped King to discover his calling to the ministry. When King was seventeen, his father arranged for King's first sermon in front of a large crowd at the family's church. It was such a success that King was ordained and made assistant pastor of Ebenezer Baptist Church in 1947. He graduated from Morehouse College in 1948 with a bachelor of arts degree. He received a bachelor of divinity degree from Crozer Theological Seminary in Chester, Pennsylvania, in 1951. King was then accepted at Boston University's graduate school, finishing his doctorate in 1955. In graduate school King met a music teacher, Coretta Scott. They married in 1953 and eventually had four children. He felt that his destiny lay in the South, despite his wife's reservations about leaving the more liberal North. He took a position preaching at Dexter Avenue Baptist Church in Montgomery, Alabama, at the end of 1954.

The Montgomery bus boycott

In Montgomery, Alabama, King found a receptive audience for his sermons. The community would follow his teachings and lend him the manpower needed to effect change. He became a member of the National Association for the Advancement of Colored People (NAACP) in 1955. The group had just won the *Brown v. Board of Education of Topeka, Kansas* case (1954), which proved that segregated schools were "inherently unequal." King's growing sense of duty toward the civil rights movement propelled him to organize and lead a 382-day boycott of the local bus system. The boycott was sparked by the refusal of a black woman, Rosa Parks (1913–), to give up her seat to a white person on December 1, 1955.

On December 5, 1955, Montgomery's buses were empty. King was voted to head the negotiations, but the situation did not quickly change. King's family was constantly bothered with threatening phone calls. He was arrested on January 26, 1956 for driving 30 mph in a 25 mph zone. Then, King's home was bombed on January 30. He was released from jail fairly quickly on the speeding charge, and no one was hurt in the bomb blast. However, his family's safety had been compromised. Nevertheless, King remained steadfast in his convictions. On March 22, 1956, the state of Alabama found King guilty of inciting a boycott. His charge was later repealed when the U.S. Supreme Court ruled on November 13 that segregation on buses was illegal. On December 21, 1956, Montgomery's buses were officially desegregated.

President of the Southern Christian Leadership Conference

King became the first president of the Southern Christian Leadership Conference (SCLC). Created in 1957, the SCLC had its headquarters in Atlanta. This group of black leaders was organized to coordinate the civil rights movement in the South. It sought to help to promote such causes as desegregation and

Civil Rights Timeline of the 1960s

1960 The sit-in protest movement against racial segregation at restaurants and stores begins at a Woolworth's department store lunch counter in Greensboro, North Carolina.

1961 Blacks and whites ride buses together on Freedom Rides to the South from Washington, D.C., challenging segregation on public transportation.

1962 Riots break out when James Meredith enrolls as the first black student at the University of Mississippi. The U.S. Supreme Court rules that segregation on public transportation is illegal.

1963 Demonstrations take place in Birmingham, Alabama. NAACP Mississippi Field Secretary Medgar Evers is murdered. The March on Washington, D.C., features the Rev. Dr. Martin Luther King Jr.'s inspiring "I Have a Dream" speech.

1964 The Civil Rights Act is signed into law by President Lyndon B. Johnson. The bill makes segregation and discrimination illegal.

1965 Black nationalist Malcolm X is murdered. Civil rights activists march from Selma to Montgomery, Alabama, where the nonviolent protest is brutally broken up by state troopers. The Voting Rights Act becomes law, making it easier for blacks to vote.

1968 Rev. Dr. Martin Luther King Jr. is assassinated. Another Civil Rights Act passes, making discrimination in housing practices illegal. Staunch civil rights supporter Robert F. Kennedy, brother of deceased U.S. president John F. Kennedy, is also assassinated.

increasing black voters and their participation in elections. On September 3, 1958, King was arrested for loitering at the Montgomery courthouse. He refused bail, preferring to draw attention to his unlawful arrest. The court released him on the basis that the government would prefer not to spend the money on his upkeep. Shortly after King's release, a black woman stabbed him in the chest during a book-signing event for his history of the Montgomery bus boycott, *Stride Toward Freedom*.

King recovered quickly, but if the stab wounds had been slightly to the left or right, he would have died. Stunned by his brush with death, King decided in early 1959 to fulfill a lifelong wish to travel to India. He paid his respects at the grave of Mohandas Karamchand Gandhi (1869–1948), the Indian activist. Gandhi's nonviolent protests helped India win independence from Britain in 1947. The peaceful activism of Gandhi, whose life was cut short by assassins in 1948, had greatly inspired King in his civil rights work. According to King biographer Stephen B. Oates in *Let the Trumpet Sound: The Life of Martin Luther King, Jr.*: "He came home with a deeper understanding of nonviolence and a deep commitment as well. For him, nonviolence was no longer just a philosophy and a technique of social change; it was now a whole way of life." When King returned to the United States, he became co-pastor with his father at the family's Ebenezer Baptist Church in Atlanta, where he could also remain active in the SCLC.

Sit-ins and freedom rides

Between 1957 and 1968, King traveled frequently and wrote several books about his experiences. He helped coordinate the "sit-ins" of 1960, in which groups of blacks refused to move from the white sections of stores and restaurants. King also was instrumental in the Freedom Rides that began on Southern buses during 1961, forcing the racial mixing of public transportation. These forms of nonviolent protest often caused an alarming amount of violent opposition from whites, including beatings and mass arrests. King and several other black leaders met with President **John F. Kennedy** (1917–1963; served 1961–63; see entry) in 1963 to plead the case for civil rights legislation that would end the need for protest and the resulting violence. However, Kennedy was not yet open to the idea.

On April 3, 1963, the Birmingham Movement began, in which blacks demonstrated for desegregated stores and fair store hiring practices. King was arrested. While in jail he wrote the now famous "Letter from a Birmingham Jail" on old newspaper and pieces of toilet paper. This time Kennedy took notice and sent the FBI to assure King's safety. The protests continued into May, with thousands of blacks of all ages marching through the streets of Birmingham. Police used dogs and water hoses to try to subdue the masses. On May 10, 1963, the demands of the protestors were met, due in no small part to the support of

Martin Luther King Jr. stares through the bars of his cell in the Birmingham jail.
© *Bettmann/Corbis.*
Reproduced by permission.

the Kennedy administration. King also spoke during the March on Washington on August 28, 1963, rallying supporters with his "I Have a Dream" speech. In the speech, as quoted in the *Seattle Times,* King stated: "I have a dream that one day this nation will rise up and live out the true meaning of its creed. 'We hold these truths to be self-evident that all men are created equal.' I have a dream that one day out in the red hills of Georgia the sons of former slaves and the sons of former slaveowners will be able to sit down together at the table of brotherhood."

The Civil Rights Act passed in 1964, formally protecting the rights of blacks as equals of whites. King won the Nobel Peace Prize on December 10, 1964. He traveled to Norway to accept the award and donated the prize money to further the civil rights movement. Upon his return, he led the Selma-Montgomery Freedom March in support of voter registration in March 1965. In response, President **Lyndon B. Johnson** (1908–1973; served 1963–69; see entry) signed the Voting Rights Act of 1965, which provided federal regulation of the voting process. Although he had already accomplished a great deal, King continued to work to protect and expand the rights of Americans, regardless of race.

Soon, however, his life was violently cut short. After King traveled to Memphis, Tennessee, in 1968 to support a sanitation workers' strike, James Earl Ray (1928–1998) shot and killed King with a bullet through the neck. The assassination occurred on April 4 while King stood on the balcony of a hotel. King continues to be remembered as one of the great heroes of the twentieth century. His January birthday has become a national holiday in the United States.

For More Information

Books

Bennett, Lerone, Jr. *What Manner of Man: A Biography of Martin Luther King Jr.* Chicago, IL: Johnson, 1964.

Haskins, James. *The Life and Death of Martin Luther King Jr.* New York: Beech Tree Books, 1992.

January, Brendan. *Martin Luther King Jr.: Minister and Civil Rights Activist.* Chicago, IL: Ferguson Publishing, 2000.

King, Coretta Scott. *My Life with Martin Luther King Jr.* New York: Holt, Rinehart & Winston, 1969, revised, 1993.

King, Coretta Scott, ed. *The Words of Martin Luther King Jr.* New York: Newmarket Press, 1983.

Oates, Stephen B. *Let the Trumpet Sound: The Life of Martin Luther King, Jr.* New York: Harper, 1982.

Pettit, Jayne. *Martin Luther King Jr.: A Man with a Dream.* New York: Franklin Watts, 2001.

Wukovits, John F. *Martin Luther King Jr.* San Diego, CA: Lucent Books, 1999.

Web Sites

"I Have a Dream." *The Seattle Times.* http://seattletimes.nwsource.com/mlk/king/words/dream.html (accessed August 2004).

The King Center. http://www.thekingcenter.org (accessed August 2004).

The National Association for the Advancement of Colored People. http://www.naacp.org (accessed August 2004).

Timothy Leary

Born October 22, 1920
Springfield, Massachusetts

Died May 31, 1996
Beverly Hills, California

Psychologist, philosopher, teacher,
writer, lecturer, LSD advocate

Timothy Leary, a psychologist and former Harvard University professor, was one of the most controversial figures on the American countercultural or anti-authoritarian scene during the 1960s. He led experimentation with hallucinogenic, or mind-altering, drugs. He advocated the use of such drugs as consciousness-raising tools—a way to open people's minds to new ways of viewing reality. Leary urged a new generation of Americans to "turn on, tune in, [and] drop out," in a 1966 interview in *Playboy* magazine.

A rebellious soul

Timothy Leary was born in Springfield, Massachusetts, on October 22, 1920. Between 1938 and 1943 he attended Holy Cross College, the U.S. Military Academy at West Point, and the University of Alabama. During Leary's college years, his rebellious spirit was stirred as he realized that he was being taught to follow rules and orders blindly rather than to ask questions and think for himself. In 1944 he married Marianne Busch and they eventually had two children.

"I want to get back in. I think I belong in American society. I think that a society that imprisons its philosophers is playing with very bad magic. You can't imprison ideas."

—Timothy Leary, speaking while confined in Folsom Prison.

Timothy Leary. *AP/Wide World Photos. Reproduced by permission.*

Marianne died in 1955 and Leary went on to marry (and divorce) several more times.

After serving in the U.S. Army during World War II (1939–45), Leary earned a PhD in psychology from the University of California at Berkeley in 1950. He taught there through 1955 and then became director of psychological research at the Kaiser Foundation Hospital in Oakland, California. He accepted a teaching position at Harvard University in 1959.

"Magic" mushrooms

Leary had long been interested in the workings of the mind, the evolution of consciousness, and the manner in which the mind and body interact. In 1960, while traveling through Mexico, he began eating mushrooms containing psilocybin, a hallucinogenic substance. Such substances cause hallucinations or mental images that are not connected to reality. Traditionally, these "magic" or "sacred" mushrooms had been consumed by Mexicans during religious rituals. Leary noted in his autobiography, *Flashbacks,* that while under the influence of the mushrooms he "gave way to delight" as he came to realize that "this world—so manifestly real—was actually a tiny stage set constructed by the mind." He referred to his initial consumption of the mushrooms as "the deepest religious experience of [his] life."

Upon his return to Harvard, Leary began the Harvard Psilocybin Project. He researched and assembled data on the effect of the psilocybin mushroom on humans. Working with Richard Alpert (1931–; later known as Baba Ram Dass), a Harvard colleague, Leary experimented on graduate students, inmates at a state prison, divinity students, friends, and acquaintances. Among those who ate the mushrooms were such noted writers as Aldous Huxley (1894–1963), Arthur Koestler (1905–1983), Allen Ginsberg (1926–1997), Robert Lowell (1917–1977), Jack Kerouac (1922–1967), and William S. Burroughs (1914–1997).

LSD experiments

In 1962 Leary took his first dose of lysergic acid diethylamide, more commonly known as LSD and nicknamed "Acid." LSD is a synthetically produced hallucinogenic drug that was discovered in 1938 by Dr. Albert Hoffman, a Swiss researcher. LSD was a powerful drug, far stronger than psilocybin. Leary described his initial LSD use, also called a "trip," as "something different. It was the most shattering experience of my life," as quoted on the *Timothy Leary* Web site. He became fascinated with the drug and began conducting experiments in which he recorded the manner in which it altered human consciousness and behavior. As he explored the drug and its effects, Leary came to believe that the use of LSD resulted in a heightened spirituality and sense of oneness with the world. He also concluded that it could be beneficial as a potential cure for alcoholism and a range of psychological disorders, including schizophrenia.

Leary's support of LSD and experimentation with students was controversial. In particular, the parents of many of his subjects were disturbed to learn that their offspring were taking drugs. Such parents had sent their children to Harvard to earn degrees and become the future leaders of America. Parents were concerned that their children were perhaps even getting involved in a subculture that embraced meditation and practiced Eastern religions.

In 1963, a nervous Harvard administration fired the professor-researcher. Leary and Alpert (who also lost his job at the university) then established the International Foundation for Internal Freedom. Based in Mexico, the foundation was a research organization that Leary and Alpert planned to use to further experiment with LSD and other psychedelic, mind-altering drugs. Almost immediately, the foundation was shut down by the Mexican government. Next, the pair founded the Castalia Institute in Millbrook, New York. Here, Leary and Alpert took the drugs themselves and supervised their use among friends and celebrities. Leary believed in taking the drug in a controlled setting to minimize the chance of having a "bad trip." During such episodes, the hallucinations are terrifying and cause dangerous actions. Leary claimed that LSD allowed the individual user to become conscious of knowledge and spiritual awareness that was contained in the brain by way of cellular energy. He became convinced that the drug was a key component in the ongoing development of human intelligence.

Arrest and appeal

In 1965 Leary traveled to India and converted to the Hindu religion. This gave an increased sense of spirituality to

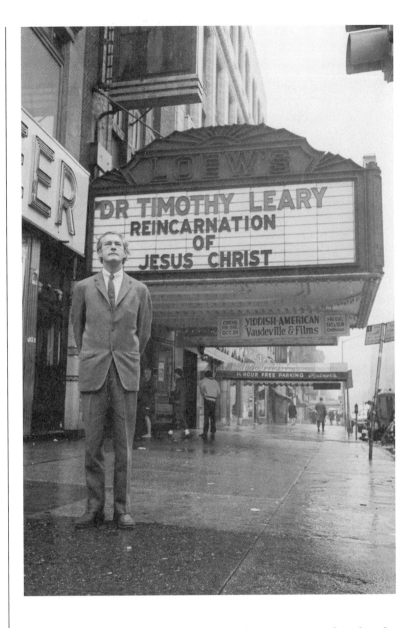

Timothy Leary stands near a theater marquee where he will speak in conjunction with his new psychedelic religious group, the League of Spiritual Discovery.
© Bettmann/Corbis. Reproduced by permission.

his beliefs about psychedelic drugs. That same year, his daughter was arrested for possession of marijuana while crossing the border from Mexico to Texas. Leary accepted responsibility for her situation and was found guilty of marijuana possession. He was sentenced to thirty years in jail. He appealed the verdict, arguing that the Marijuana Tax Act, one of the laws that supposedly had been broken, was unconstitutional. The case eventually went to the U.S. Supreme Court, which in 1969 ruled that the act was unconstitutional. The court noted that individuals neglecting to pay tax on marijuana brought into the United States would be incriminating themselves by admitting that they possessed the illegal substance.

During this period, Leary also appeared and spoke at rallies protesting the Vietnam War (1954–75). He joined in the recording of "Give Peace a Chance" with singer John Lennon and his wife, Yoko Ono. He established the League of Spiritual Discovery, which advocated the use of LSD. He wrote two books, both published in 1968. In the *Politics of Ecstasy,* he explained his belief that the use of psychedelic drugs made spiritual awareness possible. *High Priest* described his experiences while on hallucinogens. He frequently gave lectures and coordinated staged multimedia programs in which he preached about the benefits of psychedelic drugs.

"Turn on, tune in, drop out"

By this time, Leary had become the unofficial national spokesperson for LSD and the psychedelic movement. This movement involved young people who saw drug use as a means of announcing their rejection of mainstream American culture. He urged people to "turn on, tune in, drop out," which became one of the catchphrases of the psychedelic era. The saying was being repeated among those young Americans who were questioning their parents' standards and way of life. Even though Leary was old enough to be their father, many young people admired him. They liked his openness, his fascination with consciousness-expanding drugs, and his passion and zest for life.

As more and more young people experimented with LSD—untold thousands tried the drug—the attention surrounding Leary greatly increased. In particular, older, conservative Americans viewed him as nothing less than a menace to society. Accounts of "bad trips" among LSD users, including some that led to severe injury and death, only added to the controversy.

In 1970, Leary was again convicted of possessing marijuana, which two years earlier had been found by police in a borrowed automobile he was driving. This time his sentence

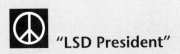

"LSD President"

During the mid-1960s, Timothy Leary was at the height of his fame as the guru of psychedelic drugs. He offered a series of predictions about the impact LSD and other hallucinogens would have on mainstream American society.

Leary claimed in a widely quoted *Playboy* interview that newly developed psychedelic drugs were "really going to revolutionize our concepts of ourselves and education." In this regard, hallucinogens would be commonly used as educational tools in all public and private schools. These drugs would instruct children to be more in touch with their sense organs. In fact, any individual of any age who was concerned with intellectual pursuits would regularly consume LSD, or "drop acid." In 1967, Leary predicted that, within fifteen years, Americans would elect an "LSD President" and there would be a "pot-smoking Supreme Court."

Of course, none of these prophesies came true.

was ten years behind bars, to be served consecutively with a second ten-year sentence connected to the earlier Texas arrest. Leary was imprisoned in a minimum-security prison in San Luis Obispo, California, and he immediately began planning his escape. He fled by climbing to a rooftop and up a telephone pole, crawling on a cable that went across the prison yard and on a barbed wire fence, and then jumping onto a roadway.

Fugitive

Once a guru of the counterculture, Leary now was a fugitive, an escaped criminal, from justice. He escaped first to Algeria and then to Switzerland and Afghanistan. In 1973 he was re-arrested in Afghanistan by U.S. Drug Enforcement Administration agents. He was sent back to prison in California and released three years later. His early discharge reportedly came about after he agreed to offer the authorities information on political radicals he had met and with whom he had conferred while overseas.

After his release from prison, Leary became fascinated by a range of subjects, including cyber-culture, computers, virtual reality, and space colonization, along with the workings of the human mind and body. He spent his last years exploring these topics as well as lecturing and writing essays. He replaced "turn on, tune in, drop out" with a new adage: "Just say know," a take-off on First Lady Nancy Reagan's "Just say no" anti-drug campaign, according to *Flashbacks*. For Leary, gaining complete knowledge was always preferable to simple rejection of something an authority figure says is dangerous.

Upon learning in the early 1990s that he had contracted prostate cancer and was terminally ill, Leary decided to document his death. He claimed that he eagerly looked forward to his passing and viewed it as "the ultimate trip." He died peacefully at his California home on May 31, 1996, surrounded by friends. Video cameras recorded his death, and his final words were reported to be, "Why not? Why not? Why not?," according to a *New York Times* obituary.

To some, Leary was a public nuisance, a corruptor of youth. In fact, in the early 1970s President Richard Nixon (1913–1994; served 1969–74) had once called him "the most dangerous man in America," according to the *New York Times*. To his fellow drug users, he was a visionary who saw the potential of the human mind. Both hated and loved, Leary was a symbol of the more decadent experimentalism of the 1960s.

For More Information

Books

Forte, Robert, ed. *Timothy Leary: Outside Looking In*. Rochester, VT: Park Street Press, 1999.

Leary, Timothy. *Change Your Brain*. Berkeley, CA: Ronin Press, 2000.

Leary, Timothy. *Changing My Mind, Among Others: Lifetime Writings*. Englewood Cliffs, NJ: Prentice-Hall, 1982.

Leary, Timothy. *Flashbacks: An Autobiography*. Los Angeles, CA: J. P. Tarcher, 1983.

Leary, Timothy. *Politics of Ecstasy*. New York: Putnam, 1968.

Leary, Timothy. *Politics of Self-Determination*. Berkeley, CA: Ronin Press, 2000.

Leary, Timothy. *Your Brain Is God*. Berkeley, CA: Ronin Press, 2000.

Periodicals

Mansnerus, Laura. Obituary, *New York Times* (June 1, 1996).

"Playboy Interview: Timothy Leary." *Playboy* (September 1966).

Web Sites

Timothy Leary Archives. http://www.leary.com/archives/index.html (accessed August 2004).

Vince Lombardi

Born June 11, 1913
New York, New York

Died September 3, 1970
Washington, D.C.

Football coach

V ince Lombardi, considered by many to be America's greatest football coach, was in many ways more connected to an earlier era. He achieved his greatest fame in a culture that placed increasing value on youth, individuality, and rebelliousness. Yet Lombardi championed teamwork, faith, and discipline. Lombardi rose to national fame after he took charge of the unlucky Green Bay Packers professional football team. In just eight years, he led the team to four league championships and two Super Bowls. During the 1960s, Lombardi became a national folk hero. His pithy comments about winning and losing were heard and discussed across the nation. For every American who sought to be part of the anti-establishment or counterculture movement, there was at least one other who agreed with Lombardi's widely quoted statement: "It is and always has been an American zeal to be first in anything we do, and to win, and to win, and to win."

Strict Catholic upbringing

Lombardi was born into an Italian American family that had lived out the immigrant dream of doing well finan-

"I firmly believe that any man's finest hour, the greatest fulfillment of all that he holds dear, is the moment when he has worked his heart out in a good cause and lies exhausted on the field of battle—victorious."

—*Vince Lombardi.*

Vince Lombardi.
© *Bettmann/Corbis.*
Reproduced by permission.

cially in the United States. His father, Enrico, had come to the country from Italy with his parents in 1892, when he was just two years old. A fifth-grade dropout, Enrico "Harry" Lombardi was a hard worker who built a successful wholesale meat business with his brother in Brooklyn, New York. He married an Italian American girl, Matilda Izzo, in 1912. On June 11, 1913, they had their first son, Vincent. The family grew to include five children. Vince was seventeen years old when his youngest brother was born.

Lombardi biographer Michael O'Brien wrote in *Vince: A Personal Biography of Vince Lombardi,* that "The Lombardis' experience resembled that of most Italian Americans: the supportive, tight-knit family, the nearby relatives, faith in the Catholic Church, and the bitter taste of discrimination." But unlike many children of immigrants, the Lombardis were not poor. They lived in comfortable middle-class neighborhoods, first in Brooklyn, New York, and later in Englewood, New Jersey.

Harry Lombardi was strict and disciplined his children. A perfectionist in all things, he was a devout Catholic. Lombardi remembered that his father taught him that "before you can exist as an individual, the first thing you have to accept is duty, the second thing is respect for authority, and the third … is to develop a strong mental discipline," as quoted by O'Brien. These values were confirmed by Lombardi's education at Catholic schools. For a time Lombardi believed that he would enter the priesthood. He enrolled at the Cathedral College of the Immaculate Conception Preparatory Seminary at the age of fifteen. Within two years, however, Lombardi dropped his dream of becoming a priest and transferred to St. Francis Preparatory School. There, he began to pursue a new vocation: football.

Majors in football

Lombardi was a good student at St. Francis, but he was an even better football player. However, he stood only 5 feet 8 inches tall and barely topped 170 pounds. He made up for his lack of size with a determination and ferocity that sometimes stunned his teammates. He won a scholarship to Fordham University, then the nation's largest Catholic university. Football in the 1930s was a tough, sometimes brutal game. Helmets had no facemasks, and padding was minimal. The plays were simple, with few complicated blocking schemes or pass routes. The best teams were those that simply blocked and tackled better than their opponents. Fordham was one the best. Under coach Jim Crowley, the Fordham Rams beat some of the top teams in the country. Though small, Lombardi was a hard-hitting offensive guard on a line that was nicknamed the "Seven Blocks of Granite." It is widely considered the best offensive line in college football history. The Rams came up one game shy of an undefeated season in 1936. It was Lombardi's senior year when they narrowly lost their last game of the year.

Although stories once circulated that Lombardi graduated with distinction from Fordham, in truth he was a fairly average student, earning mostly Bs and some Cs. According to David Maraniss, author of *When Pride Still Mattered: A Life of Vince Lombardi,* "The highlight of his academic career was an A on the final exam in ethics, which was the school's most rigorous course." In truth, academics were not that necessary for the career that Vince Lombardi had in mind. It was clear to everyone who knew him that he would become a football coach.

At Fordham, Lombardi met the woman who would become his companion for life: Marie Planitz. Lombardi and Planitz were an odd pair. She was the reserved daughter of a tight-lipped German stockbroker, he the rough, unrefined son of a meat seller. The two met in 1935, dated through college, and were married on August 31, 1940. They eventually had two children, Vincent Thomas and Susan.

Rises through the coaching ranks

Following his graduation from college, Lombardi worked for a brief time at a finance company and took law classes in the evening. However, he felt no calling for a life away from football. In 1939 he accepted a position as teacher and assistant football coach at St. Cecelia High School in Englewood, New Jersey. By day he taught Latin, algebra, physics, and chemistry, but in the afternoons he taught his favorite subject: football.

Lombardi became head coach at St. Cecelia in 1942. Over the course of four seasons his teams compiled a record of 39 wins, 7 losses, and 5 ties, with 6 state football championships. In one stretch his boys went 32 games without defeat and ran up 25 victories in a row. It was at St. Cecelia that Lombardi developed his distinctive coaching style. He demanded that his players perfect the basic skills of blocking and tackling. He tolerated no changes from his game plan. Some players complained that Lombardi made them play like robots, but most enjoyed the discipline that Lombardi provided—especially because it brought victory. At St. Cecelia, Lombardi also coached the basketball team to a state title.

With his winning record as ample proof that he could coach, Lombardi was hired in 1947 by Fordham, the university he had earlier attended. He served as the freshman football coach and moved up to assistant at the varsity level the next year. In 1949 Lombardi was hired by coach Earl "Red" Blaik to join his coaching staff at West Point, the Army's military academy. Blaik was a coaching legend, and his winning ways continued at West Point. Lombardi coached the offensive line, and he soaked up Blaik's coaching style, which stressed rigid organization and careful preparation. He also borrowed some of Blaik's favorite and famous expressions, such as "There is no substitute for victory" and "You have to pay the price."

Lombardi left West Point in 1954 to join the coaching staff of the New York Giants, a National Football League (NFL) professional team. The Giants were coached by Jim Lee Howell, who placed Lombardi in charge of the offense. New assistant coach Tom Landry was in charge of the defense. The coaches inherited a low-scoring team with a record of three wins to nine losses in the previous season. At first Lombardi's emotional, hard-driving style did not sit well with professional players, who resented being pushed so hard. Yet Lombardi managed to teach his players the importance of basic skills and flawless execution. His burning desire to win was hard to resist. The Giants soon became an NFL powerhouse. Coaches Lombardi and Landry were seen as rising stars in the coaching ranks. It was not long before Lombardi got the chance to be head coach of his own pro team.

Rebuilding the Packers

Vince Lombardi entered pro football at a time when the game was changing dramatically. It was overtaking both college football and major league baseball as America's favorite sport. Football, with its hard-hitting action, was well suited to television. Beginning in 1955 the CBS network began to televise games to a national audience. In 1956 a new sports magazine, *Sports Illustrated,* offered regular coverage of pro football. Attendance at NFL games grew from an average of 25,353 in 1950 to 40,106 in 1960. Big name teams such as the New York Giants, the Chicago Bears, and the Los Angeles Rams now had the money to build solid teams with star players. But teams from smaller cities, such as Green Bay, Wisconsin, struggled to stay competitive.

The Green Bay Packers were one of the NFL's original teams, with a history that stretched back to 1919. Ever since 1947, however, the Packers had failed to post a winning record. The residents of Green Bay were said to be the most devoted fans in the entire league. They were hungry for a winner and desperate for a winning coach. So, when Vince Lombardi asked for complete control of the team as both coach and general manager, the team's executive board gladly agreed. Lombardi became the coach of the Packers in February of 1959, beginning what would become the most legendary career of any coach in pro football.

Not long after taking charge of the Packers, Lombardi began his mission of rebuilding the team from the ground up. "We're not just going to start with a clean slate," he declared, according to Maraniss. "We're going to throw the old slate away." Lombardi remodeled the team's facilities, declaring that "you had to look good to play good." He schooled the assistant coaches in his system of play so that everyone in the organization operated from the same understanding of how the game should be played. And when he first met with his players, he insisted that they forget all the bad habits that they had learned while losing and remake themselves as a disciplined, winning team.

Lombardi recognized that the Packers did not have the greatest talent in the league. Thus, he set out to create a winning team by working harder than everybody else. He drove his players and his coaches to the point of exhaustion. The only person he drove harder was himself. It was not uncommon for Lombardi to work seventeen, eighteen, or even nineteen hours a day. Slowly, one by one, the players on the team came to believe in Lombardi, but more importantly they came to believe that they could win. When they opened the 1959 season against the Chicago Bears with a nine to six victory, the Packers lifted Lombardi atop their shoulders and carried him off the field.

The Lombardi legend

In his first season with the Packers, Lombardi helped his team to achieve its first winning record in years, seven wins to five losses. The next year the Packers played in the division championship, only to lose to the Philadelphia Eagles. Close was not good enough for Lombardi nor for the Packer faithful. They wanted more. Behind the passing of quarterback Bart Starr (1934–) and the skill of "golden boy" running back Paul Hornung (1935–), the Packers dominated the NFL throughout the fall of 1961. They met Lombardi's former team, the New York Giants, in a championship game that was seen by a record 55 million viewers. The Packers destroyed the Giants thirty-seven to zero, playing a game that many sportswriters described as near perfection.

For the next six years, the Packers were the kings of the NFL. They won championships again in 1962, 1965, and 1966. In 1967 they won the first Super Bowl, the new championship match that followed the merger of the NFL with the rival American Football League (AFL). As the coach of the most dominant team in a sport that continued to grow in popularity, Lombardi became an icon of success in Green Bay and throughout the nation. Lombardi was distinctive in his appearance and public demeanor. He was a man who became known for his earthy quotes about the importance of hard work and winning. He emphasized teamwork over individuality. With these traits, Lombardi provided great material for the sportswriters who helped change Lombardi from coach into legend.

The 1960s were a decade of popular celebrities—such as The Beatles, **Muhammad Ali** (1942–; see entry), and even President **John F. Kennedy** (1917–1963; served 1961–63; see entry). These celebrities were young, photogenic, and "cool." However, Lombardi was middle-aged and square (both physically and morally). He wore thick glasses and had a big

Joe Namath: The Anti-Lombardi from the AFL

Green Bay Packers coach Vince Lombardi stood for the old-time National Football League (NFL) values of teamwork, discipline, and keeping the coach in control of the game. In contrast, Joe Namath (1943–), the controversial quarterback of the upstart New York Jets of the American Football League (AFL), stood for the values that were transforming American football and American culture. Namath had signed with the New York Jets in 1965 for the then-huge salary of $427,000 a year. He soon distinguished himself with his flashy style of play and his love for the outrageous. His famous "guarantee" that his Jets would win Super Bowl III in 1969 is widely thought to have announced a new age in American sports: the age of the brash celebrity athlete.

Namath was an excellent football player. Born in Pennsylvania in 1943, he played his college ball under legendary coach Paul "Bear" Bryant (1913–1983) at the University of Alabama. Namath was a controversial player while at Alabama. He rejected the racist attitudes of the South and openly befriended black teammates. He was once suspended from the team for directing traffic while intoxicated. The New York Jets of the AFL were the perfect professional team for Namath, for the team did not shy away from the media attention sought by their popular and handsome quarterback. Nicknamed "Broadway Joe" by the New York press, he quickly became known as a ladies' man. But he always played well on Sunday.

Namath led the Jets to the AFL title in 1968. His team prepared to play the NFL champion Baltimore Colts in the third title match between the champions of the rival leagues. Many football observers, including Lombardi, believed that the AFL was an upstart league whose teams would fail in direct competition with the NFL teams. After all, Lombardi's Packers had soundly defeated AFL teams in the first two Super Bowls. Yet Namath led his Jets to a stunning 16 to 7 upset of the heavily favored Colts, lending the AFL instant credibility. Soon thereafter the two leagues merged. Namath continued his career with the Jets until 1976, although he never again reached the heights of the 1969 season. He retired in 1977 after a final season with the Los Angeles Rams.

toothy grin. He laughed too loud and pushed too hard. He was the farthest thing from slick. Yet, somehow this fact was what made him so endearing. He treated every one of his players the same whether they were white or black. According to his famous quote, cited on the *Vince Lombardi* Web site, he treated all players "like dogs." He demanded commitment to the high ideals of hard work and sportsmanship from everyone around him, and he was rewarded with great loyalty.

At a time when rock 'n' roll music, the anti-war movement, and an increased expression of sexuality claimed so much of the public's attention, Lombardi worshiped the old-fashioned values of hard work and winning. And people thrilled to his statements on these topics. "Winning is not a sometime thing; it's an all the time thing," said Lombardi in one of his most famous speeches, quoted on the *Vince Lombardi* Web site. "You don't win once in a while; you don't do things right once in a while; you do them right all the time." He convinced his players that they could conquer any challenge if only they willed themselves to do so. When the Packers won, people believed that perhaps Lombardi was right. These values made Lombardi a national hero. Interestingly, the quotation most often attributed to Lombardi—"Winning isn't everything, it's the only thing"—was not his, according to the Green Bay Packers Web site. It was actually a line from a 1953 John Wayne movie. Lombardi is quoted as saying: "Maybe winning isn't everything, but it sure comes way ahead of whatever is second." The coach also noted that the important thing was making the effort to win.

Life after the Packers

The pressure of building a winning football program began to wear on Lombardi by the mid-1960s. The stress only increased after the merger of the NFL with the AFL before the 1967 season. Lombardi was determined that the Packers would prove their dominance, which they did by defeating the AFL team and winning a third straight championship. Throughout the 1967 season Lombardi drove himself harder than ever before. "Nobody will ever know the kind of pressure it was," his wife, Marie, remembered, as quoted by O'Brien. On January 14, 1968, the team won its second Super Bowl in a row. By this time, Lombardi was worn out by nearly eight months of constant work. Two weeks later, on February 1, he announced his retirement as coach of the Packers, although he would retain the title of general manager.

Lombardi relaxed for a time. He played golf and cards, gave speeches, and accepted awards. He worked hard as the

The Green Bay Packers carry coach Vince Lombardi off the field after defeating the Oakland Raiders in Super Bowl II in 1968. *AP/Wide World Photos. Reproduced by permission.*

general manager of the Packers. In the end, however, Lombardi missed coaching. He did not want to undermine Phil Bengston, his replacement as coach of the Packers, but he longed to return to the field. So, Lombardi negotiated an uneasy departure from Green Bay to take over the head coach position for the then-lowly Washington Redskins. Fans and sportswriters in the nation's capital were thrilled and hoped that Lombardi would turn their players into a winning team too.

Lombardi began to work his magic with the Redskins right away, leading them to their first winning season in a decade in 1969. But all was not right with the tough coach. Early in 1970 Lombardi was plagued by a recurring illness that was soon discovered to be intestinal cancer. As his illness became public, Lombardi received many letters of support, up to five hundred letters a day. He died on September 3, 1970.

Lombardi's death was greeted with great sorrow. Thousands of people attended memorial services for the beloved coach in New York and Washington, D.C. He was given the NFL's Distinguished Service Award in 1970 and named to the NFL Hall of Fame in 1971. The trophy awarded to NFL Super Bowl champions has been known as the Lombardi Trophy since 1971. His influence continued to be felt for years thereafter, as players and assistant coaches moved on to coaching careers of their own. Lombardi was one of the most influential coaches in the history of football and an important figure in the cultural life of America in the 1960s.

For More Information

Books

Dowling, Tom. *Coach: A Season with Lombardi.* New York: Norton, 1970.

Kramer, Jerry, with Dick Schaap. *Instant Replay.* New York: New American Library, 1970.

Lombardi, Vince, and W. C. Heinz. *Run to Daylight!* Englewood Cliffs, NJ: Prentice-Hall, 1963.

Maraniss, David. *When Pride Still Mattered: A Life of Vince Lombardi.* New York: Simon & Schuster, 1999.

O'Brien, Michael. *Vince: A Personal Biography of Vince Lombardi.* New York: Morrow, 1987.

Web Sites

Packers.com. http://www.packers.com (accessed August 2004).

Vince Lombardi. http://www.vincelombardi.com/home.html (accessed August 2004).

Maharishi Mahesh Yogi

Born October 18, 1911
Uttar Pradesh, India

Spiritual teacher in Hinduism

Maharishi Mahesh Yogi had a very successful career following his own spiritual path. His teachings are based on a mixture of Vedic science, the Hindu religion, and the ancient practice of meditation. Vedic science is drawn from ancient Hindu culture. During the 1960s, Maharishi's philosophies spoke of a higher consciousness and daily spiritualism. His teachings attracted many Americans who felt that these aspects were missing from traditional Western religions and lifestyles. Maharishi also supported nonviolence as a means to social unity, a crucial concept for many rebelling groups during the 1960s. As the United States was fighting the unpopular Vietnam War (1954–75), many people called for peace. Transcendental meditation promised a new world order without conflict, based on supposedly scientific theories. Maharishi's transcendental meditation movement gained approximately four million followers from the 1960s through the early 2000s, forming a worldwide organization.

"Through transcendental meditation, the mind unfolds its potential for unlimited awareness, transcendental awareness, unity consciousness—a lively field of all potential, where every possibility is naturally available to the conscious mind. The conscious mind becomes aware of its own … infinite potential."

—*Maharishi Mahesh Yogi.*

Maharishi Mahesh Yogi.
AP/Wide World Photos.
Reproduced by permission.

Studying the Vedic texts

He was born Mahad Prasad Varna on October 18, 1911, in northern India's state of Uttar Pradesh. Maharishi Mahesh Yogi grew up surrounded by the Hindu religion. He graduated from Allahabad University with a degree in physics and spent thirteen years being taught by Swami Brahmananda Saraswati Maharij, also known as Guru Dev. His teacher taught him the Vedic science of consciousness, based on the most ancient of Hindu texts. The Vedic hymns are religious songs that describe the various fire sacrifices made to more than thirty-three Hindu gods and the meditations that occur before these ceremonies. Maharishi and his mentor played an important role in restoring these ancient Vedic texts. After Guru Dev's death in 1953, Maharishi took a vow of silence for two years in the Himalayan mountains. During that time, he improved his meditation skills and understanding of transcendental philosophy.

In 1957 Maharishi started his mission in Madras, India. He aimed to create a "Heaven on Earth" by easing human suffering, according to the *Maharishi Vedic University* Web site. This mission was also called the Spiritual Regeneration Movement. Finding happiness, according to Maharishi, included learning about the seven states of consciousness, which could be found by meditating two times a day, twenty minutes at a time. Meditation allowed people to settle their minds and look inward. While doing so, stress and fatigue faded and were replaced by a feeling of well-being. Maharishi believed that the act of meditation could bring about great healing.

Maharishi explained the power of meditation to interviewer Kathy Juline in *Science of Mind*. He observed that: "Scientific experiments with people who practice transcendental meditation indicate that it tends to produce normalization in all areas of life. It reduces stress, improves health, enriches mental functioning, enhances personal relationships, and increases job productivity and job satisfaction." He believed that these benefits extend from the body outward to the surrounding community. Meditation could heal social and political rifts and even reduce crime rates, according to Maharishi. It was this community-wide idea that he sought to spread around the world.

Followers in the United States

Maharishi first traveled to the United States on January 29, 1959. He visited San Francisco, California, for two months and shared his philosophy with hundreds of Americans. The *San Francisco Chronicle* described his visit that winter in the first article on transcendental philosophy published in the United States. Maharishi brought his message to Los Angeles and New York before taking his message to the rest of the world. His second world tour took place in 1967, when he spoke at major American universities such as Yale and the University of California at Berkeley. By the late 1960s Maharishi had gained a large following, including such celebrities as The Beatles, philosopher Marshall McLuhan, actors Jane Fonda and Mia Farrow, and football star Joe Namath. Many of Maharishi's famous and wealthy followers visited him at his ashram, or center for yoga, in Rishikesh, India.

The Beatles and transcendental meditation

George Harrison (1943–2001), guitarist for The Beatles, was especially touched by the ideas of Maharishi Mahesh Yogi. Already interested in Eastern religions, Harrison had learned how to play a sitar, a stringed instrument native to India, from musician Ravi Shankar. The instrument was first heard in The Beatles' song *Norwegian Wood*. The sitar sound was soon copied by other popular bands of the 1960s. Harrison's interest in Indian music then opened his mind to the teachings of Maharishi, who played a large role in The Beatles's philosophy from 1967 to 1968. The Beatles even visited Maharishi's ashram in India, but the spiritual link was short lived.

After claims surfaced in 1968 that Maharishi had molested a female student, The Beatles distanced themselves from the guru. Only Harrison remained interested in his teachings. According to Beatle Paul McCartney, quoted by Paul Saltzman in *The Beatles in Rishikesh:* "We made a mistake. We thought there was more to him than there was. He's human. We thought at first that he wasn't." Maharishi's alleged sexual misconduct, and the hint that he expected monetary compensation from The Beatles, soured the relationship. Yet Harrison, ever a believer in transcendental meditation, produced a record by the Hari Krishna Temple group of London and donated a mansion in England for use by followers of the Hindu

The Beatles (from left, John Lennon, Paul McCartney, Ringo Starr, and George Harrison) join Maharishi Mahesh Yogi (center) for a weekend of meditation in 1967. *AP/Wide World Photos. Reproduced by permission.*

religion. He also gave many concerts to benefit the Natural Law party, which followed Vedic science, and to support survivors of the 1971 Bangladesh flood.

The Beatles, one of the most influential bands of the 1960s, gained inspiration from Maharishi Mahesh Yogi and transcendental philosophy. At the same time, Maharishi's theories of transcendental meditation gained increased publicity through his association with the band. However, Maharishi's popularity in mainstream culture waned shortly after The Beatles lost interest in his teachings. He moved back to India in 1970.

Scientific studies support transcendental meditation

The first scientific study of transcendental meditation took place in 1968 at the University of California at Los An-

Eastern Religion in American Thought during the 1960s

During the 1960s many youths turned from mainstream Protestant or Catholic religions to Eastern mystic religions such as Zen Buddhism and the practice of transcendental meditation. San Francisco and its Haight-Ashbury neighborhood was a hotbed of social and religious change and was also Maharishi Mahesh Yogi's starting point in the United States.

Most of Maharishi's followers in the United States could be characterized as hippies. They were mostly young adults who rebelled against U.S. involvement in Vietnam, authority figures, blindly accepting traditional values, and greed and materialism. They embraced new lifestyles that were very different than those of their parents. This included living in communes, places where groups of young people attempted to live together and be self-sufficient through farm-ing the land and sharing worldly goods. Whole communities, especially of hippie students, organized around the practice of the Hindu religion, such as the Hari Krishna groups. Vegetarianism, environmentalism, incense (especially patchouli), and meditation meetings also became popular, as did the use of mind-altering psychedelic drugs.

Some believed that the use of drugs helped them experience a form of religious enlightenment, especially when the drugs were used in combination with transcendental meditation techniques. But many felt that Eastern religions were very powerful without drugs. Some elements of Eastern religions persisted into the early 2000s in American culture. These included the popular practice of yoga, holistic medicine, and the idea of a living world, or "Gaia," that needs environmental stewardship.

geles. It was conducted by physiology graduate student Robert Keith Wallace. The findings of his doctoral study, titled "The Physiological Effects of Transcendental Meditation: A Proposed Fourth Major State of Consciousness," were published in *Science* magazine and *Scientific American* in 1970 and 1972, respectively. Wallace's study supported the theories that Maharishi Mahesh Yogi had been teaching for more than a decade. Wallace found that daily meditation created a positive physical effect on the human body.

Maharishi was looking for a more effective way to get his message to people during the 1970s. Thus, he created a new philosophy called the Science of Creative Intelligence (SCI). He trained teachers to spread his views of the world. SCI classes were provided at major universities around the United States beginning in 1971. Maharishi International

University opened its doors in 1974 in Fairfield, Iowa, its sole aim being to teach the Science of Creative Intelligence.

The 1970s saw several advances in Maharishi's plan for worldwide enlightenment. In 1976 he created the World Government for the Age of Enlightenment. He also introduced the concept of Yogic Flying. According to believers, Yogic Flying occurs when a person meditates and achieves a certain level of consciousness that allows the body to lift briefly off the ground. This intense form of meditation supposedly provided a positive influence on society as a whole. Called the Maharishi Effect, it was supposed to decrease the severity of conflict worldwide. In 1984 a group of seven thousand Yogic Flyers gathered in Fairfield, Iowa, to test the Maharishi Effect. Seven thousand was symbolic as it was the square root of 1 percent of the world's population at that time. The amount was supposedly the mathematical number needed to have an effect. Believers reported that their group activity significantly decreased the number of international conflicts. However, critics disagreed.

Maharishi's activities continued into the twenty-first century. On July 21, 2001, he incorporated his own city near Fairfield, Iowa, called Maharishi Vedic City. On February 24, 2002, he released his own currency, the Raam Mudra, for use in his city and universities. Institutions supported by Maharishi Mahesh Yogi included Maharishi International University, Maharishi University of Management, Maharishi Global Construction Company, Maharishi Global Development Fund, The Maharishi Channel, Maharishi Open University, and Maharishi Vedic University. On his Web site, he addresses issues such as global terrorism and war.

For More Information

Books

Campbell, Anthony. *Seven States of Consciousness: A Vision of Possibilities Suggested by the Teaching of Maharishi Mahesh Yogi*. London: Gollancz, 1973.

Maharishi Mahesh Yogi. *The Science of Being and Art of Living*. New York: Allied Publishers, 1963.

Nidich, Sanford I., and Randi Jeanne. *Growing Up Enlightened: How Maharishi School of the Age of Enlightenment Is Awakening the Creative Ge-*

nius of Students and Creating Heaven on Earth. Fairfield, IA: Maharishi International University Press, 1990.

Olson, Helena, and Ronald Olson. *His Holiness Maharishi Mahesh Yogi: A Living Saint for the New Millennium: Stories of His First Visit to the USA.* Herndon, VA: Samhita Publications, 2001.

Saltzman, Paul. *The Beatles in Rishikesh.* New York: Viking Press, 2000.

Periodicals

Wallace, R. K. "Physiological Effects of Transcendental Meditation." *Science* 167 (1970): pp. 1751–54.

Wallace, R. K., et al. "The Physiology of Meditation." *Scientific American* 226 (1972): pp. 84–90.

Web Sites

Creating Heaven on Earth: Reviewed Links Promoting the Knowledge of His Holiness Maharishi Mahesh Yogi. http://www.alltm.org/index.html (accessed August 2004).

Juline, Kathy. "Settled Mind, Silent Mind: An Interview with Maharishi Mahesh Yogi." *Science of Mind: The Transcendental Meditation Program.* http://www.tm.org/news/science_mind.html (accessed August 2004).

Maharishi Vedic University. http://www.maharishi.org/ (accessed August 2004).

Malcolm X

Born May 19, 1925
Omaha, Nebraska

Died February 21, 1965
New York, New York

Black Muslim leader

"We declare our right on this earth ... to be a human being, to be respected as a human being, to be given the rights of a human being, in this society, on this earth, in this day, which we intend to bring into existence, by any means necessary."

—Malcolm X.

Malcolm X. *AP/Wide World Photos. Reproduced by permission.*

Malcolm X was one of the most charismatic and controversial public figures of the 1960s. As a minister in the Nation of Islam (also known as the Black Muslims), an American religious sect, he preached that whites were "devils" and supported the separation of the races. After breaking with the organization, he traveled to Mecca, the holiest city of Islam, located in Saudi Arabia. His experiences during this journey changed his thinking. He became more optimistic about finding a common ground between the races. Along with other leaders of the decade, including President **John F. Kennedy** (1917–1963; served 1961–63; see entry), **Martin Luther King Jr.** (1929–1968; see entry), and Robert Kennedy (1925–1968), he was killed by assassin bullets.

Tragic childhood

Malcolm X was born Malcolm Little in Omaha, Nebraska, on May 19, 1925. His father Earl, a Baptist minister, was a civil rights activist. Earl was a supporter of Marcus Garvey (1887–1940), who was then leading a "back to Africa" movement among African Americans. When Malcolm was six years old, Earl Little's lifeless body was discovered stretched across trolley tracks in Lansing, Michigan, where the family had settled. The authorities determined that Little's death was accidental, but the family believed he died at the hands of the Black Legion, a group like the Ku Klux Klan that terrorized black citizens. Louise Little, Malcolm's mother, was devastated by the loss and eventually had to be committed to a mental institution.

Young Malcolm was an excellent student. However, he became uninterested in his studies when a teacher discouraged him from thinking that he could become a lawyer. The sole reason the educator gave was Malcolm's ethnicity. The teacher advised Malcolm to be "realistic" about his career goals, according to *The Autobiography of Malcolm X.* In those days, society limited the career opportunities available to blacks, Hispanics, women, and other minorities.

Disheartened, the youngster left school, drifted to Boston and New York, and became first a small-time criminal and then a drug dealer, pimp, and gambling syndicate operator. In 1946, when he was three months shy of his twenty-first birthday, he received a ten-year prison sentence for burglary.

Black separatism

While in jail, Malcolm began studying the philosophy of Elijah Muhammad (1897–1975), head of the Nation of Islam. An Islamic religious group, the Nation of Islam was created to reclaim the dignity and power of the black community. Elijah claimed that blacks were racially superior to whites and that black Americans were kept powerless by a white-ruled society. Elijah frequently referred to whites as inherently evil "blue-eyed devils" because of their oppression of blacks, according to *Malcolm X: By Any Means Necessary: A Biography.* In order for blacks to control their own destiny, Elijah argued that they needed to establish their own independent nation. Malcolm became a faithful follower of Elijah and changed his name to Malcolm X. The "X" symbolized the unknown surname of his ancestors' African tribe. Africans who were captured, brought to the United States, and sold as slaves were given the last names of their owners. Little had been the surname of his family's slave masters.

Malcolm was paroled from prison in 1952 and was named a Nation of Islam minister as well as the organization's national spokesperson. His intellect and enthusiasm quickly placed him in the upper rank of the organization. He established Nation of Islam mosques and recruited thousands of new members across the country. His clear and forceful public presence made him an effective Nation of Islam representative. His growing skill as a speechmaker and spokesperson led him to become the organization's lieutenant with the highest national profile in the late 1950s. Although he remained devoted to Elijah Muhammad, whom he respected and considered his teacher, Malcolm gained fame and popularity. Soon, his presence even began to overshadow that of the Nation of Islam leader.

Dr. Martin Luther King Jr. (left) poses with Malcolm X in 1964. Both black leaders were assassinated before the end of the decade.
© *Bettmann/Corbis.*
Reproduced by permission.

Different approaches to civil rights

During the 1960s the civil rights movement was expanding across the United States. Conflict arose with regard to the methods by which blacks might best fight for equality. Some black leaders, most famously Martin Luther King Jr., felt that blacks and whites could work together in a non-violent manner to achieve racial equality. Others, such as Malcolm X, were far more radical. Malcolm was convinced that racial hatred lay deep within white people and that even the most well-meaning whites were not to be trusted. For this reason, he believed blacks needed to separate themselves from the American white population. Furthermore, Malcolm advised blacks to take up arms and defend themselves when confronted by violent, racist whites.

The more moderate civil rights leaders urged blacks to vote in elections, organized voting rights drives in the American South, and attempted to integrate or mix the races in schools across the country. Malcolm, however, suggested that black

Americans resist participating in elections and remain separate from whites. These stances made Malcolm and the Nation of Islam a threat to the American establishment. Federal Bureau of Investigation (FBI) agents secretly joined and spied on the organization, and they specifically targeted Malcolm for observation. An undercover agent even became one of his bodyguards.

A rift in the ranks

Malcolm X had been a by-the-book follower of the Nation of Islam, which required that members must take a firm vow not to have sex before marriage. Also, once married, members were to remain faithful to their spouses. In 1963, a conflict occurred between Malcolm and the Nation of Islam when he learned that Elijah Muhammad had been sexually involved with six women and had fathered children with several of them.

Previously, Elijah had criticized and even cast out Muslims who had disobeyed the sect's rules. Malcolm was outraged by what he considered to be Elijah's double standards. Additionally, Elijah asked Malcolm to keep silent about the affairs. Malcolm declined because he felt betrayed by the man he considered to be both a teacher and a prophet. In fact, he was coming to view the Nation of Islam and its leader as corrupt.

After the assassination of John F. Kennedy in November 1963, Malcolm X, in a much-publicized declaration, claimed that the president's murder was an example of "chickens coming home to roost," as quoted in *Malcolm X: By Any Means Necessary: A Biography*. He was suggesting that white Americans promoted violence against minorities and, in so doing, created a culture that allowed for the killing of their president. The insensitive nature of Malcolm's observation caused a firestorm of controversy. Elijah Muhammad suspended him from the Nation of Islam, ordering him not speak publicly for three months. Malcolm, however, suspected that the action was not in response to his comments on the Kennedy assassination. He thought it might be linked to his refusal to conform within the organization's power structure.

A change in philosophy

In March 1964, Malcolm stopped being a member of the Nation of Islam and established the Muslim Mosque, Inc.,

"Spirit of True Brotherhood"

In 1964, Malcolm X visited Mecca, the birthplace of the prophet Muhammad in c. 570 in Saudi Arabia. At that time, he wrote a letter which described his transformation from racial separatist to integrationist.

The letter, reproduced in his autobiography, began: "Never have I witnessed such sincere hospitality and the overwhelming spirit of true brotherhood as practiced by people of all colors and races here in this Ancient Holy Land.... For the past week, I have been utterly speechless and spellbound by the graciousness I see displayed all around me by people of all colors."

He remarked that their skin tones ranged from "blue-eyed blonds to black skin Africans." He noted that: "...we were all participating in the same rituals, displaying a spirit of unity and brotherhood that my experiences in America had led me to believe never could exist between the white and non-white."

Malcolm X explained that his observations during his visit to Mecca caused him to re-evaluate his beliefs. "The true Islam has shown me that a blanket indictment of all white people is as wrong as when whites make blanket indictments against blacks," he noted, as quoted in *Contemporary Black Biography.* Malcolm X realized that this change of heart would shock those familiar with his ideas, but reminded readers of his autobiography that he has "always kept an open mind."

his own religious group, and the Organization of Afro-American Unity. He also traveled to Mecca, a city in Saudi Arabia and the birthplace of the prophet Muhammad (c. 570–632), the founder of Islam. The journey greatly expanded Malcolm's understanding of Islam and changed his life. He met and got to know people of all races, whom he observed praying side by side as Muslims. He came to see the possibility that he might share a friendship with whites and returned home with a very different point of view with regard to relationships between the races.

Malcolm now believed that good and evil could not be defined strictly by black and white. Some blacks were capable of being insincere, while some whites were well meaning and kindhearted. Malcolm radically altered his message, stressing a newfound belief that the races could and should coexist. He suggested that blacks could improve their economic and political status by working through established channels. He declared that he was eager to join and support black and progressive white organizations and to work together for equality. He also chose a new name: El-Hajj Malik El-Shabazz.

That summer, he embarked on a second international journey, during which he met with the leaders of several African nations. These encounters transformed him into a committed internationalist, someone who believed in the joining together of all exploited peoples across the globe.

The conflict between Malcolm X and the Nation of Islam now was both well known and deeply philosophical. Those FBI agents who had secretly joined the organization learned that a plot to murder Malcolm X was in the planning stages. Malcolm X suspected his life was in danger as well. On February 14, 1965, his Queens, New York, home, which he shared with his wife, Betty, and four children, was fire-bombed, but no one was injured.

A tragic end

Exactly one week later, as he began a speech at the Audubon Ballroom in Harlem, New York, three assassins—all members of the Nation of Islam—charged the stage and shot Malcolm. Fifteen bullets entered his body. He was rushed to Columbia Presbyterian Hospital but was dead on arrival.

In death, Malcolm X was remembered for his passion-ate efforts in the quest for African American equality. He also won respect for expanding his approach to race relations. His 1965 book, *The Autobiography of Malcolm X,* which was pub-lished after his death, charted the many stages of his life. In particular, his message of black pride and empowerment was meaningful to his readers. At the same time, his rage against racism arguably was a contributing factor in the race riots that exploded in America's black ghettos during the long, hot summers of the late 1960s. Malcolm's beliefs also greatly af-fected several emerging political action groups of the era, from the activist Student Non-Violent Coordinating Commit-tee (SNCC) to the militant Black Panther Party.

In 1992, almost three decades after the death of Mal-colm X, African American filmmaker Spike Lee made the much-praised film biography, *Malcolm X,* starring Denzel Washington.

For More Information

Books

Benson, Michael. *Malcolm X*. Minneapolis, MN: Lerner Publications, 2002.

Brown, Kevin. *Malcolm X: His Life and Legacy*. Brookfield, CT: Millbrook Press, 1995.

Malcolm X. *Malcolm X Talks to Young People: Speeches in the U.S., Britain, and Africa*. New York: Pathfinder, 1991.

Malcolm X, with the assistance of Alex Haley. *The Autobiography of Malcolm X*. New York: Grove Press, 1965.

Myers, Walter Dean. *Malcolm X: By Any Means Necessary: A Biography*. New York: Scholastic, 1993.

Stine, Megan. *The Story of Malcolm X, Civil Rights Leader*. New York: Dell, 1994.

Periodicals

Wilson, August. "The Legacy of Malcolm X." *Life* (December 1992): p. 84.

Web Sites

Malcolm. http://www.brothermalcolm.net (accessed August 2004).

"Malcolm X." *Contemporary Black Biography.* http://www.galenet.com/servlet/BioRC (accessed August 2004).

Malcolm X Museum. http://www.themalcolmxmuseum.org (accessed August 2004).

The Official Web Site of Malcolm X. http://www.cmgww.com/historic/malcolm/index.htm (accessed August 2004).

Ralph Nader

Born February 27, 1934
Winsted, Connecticut

Consumer advocate, lawyer, author

Best known for his role in shaping the consumer support movement of the 1960s, Ralph Nader was also the founder of the Public Interest Research Group (PIRG). He was the man who remade the Federal Trade Commission (FTC), the government agency charged with promoting business competition and protecting consumers from unfair or harmful business practices. Nader touched every aspect of American consumers' lives by demanding that companies provide safe products and by forcing the federal government to regulate corporations. He also created a new form of social activism in the 1960s that was very different from the sit-ins, rallies, and riots that marked the decade. Nader encouraged students to politely and persistently dig up the facts on corporate and governmental abuses and to use that information to create change through political means.

An early calling to civic duties

Ralph Nader was born in 1934 to Lebanese immigrants Rose and Nathra Nader. His parents viewed their American cit-

"It is clear Detroit today is designing automobiles for style, cost, performance and calculated obsolescence, but not—despite the 5,000,000 reported accidents, nearly 40,000 fatalities, 110,000 permanent disabilities and 1,500,000 injuries yearly—for safety."

—*Ralph Nader.*

Ralph Nader. *AP/Wide World Photos. Reproduced by permission.*

izenship as a blessing and a serious responsibility. They made sure that their children held the same view by talking about politics at the dinner table. Nader's civic duties were clear from the time he was a child, so it was natural for him to study related subjects in college. He majored in Far Eastern studies and economics at Princeton University in New Jersey, receiving a bachelor's degree with high grades in 1955.

At Princeton, Nader noticed several dead birds on the campus. He realized that the birds' deaths were caused by the use of dichlorodiphenyltrichloroethane, commonly called DDT (a poison that was later made illegal). Nader attempted to stop the use of the chemical, despite the school's claims that DDT was safe. Surely, according to the school paper, the well-respected scientists hired by Princeton University would know if DDT was a hazardous chemical.

Nader also had suspicions about the meat packing industry, ideas that he picked up from Upton Sinclair's famous 1906 novel, *The Jungle*. Nader later led an unpopular crusade against a local hot dog vendor. Sinclair described the unsafe and unsanitary conditions at meat packing plants, for workers and consumers alike. He detailed the ingredients used in secondary meats like sausages, bologna, and hot dogs. The book contributed to the passage of one of the nation's first consumer protection laws. Nader's enthusiasm for the safety of the consumer only increased following his first unsuccessful attempts to cause change. Although some saw Nader as an idealistic student at this stage in his life, his ideas gained wider approval in the following years, especially after the publication of his first book.

Ralph Nader battles General Motors

Nader entered Harvard University's school of law in Cambridge, Massachusetts, in 1955, graduating with honors in 1958. At Harvard, Nader studied the engineering design of automobiles. He wrote an article for the *Nation* titled "The Safe Car You Can't Buy," which was published in 1959. For several years after graduation from Harvard, Nader attempted to work as a conventional lawyer in Hartford, Connecticut. He also took extended leaves of absence to travel around the world, to Cuba, Russia, and Chile, writing freelance articles

The Rise of Consumerism

Before 1965 most consumer reforms only took place after some tragic accident occurred. Consumers themselves rarely instigated these reforms. Instead, when it suited them, congressmen and senators occasionally looked into their constituents' complaints. Journalists rarely investigated such stories. This made challenging wealthy and powerful corporations difficult.

But during the 1960s, news organizations began taking an interest in such stories. Investigative reporters became very popular with the public. It was at this time that Ralph Nader focused attention on how people's purchases affected their own and others' lives. He showed how corporations and government agencies helped or hurt consumers' abilities to make good buying decisions. Information became a very powerful tool in the hands of consumers. Armed with the facts about product safety and performance, consumers could make more informed decisions about the item being offered for sale. In 1971, the word *consumerism* first appeared in *Webster's Third International Dictionary.* Webster's defined the term as "the promotion of consumer's interests (as against false advertising or shoddy goods)."

about international politics for the *Harvard Law School Record.* In 1963 Nader decided to shift his career to focus on politics. He hitchhiked to Washington, D.C., to start his new job as consultant to the U.S. Department of Labor and adviser to Senator Abraham Ribicoff (1910–1998). Senator Ribicoff chaired a Senate subcommittee that focused on the role of the government regarding automobile safety issues, a topic that already held Nader's interest.

Nader continued to research auto safety and began writing a book about the faulty construction of the General Motor's car, the Corvair. Nader's first big attack on corporate America, the book *Unsafe at Any Speed: The Designed-in Dangers of the American Automobile* (1965) did not sell well initially. Still, General Motors tried to discredit him. They hired private detectives to follow Nader to see if they could uncover anything negative about him. The press learned of this harassment and reported the story. Nader sued for invasion of privacy. The resulting publicity caused sales of the book to skyrocket. In 1966 Senator Ribicoff held a press conference to share the findings of Nader's investigations into the automobile industry.

Between 1960 and 1966, approximately one out of five cars was recalled for safety issues. However, consumers were not warned of faults immediately. In fact, even major problems were fixed only when customers happened to bring in their cars for regular maintenance. In Ribicoff's words, quoted by Justin Martin in *Nader: Crusader, Spoiler, Icon,* "It shatters once and for all the myth that accidents are ... caused by bad driving. From now on we must be concerned, not just with the 'nut behind the wheel' but with the nut in the wheel itself, with all parts of the car and its design." Nader won a personal apology from then-president of General Motors James Roche and a $425,000 settlement.

Nader's importance in American culture was increased after the settlement of this famous case. Nader received the Neiman Fellows award in 1956, and the U.S. Junior Chamber of Commerce named him one of ten Outstanding Young Men of the Year in 1967. He had gained the attention of the nation and motivated concerned consumers to demand adequate services from corporations and governments.

Nader's Public Interest Research Groups advocate consumer safety

With his newfound popularity and a full bank account, Nader started the first Public Interest Research Group (PIRG) in Washington, D.C. He supported automobile safety laws such as the Traffic Safety Act (1966) that made seat belts mandatory in American cars. A large number of young people wanted to work with Nader, including college students. This growing number of young volunteers was called "Nader's Raiders" by *Washington Post* reporter William Greider. Nader and his Raiders supported the passage of bills that included the Freedom of Information Act (1966) and related "Sunshine Laws," a group of laws geared to make government policy-making a more open and visible process. He also pushed for the Clean Air Act (1970) and the Safe Drinking Water Act (1974). These acts helped improve citizen access to government information and reduced the amount of air and water pollution caused by American industries.

Nader released a highly critical report on the Federal Trade Commission (FTC) in 1969. The document caused

Congress to investigate and reevaluate the functioning of the agency. The FTC was supposed to protect American consumers. However, from its beginnings in 1914, it had limited itself merely to regulating corporate mergers and controlling deceptive interstate advertising. Nader and his Raiders found in the FTC's own records that only 1 in 125 consumer complaints had ever resulted in action from the commission. In the report, Nader's Raiders rated the performance of the FTC as "shockingly poor," as quoted on the FTC's Web site. Senator Abraham Ribicoff praised the group's work. As noted on *The Nader Page,* the senator stated: "Bureaucracy being what it is, I am fascinated by your ability to get in so deep, and get so much information. I am sure that you gentlemen are the envy of the large number of reporters here." Commissioner Paul Rand Dixon, who was head of the FTC, resigned. After some major restructuring, the organization waged several successful cases against Coca-Cola and McDonald's for false advertising.

Ralph Nader discusses car safety as he stands on an overpass above I-495 near Washington, D.C., in 1967. *AP/Wide World Photos. Reproduced by permission.*

To increase corporate and government accountability to citizens, Nader opened the Center for Study of Responsive Law in 1969 and began Public Citizen in 1971. The groups monitored corporate and/or legal activities to better protect citizens. By 2004, Public Citizen was comprised of seven public action groups, including Auto Safety, Congress Watch, Health Research Group, Litigation Group, Global Trade Watch, Critical Mass Energy Project, and Buyers Up (a fuel purchasing cooperative). The Center for Study of Responsive Law continued its work to inform political and corporate institutions of the needs of citizens and consumers. Nader and his volunteers also helped push for the formation of the National Highway Traffic Safety Administration (1970), the Environmental Protection Agency (1970), the Occupational Safety and Health Administration (1971), and the Consumer Protection Agency (1978). These government agencies were designed to protect consumers from wrongdoing on the part of big business.

A bid for the presidency with the Green Party

Nader broadened his campaigns for the protection of consumers to include the public good as well. He formed public interest groups, including the Consumer Project on Technology (1995), Citizen Works (2001), and Democracy Rising (2001). During the 1990s Nader supported many of the ideals of the Green Party of the United States, including the conservation of natural resources through recycling and limits on usage and pollution. He also opposed the General Agreement on Tariffs and Trade (GATT), which regulated international commerce. In 2000 Nader ran for president of the United States on the Green Party ticket, receiving almost 3 percent of the vote. Some Democrats blamed him for taking away the slim margin of votes that Vice President and Democratic presidential candidate Al Gore (1948–) would have needed to defeat Republican winner George W. Bush (1946–). Nader discounted the attacks, saying that "Gore beat Gore." He stated that those who voted for Nader would not have voted at all if he had not run for president, according to *USA Today.* On February 22, 2004, Nader announced his intention to run for president again, this time as an independent candidate. He stated in an interview with *USA Today:* "This campaign will help beat Bush because we can expose the Bush regime's vulnerabilities and failures in additional, effective ways that the Democrats are too cautious or too indentured to corporations to do by themselves."

For More Information

Books

Bowen, Nancy. *Ralph Nader: A Man with a Mission.* Brookfield, CT: Twenty-First Century Books, 2002.

Martin, Justin. *Nader: Crusader, Spoiler, Icon.* Cambridge, MA: Perseus Publishing, 2002.

Nader, Ralph. *Crashing the Party: How to Run for President and Still Tell the Truth.* New York: St. Martin's Press, 2002.

Nader, Ralph. *Unsafe at Any Speed: The Designed-in Dangers of the American Automobile.* New York: Grossman, 1965.

Nader, Ralph, and Barbara Ehrenreich. *The Ralph Nader Reader.* New York: Seven Stories Press, 2000.

Periodicals

Nader, Ralph. "The Safe Car You Can't Buy." *Nation* (April 1959).

Squitieri, Tom. "Ralph Nader Announces Run for Presidency." *USA Today* (February 22, 2004).

Web Sites

Center for Study of Responsive Law. http://www.csrl.org/ (accessed August 2004).

Citizen Works. http://www.citizenworks.org/ (accessed August 2004).

Crashing the Party: Taking on the Corporate Government in an Age of Surrender. http://www.crashingtheparty.org/ (accessed August 2004).

Federal Trade Commission. http://www.ftc.gov (accessed August 2004).

The Nader Page. http://www.nader.org (accessed August 2004).

Public Citizen. http://www.citizen.org/ (accessed August 2004).

Richard Oakes

Born 1942
St. Regis Mohawk Reservation, New York

Died September 20, 1972
Sonoma County, California

Ironworker, political activist

"We invite the United States to acknowledge the justice of our claim. The choice now lies with … the American government—to use violence upon us as before to remove us from our Great Spirit's land, or to institute a real change in its dealing with the American Indian."

—*Richard Oakes.*

Richard Oakes.
© *Bettmann/Corbis.*
Reproduced by permission.

Richard Oakes was one of the earliest leaders of the Native American rights movement that began to grow during the 1960s. In an era when many groups of people were fighting to end discrimination and claim their civil rights, the First People of the United States often felt like a forgotten minority. Oakes and those who worked with him did much to unite Indian people and to publicize their cause. Their work helped to restore Native American pride. Their efforts forced the U.S. government to take some responsibility for the destruction of Native American culture.

Born to a proud people

Oakes was born into the Mohawk tribe of the northeastern United States and southeastern Canada some time in 1942. The Mohawk are a proud people with a long history. They were one of the five nations of the Iroquois Confederacy, an alliance of native peoples created at least a hundred years before Europeans settled North America. The St. Regis Reservation, sometimes called the Akwesasne Reservation by the Indians, stretches across the Canadian-U.S. border. However, it represents only a small part of the Mohawks' ancestral land. The Mohawks have a strong tribal identity that pays little attention to the borders drawn by European immigrants.

During the late nineteenth century, the U.S. government overwhelmed various Native American peoples and gained control of most Indian territory. Native people who managed to survive the bitter wars and disease brought by white settlers lost much of their ancestral land. They were forced to live in much smaller areas that were "reserved" for them. These reservations were often filled with poverty and despair. Given little support by the government, the Native Americans living on reservations had few employment or educational opportunities. Schools were run by white educators who did little to support native culture, language, or pride. Richard Oakes found little to keep him in the reservation school, and he left when he was in eleventh grade. He continued to study throughout his life, however, and he attended community college and university classes whenever he could.

Balancing on the high steel

After dropping out of school, Oakes went to work in the construction industry. He followed a long tradition of Mohawk men by getting a job as an ironworker walking the high steel beams of skyscrapers. Beginning in the late 1800s, Mohawks had proven their skill and balance in high steel construction work. Many Mohawk men traveled throughout the country seeking construction work after that, sending money back to families on the reservation.

Oakes traveled throughout the northeastern United States, working on skyscraper construction and continuing his education. He attended Adirondack Community College and Syracuse University in northern New York State. He also met native people from many other tribes who were working to improve the status of Indians in the United States. It was during his conversations with these Indian activists that he began to develop a political awareness about the need for change in the government's treatment of Native Americans.

West Coast activism and Native American pride

During the mid-1960s, his work on construction crews finally took Oakes across the country to California. There, he continued to visit other Native American groups and to learn about their struggles. He made his home in San Francisco and enrolled in San Francisco State University. In 1969, he married Annie Marufo, a member of the Pomo nation. Marufo already had five children, and Oakes adopted them as his own.

In the 1960s, San Francisco was buzzing with activism. College campuses were centers of radical political energy. Oakes was a large, handsome man who drew people to him with his charm, humor, and sincerity. Soon he was the center of a passionate group of young Native American radicals, many of whom were university students. Since they came from many different tribes and from all over the country, they named their group Indians of All Tribes (IAT).

The members of IAT felt that the needs and struggles of native peoples had been forgotten and pushed aside for too long. During the fall of 1969 they began to seek a way to draw public attention to the injustices that Indians suffered, both in the past and in the present. They wanted to make a public point with drama and humor. The idea that finally came to them had been sitting in plain sight all along, right in the bay across from the city: Alcatraz Island.

Claiming Alcatraz

Alcatraz Island is little more than a giant rock in the middle of San Francisco Bay. It was once a frontier fortress where leaders from the Hopi and Modoc nations had been imprisoned during the 1800s. From 1934 to 1963, the island had been home to a high-security federal prison. The federal government had not used the land and buildings since the prison was shut down.

An 1868 treaty between the U.S. government and the Lakota Sioux stated that Indians could reclaim federal land and buildings that were no longer being used by the federal government. Thus, the members of IAT plotted to take over

and occupy Alcatraz Island. A group of Native Americans had the idea of claiming Alcatraz five years earlier, but the occupation had only lasted a few hours. Oakes and his group intended to attempt something much larger.

On November 21, 1969, a group of nearly eighty Indians took a chartered boat to Alcatraz Island. When the boat's captain appeared reluctant to land on the island, Oakes dramatically took leadership by diving into the bay and swim-

The End of the Occupation

The Native American occupation of Alcatraz lasted nineteen months. During that time, more than 15,000 people visited the island, mostly Native Americans from across the United States. Occupiers set up a decision-making council, a nursery, and a radio station (Radio Free Alcatraz). Native Americans and other activists on the outside raised money and sent supplies to the occupiers. Many liberal celebrities supported the occupation as well, including actors Marlon Brando, Anthony Quinn, and Jane Fonda. The rock band Creedence Clearwater Revival contributed $15,000 to the occupation of Alcatraz.

The U.S. government did not agree to the demands. However, President **Richard Nixon** (1913–1994; served 1969–74) was reluctant to force the group off the island and did little to end the demonstration. However, in May 1970, the government did shut down electricity on the island and stopped water deliveries, which caused difficulties for those who continued the occupation. Some occupiers were arrested for theft of building materials, and others were blamed for fires that destroyed historic sites. Discouraged by negative press coverage and worsening conditions,

many left the occupation. On June 11, 1971, federal authorities removed the few who remained: six men, four women, and five children.

Although the Indian university and cultural center were never built on Alcatraz Island, the occupation and the public attention it drew to native issues had a far-reaching impact. The federal government ended its policy of breaking up tribes and granted official nation status to Indian tribes. During the occupation, 49,000 acres of land were returned to the Taos Indians. More Native Americans were hired to work at the federal Bureau of Indian Affairs. Pro-Indian legislation was passed, including the Indian Self-Determination and Education Act, the Indian Financing Act, and the Indian Health Act.

The International Indian Treaty Council honors the occupation every year when they return to Alcatraz Island for an "un-Thanksgiving" ritual. The event is a remembrance of those who sacrificed their comfort and risked their safety to demonstrate for Native American rights. It is also a protest against all the injustices still suffered by native peoples in the twenty-first century.

ming ashore. The rest of the party followed, and the occupation of Alcatraz began.

The group painted "You Are on Indian Land" on the dock. Then, the occupiers called a press conference. Well-spoken and handsome, Oakes became the spokesperson for the group. Using characteristic humor, he told reporters that the

Indians would buy the island for twenty-four dollars' worth of beads and red cloth. That was the price that European settlers had paid for Manhattan Island in New York in 1626. They wanted to create an Indian university, cultural center, and museum on the island. Oakes also criticized the government's mistreatment of native peoples, including the policy of dividing tribes, breaking treaty agreements, and giving Indian land to oil, lumber, and development corporations. Oakes triumphant yell, "We hold the Rock!," became the rallying cry of the occupiers, according to the *Alcatraz Island* Web site.

Oakes remained on Alcatraz for several months. Although he was respected and admired by many, some IAT members began to question his leadership. Quarrels arose among the occupiers. On January 5, 1970, his twelve-year-old stepdaughter Yvonne died when she fell off a staircase to the ground three stories below. Oakes and Marufo left the island for Yvonne's funeral and never returned.

Tribute to a fallen warrior

Oakes did not stop working for Indian rights, however. In response to the work of native activists, San Francisco State University created an American Indian Studies Department and made Oakes its first chairperson. Along with helping to design a program of courses for the department, Oakes continued to work directly to help in native struggles. He was committed to protecting the status of small tribes. Always dramatic by nature, he made a very public citizen's arrest of the president of Pacific Gas and Electric in June 1970 for crimes against Native Americans. Within a day, he was attacked and beaten. In 1971, he worked with the Pit River Indians of Northern California as they attempted to recover tribal land.

Oakes's activist work put him in danger more than once. Many people believe that his activism cost him his life. He was killed in the early fall of 1972 in northern California by Michael Morgan, a white man. Oakes and Morgan had argued about Indian rights a day earlier. Oakes had a reputation as being gentle and nonviolent. He was unarmed when he was shot by Morgan. Nevertheless, the man who shot him was cleared of manslaughter charges.

Oakes was one of the first in a long list of modern Native American activists who were killed. The loss of such a young movement leader angered many Indians who became more determined than ever to fight for justice and civil rights. With the political work he did during the 1960s, Oakes was one of the first Native American activists to insist publicly that Indian tribes deserve the respect and rights given to other nations. The occupation of Alcatraz that he helped plan and lead was a symbolic event that launched a movement.

Although Oakes died when he was only thirty years old, he is remembered with love and respect by many who appreciated the work he did. There are many memorials to his life. One of the earliest was a song, titled "Alcatraz (Pelican Island)," written by folksinger Malvina Reynolds in support of the occupation. In the mid-1970s, composer Charles Fox and choreographer Michael Smuin created the ballet "Song for a Dead Warrior" in honor of Oakes. In December 1988, San Francisco State University opened the Richard Oakes Multicultural Center, which features a prominent sign acknowledging that it is built on Indian land.

For More Information

Books
Smith, Paul Chaat, and Robert Allen Warrior. *Like a Hurricane: The Indian Movement from Alcatraz to Wounded Knee.* New York: The New Press, 1996.

Viola, Herman J. *After Columbus: The Smithsonian Chronicle of the American Indians.* Washington, DC: Smithsonian Books, 1990.

Periodicals
"The Angry American Indian: Starting Down the Protest Trail." *Time* (February 9, 1970): pp. 14–21.

Web Sites
"Alcatraz Is Not an Island." *Public Broadcasting System.* http://www.pbs.org/itvs/alcatrazisnotanisland/occupation.html (accessed August 2004).

Johnson, Troy. "The Alcatraz Indian Occupation." *Alcatraz Island: We Hold the Rock.* http://www.nps.gov/alcatraz/indian.html (accessed August 2004).

Madalyn Murray O'Hair

Born April 13, 1919
Pittsburgh, Pennsylvania

Died September, 1995
Near Austin, Texas

Atheist activist

Madalyn Murray O'Hair was widely known as the woman who ended prayer in American public schools in the early 1960s. She proudly accepted the label "the most hated woman in America," given to her by *Life* magazine in 1964. O'Hair became known across the nation in 1961, when she and her son William challenged the Baltimore Public Schools' practice of saying a morning prayer. Excited by the publicity she received, O'Hair became a spokesperson for the atheist cause at a time when religious belief was included in most American institutions. Atheism is the belief that there is no God. Over the next thirty-four years, she published atheist periodicals, hosted atheist radio shows, toured in a religious debate show, and created a string of atheist organizations. Angry, profane, vengeful, and persuasive, she stirred controversy and attracted attention like few others. Then she suddenly disappeared under mysterious circumstances in 1995. Investigators solved the mystery of her disappearance in 2001 when they discovered that she, her son Jon Garth, and her granddaughter had been killed in a bizarre triple murder.

"We are Atheists. As such, we are foes of any and all religions. We want the Bible out of school because we do not accept it as being either holy or an accurate historical document."

—Madalyn Murray O'Hair.

Madalyn Murray O'Hair.
AP/Wide World Photos.
Reproduced by permission.

Difficult youth

A few of the details from O'Hair's early life are known to be true: Madalyn Evalyn Mays was born on April 13, 1919, in a suburb of Pittsburgh, Pennsylvania. Her parents were John Irwin, a carpenter, and Lena Christina Scholle Mays, a homemaker. Most of the other details of her early years have been contested, with O'Hair's own recollections at odds with those of her family and friends. O'Hair later recalled a very happy, even wealthy childhood, complete with chauffeurs and fur coats. Her son William Murray disagreed with such claims, stating that her father, a carpenter, was only somewhat prosperous before he went broke in the stock market collapse of 1929.

The family suffered financial troubles during the Great Depression (1929–41), an economic crisis in which many people lost money in stocks and were unemployed. They had to leave Pittsburgh to find work. They lived briefly in Detroit and Chicago before settling near Akron, Ohio. Some historians note that John Mays was probably involved in bootlegging for a time. Bootleggers sold illegally produced alcohol. Eventually he landed a more stable job at a glass factory in Ohio.

O'Hair's family attended various churches during the early 1930s. It was at about the age of twelve or thirteen that O'Hair began to pay attention to the Bible. In *The Atheist: Madalyn Murray O'Hair,* author Bryan F. Le Beau quoted her reaction to the religious text: "[I was] completely appalled, totally turned off ... [by] the hatred, the brutality, ... the cruelty, the killing, the ugliness." She dated her complete denial in a supernatural power or God from this time. However, others who knew her claim that her atheism began later.

O'Hair graduated from high school in Rossford, Ohio. A bright student, she briefly attended the University of Toledo before returning to Pittsburgh with her family. She enrolled in the University of Pittsburgh but fell in love with and married John Henry Roths on October 9, 1941. Within two months, however, the United States entered World War II (1939–45). The conflict drew John into the Marines and Madalyn into the Women's Army Corps. O'Hair quickly gained high security clearances and assisted Allied staff in North Africa, France, and Italy. In Italy she met Captain

William J. Murray Jr. The two had a brief affair and O'Hair became pregnant.

O'Hair returned to her family to give birth to her illegitimate child and to plan how to tell her husband the news of her betrayal. They divorced soon after. Amid this stress, she apparently had another of her dramatic realizations of her resistance to the idea of God. According to her son's autobiography, quoted by Ted Dracos in *Ungodly: The Passions, Torments, and Murder of Atheist Madalyn Murray O'Hair,* she decided to stand outside in a terrific thunderstorm. There, she decided to "challenge God to strike [her] and this child dead with one of those lightning bolts." She survived this challenge, which caused her to continue her disbelief. On May 25, 1946, she gave birth to a son and named him William Murray.

Divorced, with a young son from a man she had never married, O'Hair was hardly a typical figure in post-war America. Society stressed the importance of marriage and family. O'Hair seemed to recognize that she would never fit in and developed a harsh attitude toward anyone who challenged her. She returned to school in 1948 attending Ashland College in Ohio. When her family moved to Texas to get construction work for her father, she attended South Texas College of Law. Although she finished her law degree, she was unable to pass the bar exam required to become a lawyer. So she found herself working a variety of jobs in Texas and later in Baltimore, Maryland. She never stayed at a job for long. Co-workers recalled her as a combative, disruptive person. In 1954 she once again became pregnant by a man who was not her husband and gave birth to a boy she named Jon Garth Murray. By this time she was also using Murray as her own last name.

The battle over prayer in schools

In 1959, O'Hair transferred her son William from a private school to the public Woodbourne Junior High School in West Baltimore. On the day that she arrived to enroll William in school, she saw students bowing their heads and reciting the Lord's Prayer, a prayer well known among Christians. O'Hair marched into the counselor's office and demanded to know why students were praying. She proclaimed that the practice was unconstitutional. The school defended

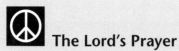 **The Lord's Prayer**

When Madalyn Murray O'Hair sought to drive prayer out of the public schools of Baltimore, Maryland, she targeted one of the most recited prayers in the Christian religion, the Lord's Prayer. Christians believe that the Lord's Prayer was originally given by Jesus to show his apostles how to pray. The prayer is recorded in the biblical book of Matthew 6:9–13, and a similar prayer is also recorded in Luke 11:2–4.

A version of the Lord's Prayer has been used by most Christian groups since the time of Christ. They believe that they can communicate directly with God through prayer. The Lord's Prayer is often the first prayer taught to children and the one prayer that every member of a Christian congregation can be expected to recite in unison. Although there are many minor variations on the Lord's Prayer, and the most-used Catholic version has an additional verse, the Lord's Prayer is as follows:

Our Father, who art in Heaven,

Hallowed be Thy Name.

Thy Kingdom come,

Thy Will be done,

On Earth, as it is in Heaven.

Give us this day our daily bread,

And forgive us our trespasses,

As we forgive those who trespass against us.

And lead us not into temptation,

But deliver us from evil.

For thine is the kingdom

And the power

And the glory

Forever and ever.

Amen.

the practice, saying that students had prayed in schools in Baltimore from its earliest days.

Prayer had been practiced in Baltimore public schools for years. In fact, in 1960 Christian prayers were being said in many public schools across America. Although this practice might seem strange to students in the early twenty-first century, it reflected the cultural and political standards of the late 1950s and early 1960s. The religious roots of American history were an important element of the war of ideas that the United States was waging with the Soviet Union, a war known as the Cold War (1945–91). For some, the Cold War was a battle between the forces of religion: the Christianity of the United States versus the atheism of the communist Soviet Union. The enthusiasm for America's religious heritage was confirmed in several ways in the 1950s. Congress added the phrase "under God" to the Pledge of Allegiance in 1954. President Dwight D. Eisenhower (1890-1969; served 1953–61) signed a law adding the phrase "In God We Trust" to the nation's currency in 1955. That phrase also became the national motto in 1956. With such widespread approval of references to God in civic life, most nonbelievers simply went along with the majority—but not Madalyn Murray O'Hair.

Beginning in the 1960 school year, O'Hair and her son William increased their conflict with the school district. The school insisted that William attend the homeroom class where prayers were said. O'Hair withdrew her son until that demand was removed. But the conflict soon spilled beyond the school system as O'Hair began to write angry letters that drew attention to her cause. In a letter to the Baltimore *Sun* newspaper, quoted in *Ungodly*, she claimed to be asking questions on behalf of the sixty-eight million Americans she said did not go to church. "When we go to a public meeting why are we subjected to prayer, in the [power] of which we do not believe? When we handle money, why, since 1955, are we confronted with money minted with In God We Trust on it? Why should our mail be stamped 'Pray for Peace'?... Is your belief so thin that you must force it upon others?" Feature articles followed, and the clash soon became national news and was broadcast on all the major television networks. O'Hair courted the press, fixing them coffee and doughnuts, and doing everything she could to promote the story.

While the press buzzed with stories of the colorful woman who challenged prayer in schools, the legal case proceeded through the court system. The school district's attorneys, unable to see the legitimacy of O'Hair's charges, scarcely mounted a defense. However, the pro-prayer case was supported by the Maryland attorney general, who claimed that the children of Maryland "had the right and the duty to bow their heads in humility before the Supreme Being," according to *The Atheist*. Prayer was also supported by the Superior Court of Baltimore and finally by the Maryland Court of Appeals. On May 15, 1962, O'Hair and Leonard Kerpelman, the only attorney she could find who would take on her controversial case for free, appealed to the U.S. Supreme Court. The high court agreed to hear the case, known in court records as *Murray v.*

Madalyn Murray O'Hair stands in front of the U.S. Supreme Court building in 1963 with sons William (left) and Jon Garth (right).
AP/Wide World Photos. Reproduced by permission.

Curlett (the school board president), in conjunction with a similar case from Pennsylvania, *Abington Township v. Schempp.*

The U.S. Supreme Court rules

The members of the U.S. Supreme Court had long recognized that the First Amendment to the Constitution was open to widely varying interpretations. The clause relating to school prayer declared that "Congress shall make no law respecting an establishment of religion, or prohibiting the free exercise thereof." This clause, called the Establishment Clause, was widely believed to indicate that there would be a separation of church and state. Previous cases had confirmed this separation of church and state. For example, religious instruction was not allowed in public schools and religious tests could not be given to candidates for public office. Yet prior to the 1962 cases, there had been no definitive ruling on prayer in school. That would soon end.

Deliberations on the *Murray* case began on February 26, 1963. However, the court did not issue its ruling until June 17, 1963. The court ruled in favor of Murray by a vote of eight to one. Thus, prayer was officially removed from American public schools. Reaction to the ruling was swift and dramatic. Several groups formed to try to create constitutional amendments that would allow prayer in school, though these never got far. Preachers and politicians across the nation spoke out against the ruling. The nation's most prominent religious figure, the evangelist Billy Graham (1918–), proclaimed "I am shocked at the … decision…. In my opinion, it is the Supreme Court that is wrong…. At a time when moral decadence is evident on every hand, when race tension is mounting, when the threat of Communism is growing, when terrifying new weapons of destruction are being created, we need more religion, not less," as quoted by Le Beau.

"The most hated woman in America"

The Supreme Court ruling was a major victory for O'Hair, who had come to believe she was the champion of American atheists. She claimed nearly complete responsibility for this major change in policy, despite the fact that much of the legal work had been done by others. In fact, O'Hair had used her battle over school prayer as a platform for what amounted to her lifelong career as an advocate for atheist causes. During the course of the battle, she took control of a small newsletter titled *The American Atheist* to spread her views and to solicit financial support. O'Hair was featured in major profiles in *Time, Newsweek,* the *Saturday Evening Post,* and other magazines. A June 19, 1964 *Life* profile titled "The Most Hated Woman in America" labeled O'Hair "America's most outspoken and militant atheist." O'Hair did not dislike these labels; in fact she enjoyed them.

In the years following the ruling, O'Hair set about building an empire around her crusade to achieve the complete separation of church and state in American life. She launched legal cases to remove religious mottoes from the currency and to remove any religious references from vows taken to attain public office. Over the years she created a string of atheist organizations, including American Atheists, the Society of Separationists, and a variety of smaller groups. She also formed a radio broadcasting network called the American Atheists Radio Series, and she published numerous books spelling out her philosophies about atheism.

O'Hair proved clever at keeping herself in the public eye. She was a guest on the premier of the *Phil Donahue Show*, a national television talk show. Donahue's show was the first of what would become the exploitative talk shows of the 1990s, such as the *Jerry Springer Show*. While the television cameras were on, O'Hair adopted the role of a combative but lovable matron. As soon as the cameras stopped rolling, she spewed curses and challenges to the audience, churning them up in anger against her. She challenged prominent evangelists such as Billy Graham to debates, and she organized boycotts when the Pope, the Catholics' top cleric, made appearances in the United States in the late 1970s. In the mid-1970s she joined with the Reverend Bob Harrington of New Orleans in a traveling debate show. The shows enjoyed some popularity—and earned O'Hair about $5,000 per show—until they were exposed by newspapers as a thinly disguised scam to raise money.

The decline of the atheist empire

As O'Hair rose to prominence and built her national network of atheist organizations, her personal life grew increasingly bizarre. Shortly after the Supreme Court ruling, O'Hair and her son were charged with assaulting police officers who had visited their home on a domestic violence call. The pair fled the state, resettling first in Hawaii and then later in Mexico. In Mexico, O'Hair fought to take control of an experimental school called Blake College, where the teachers and students found her so controlling and offensive that they eventually pushed her out. Also, in Mexico, O'Hair met Richard O'Hair, a hard-drinking American who was either a retired artist or a former CIA agent discharged from service and serving as an FBI informant. The pair married in October 1965. When the assault charges against Madalyn were finally dismissed late in 1965, the O'Hairs settled near Austin, Texas.

Austin became the home base for O'Hair's atheist empire. As early as the late 1960s, according to biographers, O'Hair, her son Jon Garth Murray, and her granddaughter Robin Murray began using the various organizations for their personal enrichment. Sympathetic atheists channeled money into the organizations. Much of that money was used to build a lavish national headquarters building, which included a library of atheist literature valued in the millions. But more and more of the money was directed into the pockets of O'Hair and Jon Garth Murray. In 1980, son William Murray, who as a teen had sided with his mother during the battle to end school prayer in Baltimore, converted to Christianity. He spoke out against the work of his mother. O'Hair voiced her displeasure at her son. She told the national media that "One could call this a postnatal abortion on the part of a mother, I guess; I repudiate him entirely and completely for now and all times.... He is beyond human forgiveness," according to Dracos.

By the late 1980s, O'Hair and her family were said to be worth millions, but they no longer had much influence on public life. American cultural life had grown to include more diversity since the early 1960s. People with minority religious viewpoints were not discriminated against in public life. The movements to gain civil rights for African Americans, women, and gays had helped make America a more tolerant place. O'Hair had largely disappeared from public life in the early 1990s. However, she again gained media attention when she, Jon Garth Murray, and Robin Murray all vanished in September 1995. There was much speculation that she had again fled the country. It was rumored that she left to escape the Internal Revenue Service, which was prosecuting her for tax evasion. However, a reporter looked into the story and helped police uncover what had happened. A former business associate of O'Hair's, mindful of her hidden money, kidnapped and killed all three of the atheists. Before murdering the trio, the killer forced them to channel $600,000 of their money to him and his accomplices. After a lengthy investigation, the killer led detectives to the bodies, hacked to pieces and buried in a shallow grave in the Texas hills. Police later determined that the murders must have occurred sometime between September 25 and 29, 1995.

For More Information

Books

Dracos, Ted. *Ungodly: The Passions, Torments, and Murder of Atheist Madalyn Murray O'Hair*. New York: Free Press, 2003.

Le Beau, Bryan F. *The Atheist: Madalyn Murray O'Hair*. New York: New York University Press, 2003.

Murray, William. *My Life Without God*. New York: Thomas Nelson, 1983.

O'Hair, Madalyn Murray. *An Atheist Epic: The Complete Unexpurgated Story of How Bible and Prayers Were Removed from the Public Schools of the United States*. Austin, TX: American Atheist Press, 1970.

Wright, Lawrence. *Saints and Sinners: Walker Railey, Jimmy Swaggart, Madalyn Murray O'Hair, Anton LaVey, Will Campbell, Matthew Fox*. New York: Vintage Books, 1995.

Web Sites

Goeringer, Conrad F. "The Murray O'Hair Family." *American Atheists*. http://www.atheists.org/visitors.center/OHairFamily (accessed August 2004).

The Smothers Brothers

Tom Smothers
Born February 2, 1937
New York, New York

Dick Smothers
Born November 20, 1939
New York, New York

American actors, comedians, and singers

Tom and Dick Smothers—known as The Smothers Brothers—crafted themselves into a musical comedy team that represented the struggles of the nation in the 1960s. The brothers' variety show reached nearly every household in the United States. Ninety percent of viewers tuned into one of the three major networks that existed in the country at the time. To this large audience, the brothers offered political satire that recognized society's uncertainty about the war in Vietnam (1954–75) and shifting opinions about drugs and sex. Despite the high ratings of *The Smothers Brothers Comedy Hour* (1967–70), host network CBS became increasingly uncomfortable with the show's content. The struggle between the Smothers Brothers and CBS helped define the role entertainment, especially television, would play in social change.

The Smothers brothers were born just before the outbreak of World War II (1939–45). Thomas B. Smothers III was born February 2, 1937, and his brother, Richard, was born November 20, 1939, both in New York City. The brothers were the sons of army officer Thomas B. and homemaker

"Mom always liked you best."

—*Tom Smothers's most famous line, delivered to his brother as part of their comedy act.*

Tom and Dick Smothers.
AP/Wide World Photos.
Reproduced by permission.

Ruth Smothers. Their father died in a Japanese prisoner of war camp in 1945, and their mother raised them.

While attending San Jose State College in the late 1950s and early 1960s, the brothers developed a singing act. At the time, folksingers were very popular. Tom and Dick teamed with Bobby Blackmore to create a group called The Smothers Brothers & God. (Blackmore played God.) The act made them so popular that neither Tom nor Dick felt it necessary to finish college. Tom abandoned his pursuit of an advertising degree in his senior year. Dick dropped out of his education major classes in his junior year. The trio started as a musical group, but the banter that Tom and Dick used to introduce songs slowly developed into a major portion of their show, making it part music and part comedy. Their first professional performance was an extended show at the Purple Onion in San Francisco in 1959. Although the group did well, after six months Blackmore left the group to move with his new bride to Australia.

Jokes prevail over music

The brothers were left on their own and wondered if they could succeed without Blackmore, their lead singer. The two spent more than a year performing in Colorado and California, perfecting their new act. They kept their music clean and folksy while they developed their comedy. Soon they learned what made audiences laugh. The two played four shows each night, and Tom made up new jokes for each show. When he started to run out of ideas, Dick suggested that he repeat some of them. At first Tom resisted, thinking that people would catch on. But Tom soon recognized that he could sing songs over and over without upsetting his audience. When he tried some of his jokes again and got another laugh, he was amazed. Their often-repeated phrase soon became "Mom always liked you best." In 1960 they signed a recording contract with Mercury Records; by 1965 they had recorded eight albums. Despite their steady production, Tom rarely wrote down his jokes.

In January 1961, the brothers were invited to perform on NBC's *The Tonight Show* with host Jack Paar. Paar jokingly complimented the two after their act, saying "I don't know

what you guys have, but no one's gonna steal it," according to Gerald Nachman in *Seriously Funny*. In the early 1960s, 90 percent of American households owned televisions and a similar percentage tuned in nightly to one of the three networks, ABC, CBS, and NBC. The Smothers Brothers' television debut was seen by a huge portion of television viewers. The show became an overnight success and the Smothers were instant celebrities. Their newfound popularity helped them to land guest appearances on such shows as *The Andy Williams Show, The Ed Sullivan Show, The Sonny and Cher Show, The Steve Allen Show,* and *Hootenany.*

Tom (left) and Dick Smothers perform a routine, blending music, humor, and political commentary. *© Neal Preston/Corbis. Reproduced by permission.*

The Smothers Brothers on television

CBS offered Tom and Dick their own show for the 1965 and 1966 season. *The Smothers Brothers Show* was a comedy in which Tom played an angel and Dick played his human brother. CBS canceled that show after one season but offered the Smothers Brothers their own variety show the next year. *The Smothers Brothers Comedy Hour* debuted on CBS opposite NBC's *Bonanza,* the top-rated show at the time. CBS hoped that the brothers' mix of clean-cut good looks, youthful comedy, and music would attract a traditional, older audience while appealing to a younger audience at the same time. The Smothers Brothers had broad, safe appeal. They "were primarily viewed as a couple of genial, middle-of-the-road entertainers who generated laughs with the dizzy siblings spats of their folksinging comedy act," reported Mike Duffy in the *Detroit Free Press.* The brothers selected a mixed group of performers to round out their show. For example, they booked established movie star Bette Davis at the same time as the up-and-coming British rock band The Who. Along with the Smothers Brothers, writers for the show included Rob Reiner and Steve Martin.

By mixing guests from different generations on the same show, the Smothers Brothers caused changes in prime-time television offerings. During the second year of the show, the brothers started to address the political and social changes in the country in ways no one had seen before. Dressed conservatively in tuxedoes or blazers with pressed pants, the brothers uttered some of the first political satire ever heard on television. CBS cautiously endorsed the brothers' brand of comedy, telling them that it was okay to make jokes about "the president as long as you do it with respect," as noted in *Seriously Funny.* For their news-driven satire, Tom played a silly, well-meaning college kid to Dick's more conservative, sensible authority figure. In one show, Dick said, "We've come a long way since that first Thanksgiving in Plymouth, when the Pilgrims sat down at the table with the Indians to eat turkey." Tom replied, "Boy, I'll say we've come a long way. Now we're in Paris, sitting down at a table with the Viet Cong, eating crow." With remarks like these, however, CBS began to feel that the brothers lacked respect and began censoring the show.

Surviving the censors

The Smothers Brothers did not bow down to network pressure. As the brothers started developing distinct opinions about the Vietnam War and social issues at home, their opinions came out in their show. Having the attention of hundreds of thousands of people every week proved an irresistible soapbox for the brothers. They and the nation were deeply moved by such events as protests erupting at the 1968 Democratic convention and the assassinations of **Martin Luther King Jr.** (1929–1968; see entry) and Senator Robert Kennedy (1925–1968). Yet when the Smothers Brothers had scheduled folksinger Pete Seeger to sing on their show, CBS censored his song because of its antiwar message. "Waist Deep in the Big Muddy" included lyrics that criticized President **Lyndon B. Johnson** (1909–1973; served 1963–69; see entry) and his policies regarding the war in Vietnam. The song describes military troops who lose their lives when their commander orders them to cross a dangerous river. CBS later allowed Seeger to perform his song after the public insisted. However, much of the Smothers' political material was never allowed to be shown.

Their opinions were too radical for CBS executives. As noted in *People Weekly,* a CBS vice president said in 1969 that the Smothers Brothers "touched nerves with those jokes." The brothers anticipated censors axing their lines and would add in offensive lines as decoys in order to slip their true message past the censors. To draw public attention to their plight, the brothers introduced satirical skits into the show that poked fun at the CBS censors. While jokes about drugs and sexuality slipped by censors, political jokes were immediately cut.

The Smothers Brothers Comedy Hour had become something unlike any show ever before seen on television. And during its second year, *The Smothers Brothers Comedy Hour* toppled *Bonanza* from its long-held top rank. But the struggles between the brothers and the network only grew, and CBS fired the brothers in their third season. The brothers, in turn, sued the network for not fulfilling their contract and received $776,000. As noted in the television documentary *Smothered* and quoted in the *Detroit Free Press,* comedian Bill Maher recalled: "The Smothers Brothers sacrificed their show because they wouldn't sacrifice their principles." (Maher lost his network show, *Politically Incorrect,* after he made some highly controversial political statements about the terrorist attacks on September 11, 2001.)

The Smothers Brothers had opened television to the new world. After *The Smothers Brothers Comedy Hour* left the

Rowan and Martin's Laugh-In

Rowan and Martin's Laugh-In (1968–73) was the top-ranked television show in 1968 and 1969. The show featured comedy skits and celebrity guests but put a new twist on the comedy-variety show format. Instead of longer segments featuring guests and musical numbers, *Laugh-In* strung rapid-fire jokes, one-liners, celebrity cameos, and dancing segments into an hour-long show. The show required several video editors to piece together the hundreds of shots that flashed, sometimes for fewer than thirty seconds, from one joke, dancer, or flashcard with a one-liner on it to another. The show created such popular phrases as "Sock it to me!" and "You bet your sweet bippy!" Each episode ended in the same way, with regulars and guests popping their heads through little doors in a wall to deliver a quick joke as the credits rolled.

Although the show focused mainly on silliness, it also dabbled with political humor. A one-liner said, "George Wallace, your sheets are ready," referring to the alignment of Alabama governor Wallace (1919–1998) with the racist attitudes of the Ku Klux Klan. But the political humor on *Laugh-In* did not seem to threaten as much as *The Smothers Brothers Comedy Hour.* Conservatives such as actor John Wayne and even President **Richard Nixon** (1913–1994; served 1969–74) appeared on *Laugh-In.*

air, *Rowan and Martin's Laugh-In* on NBC became the hit comedy for young audiences, using humor inspired in part by the Smothers Brothers. The brothers took a break from performing after the cancellation of their show. Tom told *People Weekly* that after the show ended "I lost my sense of humor.... Everything was deadly serious." But eventually that sense of humor returned. In addition to revamping their act and touring again, the brothers have each married and divorced several times and pursued other interests. Tom has three children and Dick has six. Dick enjoys racing cars, and Tom owns and operates a winery in California. One of the wines he produces is called "Mom's Favorite Red."

The Smothers Brothers have made guest appearances on several television shows as well as some movies. In the early 2000s, they were still performing and were considered revolutionaries in prime-time television. CBS featured a twentieth reunion for *The Smothers Brothers Comedy Hour* in 1988. During the reunion, as quoted in *People Weekly,* the brothers joked about their comeback show on CBS, the same network that had fired them in the 1960s. "'I knew they'd change their minds,' says Tom.... 'It's been 20 years though,' Dick observes."

But other than the occasional special feature, such biting political satire as their 1960s prime-time offerings was included in the early 2000s only on late-night television shows and a few cable offerings. The political climate of the early 2000s brought renewed interest in the Smothers Brothers' continuing political satire. Tom told the *Hollywood Reporter*: "Dickie and I still feel it's our job to question power and authority." He added: "It's feeling like 1968 all over again. People are questioning the patriotism and Americanism of those who speak out. We all suddenly have to watch what we say."

For More Information

Books
Nachman, Gerald. *Seriously Funny: The Rebel Comedians of the 1950s and 1960s*. New York: Random House, 2003.

Periodicals
Carr, Steven Allen. "On the Edge of Tastelessness: CBS, the Smothers Brothers, and the Struggle for Control." *Cinema Journal* (Summer 1992): pp. 3–24.

Duffy, Mike. "'Smothered' Revisits Brothers' Battle with CBS." *Detroit Free Press* (December 2, 2002).

Kaufman, Joanne. "Censors, Beware! 20 Years After They Were Banned by CBS, the Smothers Brothers Are Back in a Breakthrough Special." *People Weekly* (February 8, 1988): p. 46.

Richmond, Ray. "Timely Return for Smothers Brothers." *Hollywood Reporter* (April 14, 2003): p. 1.

Tresniowki, Alex. "Grapes without Wrath: For Winemaker and New Dad Tommy Smothers, These Are Vintage Years." *People Weekly* (August 5, 1996): p. 63.

Web Sites
The Smothers Brothers Web Site. http://www.smothersbrothers.com (accessed March 13, 2004).

Andy Warhol

Born August 6, 1928
Pittsburgh, Pennsylvania

Died February 22, 1987
New York, New York

Artist, filmmaker, publisher, entrepreneur

"Warhol may be the one person who has understood, consciously or not I don't know, that to be a star is to be a blank screen. He has lived by that. A blank screen for the projection of spectators' phantasms, dreams, and desires."

—*Thierry de Duve in* Andy Warhol, *2001.*

Andy Warhol. © *Hulton-Deutsch Collection/Corbis. Reproduced by permission.*

Andy Warhol was one of the most imaginative, thought-provoking, and influential artists of the twentieth century. He was a key figure in the development of Pop Art, an artistic movement originating in the 1960s. In Pop Art, common objects are the subject of the artwork. He inspired outrage and delight with work such as his famous *Campbell's Soup Cans* series of paintings. He was also fascinated by fame and the famous, creating silk-screen images of celebrities such as Marilyn Monroe (1926–1962), Elizabeth Taylor (1932–), and Elvis Presley (1935–1977). Above all Warhol challenged accepted ideas of what art should be and was responsible for breaking down the barrier between art and commercial design.

Becomes commercial artist in New York City

He was born Andrew Warhola on August 6, 1928, in McKeesport, a borough of Pittsburgh, Pennsylvania. His parents had emigrated from what was then Czechoslovakia. Warhol had a childhood marked by poverty. His father, Andrej Warhola, was a laborer and construction worker. Like many men during the Great Depression (1929–41), Andrej was forced to travel in search of work. As a result Warhol and his two older brothers were dependent on their mother, Julia (Zavacky) Warhola. She made artificial flowers and sold them door-to-door. Warhol attended Holmes Elementary School as well as Saturday art classes at the Carnegie Institute of Technology (later Carnegie Mellon University). After graduating from Schenley High School in 1945, he returned to the institute, enrolling as a freshman majoring in pictorial design. Despite almost failing his freshman year, he graduated with a bachelor's degree in fine art in 1949.

Soon after graduating from the institute, Warhol moved to New York City and began a career as a commercial artist. At first he shared an apartment. As he became more successful, however, he moved into his own apartment on Lexington Avenue. Warhol's mother moved in with him in 1953 and lived with him until 1971. She acted as housekeeper and cook. He worked and enjoyed the colorful, sociable lifestyle of New York's underground gay community. Warhol threw himself into many different projects. Perhaps his most famous commercial designs were the I. Miller shoes advertisements that appeared weekly in the *New York Times*. One of these advertisements won the Art Directors' Club medal in 1957. He also designed store window displays for the jeweler Tiffany and Company and numerous magazine and book covers. Along the way, he collected many awards and positive reviews.

By the late 1950s Warhol was earning $100,000 a year. He considered breaking out of the purely commercial art world and into fine art. He had already begun to sell some of his original works. He also gave away printed collections of his sketches to clients. Among the most collectable of these are the booklets *The Gold Book* (1957) and *Wild Raspberries* (1959). He continually experimented with new techniques and materials. Moreover, he began to mold his own appearance so that he became his own work of art. As his hair thinned, Warhol took to wearing bleached blond wigs. He also had plastic surgeries to reduce the size of his nose and to remove skin blemishes left over from a childhood illness. Warhol's physical image would soon become as recognizable as his best-known art works.

Working at The Factory

By 1960 Warhol was still taking on commercial projects, but only to fund his less profitable fine art. His attempt

 **Pop Art**

In the 1950s the United States entered a period of consumerism, or increased purchasing of mass-produced goods. This changed American life forever. The new era of consumerism followed the poverty of the Great Depression (1929–41) and the rationing of products during World War II (1939–45). Suddenly, consumer goods such as refrigerators, automobiles, and televisions became widely available. Mass production meant that items of all kinds became cheap to make and buy. Americans lost no time in taking advantage of these items. Pop Art was a celebration of this new materialistic culture. It made art from mass-produced objects, the media, and the world of glamour. It was first given a name by the British critic Lawrence Alloway in the journal *Architectural Digest* in 1958.

Pop Art became an alternative to the artistic style known as Abstract Expressionism, which had dominated the art world for most of the 1940s and 1950s. It made stars of such artists as Jackson Pollock (1912–1956) and Mark Rothko (1903–1970). It was serious and philosophical; most people found it difficult to understand. Other artists such as Robert Rauschenberg (1925–), Roy Lichtenstein (1923–1997), David Hockney (1937–), and Andy Warhol drew inspiration instead from comic strips, advertising, packaging designs, and everyday scenes. Lichtenstein became famous for blowing up newspaper comic strips to enormous size. Hockney is well known for his gaudy paintings of empty swimming pools. Warhol, who is thought by many to be the most important Pop artist of all, recreated Campbell's soup cans and Brillo boxes on canvas and as sculptures.

Pop Art used humor to challenge conventional ideas of what the subject of art could be. It drew on images from the media, entertainment, and Hollywood. Lichtenstein's enormous newspaper comic strips often appeared on the walls of public buildings. Placing Pop Art in strange contexts changed the way celebrities and other popular images were seen. It encouraged the audience to look at them in new ways. This was the central idea in the Pop Art revolution: that popular, mass-produced images and designs could become art if they were treated as art, regardless of their subject matter. Andy Warhol is widely quoted as saying: "Everything is beautiful. Pop is everything."

to sell paintings similar in style to the large-scale comic strips of Roy Lichtenstein (1923–1997) failed. In 1962 Warhol exhibited his series of thirty-three *Campbell's Soup Cans* paintings. First appearing at the Ferus Gallery in Los Angeles, the series consisted of canvases depicting soup cans stacked up in rows. The cans were realistically drawn; Warhol presented them in a strikingly plain way. This work had a dramatic ef-

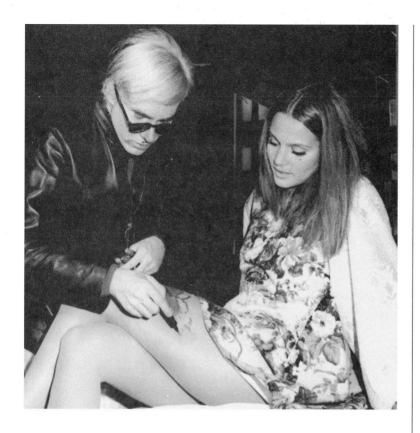

Underground, for example, were promoted by Warhol between 1966 and 1968. He even produced their first album, which was called *Andy Warhol*. The Velvet Underground became the house band at Warhol's nightclub, known as The Exploding Plastic Inevitable. Many of Warhol's followers worshipped him. However, Warhol often exploited their loyalty and treated them as a big joke. One of them, Valerie Solanis, shot and seriously wounded Warhol on June 3, 1968, claiming that he had too much control over her. Warhol was clinically dead for a short time, but doctors managed to save his life. Warhol later recalled in his book *POPism*: "I couldn't figure out why, of all the people Valerie must have known, I had to be the one to get shot. I guess it was just being in the wrong place at the right time. That's what assassination is all about."

By the 1970s Warhol was one of the most influential and respected of all living artists. Although his best work was completed during the 1960s, nothing he did failed to sell. In the early 1970s he could charge more than $25,000 for a single portrait. Warhol himself had become famous around the world. He socialized with music and movie stars and was entertained at lavish receptions by world leaders, including American presidents and the shah of Iran. He acted as host at Studio 54, a notorious New York nightclub, and lived a high-profile life of parties, movie premiers, and glittering social events.

Warhol died on February 22, 1987, from complications following a routine gall bladder operation. He left an estate valued at over $220 million. As an artist Warhol revolutionized the art world and helped narrow the gap between art and design. But perhaps his greatest achievement was his understanding of fame and the media. In the early 2000s the Warhol "brand" was familiar to millions. His *Marilyn* silk-screen portraits graced objects from T-shirts to coffee cups, while exhibitions of his work drew huge crowds. Warhol's own image, with his side-parted white wig, dark glasses, and leather jacket, was among the most recognizable in the early 2000s.

For More Information

Books

Bolton, Linda. *Andy Warhol.* New York: Franklin Watts, 2002.

Hackett, Pat, ed. *The Andy Warhol Diaries.* New York: Warner Books, 1989.

McCabe, David. *A Year in the Life of Andy Warhol.* New York: Phaidon Press, 2003.

Michelson, Annette. *Andy Warhol.* Cambridge, MA: MIT Press, 2001.

Ratcliff, Carter. *Warhol.* New York: Abbeville Press, 1983.

Schaffner, Ingrid. *Andy Warhol.* New York: Henry N. Abrams, 1999.

Warhol, Andy, with Pat Hackett. *POPism: The Warhol '60s.* New York: Harcourt, 1980.

Watson, Steven. *Factory Made: Warhol and the Sixties.* New York: Pantheon Books, 2003.

Web Sites

The Andy Warhol Foundation for the Visual Arts. http://www.warholfoundation.org (accessed August 2004).

The Andy Warhol Museum. http://www.warhol.org (accessed August 2004).

Where to Learn More

Books

Altman, Linda Jacobs. *The American Civil Rights Movement: The African-American Struggle for Equality.* Berkeley Heights, NJ: Enslow, 2004.

Anderson, David L. *The Columbia Guide to the Vietnam War.* New York: Columbia University Press, 2002.

Archer, Jules. *The Incredible Sixties: The Stormy Years that Changed America.* San Diego, CA: Harcourt Brace Jovanovich, 1986.

Austin, Joe, and Michael Nevin Willard. *Generations of Youth: Youth Cultures and History in Twentieth-Century America.* New York: New York University Press, 1998.

Bloom, Alexander, and Wini Breines, eds. *"Takin' It to the Streets": A Sixties Reader.* New York: Oxford University Press, 2003.

Breuer, William B. *Race to the Moon: America's Duel with the Soviets.* Westport, CT: Greenwood Publishing, 1993.

Burner, David. *Making Peace with the 1960s.* Princeton, NJ: Princeton University Press, 1996.

Cantwell, Robert. *When We Were Good: The Folk Revival.* Cambridge, MA: Harvard University Press, 1996.

Collier, Christopher, and James Lincoln Collier. *The Changing Face of American Society: 1945-2000.* New York: Benchmark, 2002.

Dougan, Clark. *A Nation Divided.* Boston: Boston Publishing Co., 1984.

Dudley, William, ed. *The 1960s*. San Diego: Greenhaven, 2000.

Dunn, John M. *A History of U.S. Involvement*. San Diego, CA: Lucent Books, 2001.

Edelstein, Andrew. *The Pop Sixties*. New York: Ballantine Books, 1985.

Farber, David. *The Age of Great Dreams: America in the 1960s*. New York: Hill and Wang, 1994.

Farber, David, and Beth Bailey, with others. *The Columbia Guide to America in the 1960s*. New York: Columbia University Press, 2001.

Feinstein, Stephen. *The 1960s from the Vietnam War to Flower Power*. Berkeley Heights, NJ: Enslow, 2000.

Finkelstein, Norman H. *The Way Things Never Were: The Truth about the "Good Old Days."* New York: Atheneum Books for Young Readers, 1999.

Galt, Margot Fortunato. *Stop This War!: American Protest of the Conflict in Vietnam*. Minneapolis, MN: Lerner, 2000.

Gitlin, Todd. *The Sixties: Years of Hope, Days of Rage*. New York: Bantam, 1987; revised, 1993.

Goldberg, RoseLee. *Performance: Live Art since 1960*. New York: Harry N. Abrams, 1998.

Holland, Gini. *The 1960s*. San Diego, CA: Lucent, 1999.

Isserman, Maurice, and Michael Kazin. *America Divided: The Civil War of the 1960s*. New York: Oxford University Press, 2000.

Jay, Kathryn. *More Than Just a Game: Sports in American Life Since 1945*. New York: Columbia University Press, 2004.

Kallen, Stuart A. *The Kennedy Assassination*. San Diego, CA: Lucent, 2003.

Kallen, Stuart A. *Political Activists of the 1960s*. San Diego, CA: Lucent Books, 2004.

Kallen, Stuart A., ed. *Sixties Counterculture*. San Diego, CA: Greenhaven Press, 2001.

Katz, William Loren. *The Great Society to the Reagan Era, 1964-1990*. Austin, TX: Raintree Steck-Vaughn, 1993.

Lebrecht, Norman. *The Companion to 20th-Century Music*. New York: Simon & Schuster, 1992.

Levy, Debbie. *The Vietnam War*. Minneapolis, MN: Lerner, 2004.

Lobenthal, Joel. *Radical Rags: Fashion of the Sixties*. New York: Abbeville Press, 1990.

Lowe, Jacques. *The Kennedy Legacy: A Generation Later*. New York: Viking Studio, 1988.

Lucie-Smith, Edward. *Visual Arts in the Twentieth Century*. Upper Saddle River, NJ: Prentice Hall, 1996.

MacNeil, Robert, ed. *The Way We Were: 1963, the Year Kennedy Was Shot*. New York: Carroll & Graf, 1988.

Marsden, George M. *Religion and American Culture.* San Diego, CA: Harcourt Brace Jovanovich, 1990.

McCormick, Anita Louisa. *The Vietnam Antiwar Movement in American History.* Berkeley Heights, NJ: Enslow Publishers, 2000.

McWilliams, John C. *The 1960s Cultural Revolution.* Westport, CT: Greenwood Press, 2000.

Miller, Jim. *Democracy Is in the Streets: From Port Huron to the Siege of Chicago.* Cambridge, MA: Harvard University Press, 1994.

Miller, Jim, ed. *The Rolling Stone Illustrated History of Rock and Roll.* New York: Rolling Stone Press, 1980.

Miller, Timothy. *The Hippies and American Values.* Knoxville: University of Tennessee Press, 1991.

Mordden, Ethan. *Medium Cool: The Movies of the 1960s.* New York: Knopf, 1990.

Moss, George. *America in the Twentieth Century.* Upper Saddle River, NJ: Prentice-Hall, 1988.

Northrup, Cynthia Clark, ed. *The American Economy: A Historical Encyclopedia.* Santa Barbara, CA: ABC-CLIO, 2003.

O'Neill, William L. *Coming Apart: An Informal History of America in the 1960s.* Chicago, IL: Quadrangle, 1971.

Parker, Thomas, and Douglas Nelson. *Day by Day: The Sixties.* New York: Facts on File, 1983.

Roberts, Randy, and James S. Olson. *Winning Is the Only Thing: Sports in America Since 1945.* Baltimore, MD: Johns Hopkins University Press, 1989.

Schwartz, Richard A. *Cold War Culture: Media and the Arts, 1945–1990.* New York: Facts on File, 1997.

Sloman, Larry. *Steal This Dream: Abbie Hoffman and the Countercultural Revolution in America.* New York: Doubleday, 1998.

Stevens, Jay. *Storming Heaven: LSD and the American Dream.* New York: Atlantic Monthly Press, 1987.

Stern, Jane, and Michael Stern. *Sixties People.* New York: Knopf, 1990.

Summers, Harry G., Jr. *Historical Atlas of the Vietnam War.* New York: Houghton Mifflin, 1995.

Treanor, Nick, ed. *The Civil Rights Movement.* San Diego, CA: Greenhaven Press, 2003.

Tucker, Spencer C. *Encyclopedia of the Vietnam War: A Political, Social, and Military History.* 3 vols. Santa Barbara, CA: ABC-CLIO, 1998.

Turbulent Years: The 60s. Alexandria, VA: Time-Life Books, 1998.

Unger, Irwin, and Debi Unger, eds. *The Times Were a Changin'.* New York: Random House, 1998.

Uschan, Michael V. *Life on the Front Lines: The Fight for Civil Rights.* San Diego, CA: Lucent Books, 2004.

Witcover, Jules. *The Year the Dream Died: Revisiting 1968 in America.* New York: Warner Books, 1997.

Wormser, Richard. *Three Faces of Vietnam.* New York: F. Watts, 1993.

Young, Marilyn B., John J. Fitzgerald, and A. Tom Grunfeld. *The Vietnam War: A History in Documents.* New York: Oxford University Press, 2002.

Web Sites

American Presidents Life Portraits. http://www.americanpresidents.org.

"The Cuban Missile Crisis, 1962: The 40th Anniversary." *The National Security Archive.* http://www.gwu.edu/~nsarchiv/nsa/cuba_mis_cri/.

Divining America: Religion and the National Culture. http://www.nhc.rtp. nc.us/tserve/divam.htm.

Hippies on the Web: Haight-Ashbury Music and Culture. http://www. rockument.com/links.html.

John F. Kennedy Library and Museum. http://www.jfklibrary.org.

"The Living Room Candidate: Presidential Campaign Commercials, 1952-2004." *American Museum of the Moving Image.* http:// livingroomcandidate.movingimage.us/index.php.

Lyndon Baines Johnson Library and Museum. http://www.lbjlib.utexas.edu.

National Civil Rights Museum. http://www.civilrightsmuseum.org.

"The Presidents of the United States." *The White House.* http://www. whitehouse.gov/history/presidents.

The Richard Nixon Library and Birthplace. http://www.nixonfoundation.org.

The Sixties Project. http://lists.village.virginia.edu/sixties/.

The 1960s—Social Unrest & Counterculture. http://www.historyteacher. net/APUSH-Course/Weblinks/Weblinks27.htm.

Vietnam Online. http://www.pbs.org/wgbh/amex/vietnam/.

Voices of Civil Rights: Ordinary People, Extraordinary Stories. http://www. voicesofcivilrights.org.

Index

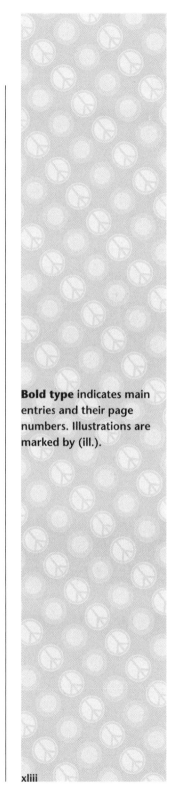